LYRA HEROICA

LYRA HEROICA

A BOOK OF VERSE FOR BOYS

SELECTED AND ARRANGED BY

WILLIAM ERNEST HENLEY

Sound, sound the clarion, fill the fife!
To all the sensual world proclaim
One crowded hour of glorious life
Is worth an age without a name.
                    Sir Walter Scott.

Granger Index Reprint Series

BOOKS FOR LIBRARIES PRESS
FREEPORT, NEW YORK

First Published 1891
Reprinted 1970

STANDARD BOOK NUMBER:
8369-6181-1

LIBRARY OF CONGRESS CATALOG CARD NUMBER:
73-128154

MANUFACTURED
BY
HALLMARK LITHOGRAPHERS, INC.
IN THE U.S.A.

TO WALTER BLAIKIE

ARTIST-PRINTER

MY PART IN THIS BOOK

W. E. H.

Edinburgh, July 1891.

PREFACE

This book of verse for boys is, I believe, the first of its kind in English. Plainly, it were labour lost to go gleaning where so many experts have gone harvesting; and for what is rarest and best in English Poetry the world must turn, as heretofore, to the several 'Golden Treasuries' of Professor Palgrave and Mr. Coventry Patmore, and to the excellent 'Poets' Walk' of Mr. Mowbray Morris. My purpose has been to choose and sheave a certain number of those achievements in verse which, as expressing the simpler sentiments and the more elemental emotions, might fitly be addressed to such boys—and men, for that matter—as are privileged to use our noble English tongue.

To set forth, as only art can, the beauty and the joy of living, the beauty and the blessedness of death, the glory of battle and adventure, the nobility of devotion—to a cause, an ideal, a passion even—the dignity of resistance, the sacred quality of patriotism, that is my ambition here. Now, to read poetry at all is to have an ideal anthology of one's own, and in that possession to be incapable of content with the anthologies of all the world besides. That is, the personal equation is ever to be reckoned withal, and I have had my preferences, as those that went before me had theirs. I have omitted much, as Aytoun's 'Lays,' whose absence many will resent; I have included much, as that brilliant piece of doggerel of Frederick Marryat's, whose presence some will regard with distress. This without reference to enforcements due to the very nature of my work.

I have adopted the birth-day order: for that is the simplest. And I have begun with—not Chaucer, nor Spenser, nor the ballads, but—Shakespeare and Agincourt; for it seemed to me that a book of heroism could have no better starting-point than that heroic pair of names. As for the ballads, I have placed them, after much considering, in the gap between old and new, between classic and romantic, in English verse. The witness of Sidney and Drayton's example notwithstanding, it is not until 1765, when Percy publishes the ' Reliques,' that the ballad spirit begins to be the master influence that Wordsworth confessed it was; while as for the history of the matter, there are who hold that 'Sir Patrick Spens,' for example, is the work of Lady Wardlaw, which to others, myself among them, is a thing preposterous and distraught.

It remains to add that, addressing myself to boys, I have not scrupled to edit my authors where editing seemed desirable, and that I have broken up some of the longer pieces for convenience in reading. Also, the help I have received while this book of 'Noble Numbers' was in course of growth —help in the way of counsel, suggestion, remonstrance, permission to use—has been such that it taxes gratitude and makes complete acknowledgment impossible.

W. E. H.

CONTENTS

**WILLIAM SHAKESPEARE (1564–1616) and
MICHAEL DRAYTON (1563–1631).**

	PAGE
I. AGINCOURT	
Introit	1
Interlude	2
Harfleur	3
The Eve	4
The Battle	6
After	10

SIR HENRY WOTTON (1568–1639).

II. LORD OF HIMSELF	11

BEN JONSON (1574–1637).

III. TRUE BALM	12
IV. HONOUR IN BUD	13

JOHN FLETCHER (1576–1625).

V. THE JOY OF BATTLE	13

FRANCIS BEAUMONT (1586–1616).

VI. IN WESTMINSTER ABBEY	15

ROBERT HERRICK (1591–1674).

VII. GOING A-MAYING	15
VIII. TO ANTHEA, WHO MAY COMMAND HIM ANYTHING	18

GEORGE HERBERT (1593-1638).

    IX. MEMENTO MORI 19

JAMES SHIRLEY (1594-1666).

    X. THE KING OF KINGS 20

JOHN MILTON (1608-1674).

    XI. LYCIDAS 21
    XII. ARMS AND THE MUSE 27
    XIII. TO THE LORD GENERAL . . . 28
    XIV. THE LATE MASSACRE 28
    XV. ON HIS BLINDNESS 29
    XVI. EYELESS AT GAZA 30
    XVII. OUT OF ADVERSITY 31

JAMES GRAHAM, MARQUIS OF MONTROSE (1612-1650).

    XVIII. HEROIC LOVE 31

RICHARD LOVELACE (1618-1658).

    XIX. GOING TO THE WARS 32
    XX. FROM PRISON 33

ANDREW MARVELL (1620-1678).

    XXI. TWO KINGS 34
    XXII. IN EXILE 39

JOHN DRYDEN (1631-1701).

    XXIII. ALEXANDER'S FEAST 40

SAMUEL JOHNSON (1709-1784).

    XXIV. THE QUIET LIFE 45

CONTENTS

BALLADS

		PAGE
XXV.	CHEVY CHASE	
	The Hunting	47
	The Challenge	49
	The Battle	51
	The Slain	54
	The Tidings	56
XXVI.	SIR PATRICK SPENS	57
XXVII.	BRAVE LORD WILLOUGHBY	60
XXVIII.	HUGHIE THE GRÆME	64
XXIX.	KINMONT WILLIE	
	The Capture	66
	The Keeper's Wrath	67
	The March	69
	The Rescue	71
XXX.	THE HONOUR OF BRISTOL	73
XXXI.	HELEN OF KIRKCONNELL	77
XXXII.	THE TWA CORBIES	79

THOMAS GRAY (1716-1771).

XXXIII. THE BARD 80

WILLIAM COWPER (1731-1800).

XXXIV. THE ROYAL GEORGE 85
XXXV. BOADICEA 86

GRAHAM OF GARTMORE (1735-1797).

XXXVI. TO HIS LADY 88

CHARLES DIBDIN (1745-1814).

XXXVII. CONSTANCY 89
XXXVIII. THE PERFECT SAILOR 90

JOHN PHILPOT CURRAN (1750-1817).

XXXIX. THE DESERTER 91

PRINCE HOARE (1755–1834).

XL. THE ARETHUSA 92

WILLIAM BLAKE (1757–1823).

XLI. THE BEAUTY OF TERROR 94

ROBERT BURNS (1759–1796).

XLII. DEFIANCE 95
XLIII. THE GOAL OF LIFE 96
XLIV. BEFORE PARTING 97
XLV. DEVOTION 98
XLVI. TRUE UNTIL DEATH 99

WILLIAM WORDSWORTH (1770–1850).

XLVII. VENICE 100
XLVIII. DESTINY 101
XLIX. THE MOTHER LAND 101
L. IDEAL 102
LI. TO DUTY 103
LII. TWO VICTORIES 105

SIR WALTER SCOTT (1771–1832).

LIII. IN MEMORIAM 107
LIV. LOCHINVAR 112
LV. FLODDEN
    The March 114
    The Attack 116
    The Last Stand 119
LVI. THE CHASE 121
LVII. THE OUTLAW 126
LVIII. PIBROCH 129
LIX. THE OMNIPOTENT 130
LX. THE RED HARLAW 131
LXI. FAREWELL 133
LXII. BONNY DUNDEE 134

CONTENTS

SAMUEL TAYLOR COLERIDGE (1772-1834).
LXIII. ROMANCE 136

WALTER SAVAGE LANDOR (1775-1864).
LXIV. SACRIFICE 138

THOMAS CAMPBELL (1777-1844).
LXV. SOLDIER AND SAILOR 140
LXVI. 'YE MARINERS' 143
LXVII. THE BATTLE OF THE BALTIC . . 144

EBENEZER ELLIOTT (1781-1846).
LXVIII. BATTLE SONG 146

ALLAN CUNNINGHAM (1785-1842).
LXIX. LOYALTY 147
LXX. A SEA-SONG 148

BRYANT WALLER PROCTOR (1787-1874).
LXXI. A SONG OF THE SEA 149

GEORGE GORDON, LORD BYRON (1788-1824).
LXXII. SENNACHERIB 150
LXXIII. THE STORMING OF CORINTH
    The Signal 151
    The Assault 153
    The Magazine 156
LXXIV. ALHAMA 160
LXXV. FRIENDSHIP 164
LXXVI. THE RACE WITH DEATH . . . 165
LXXVII. THE GLORY THAT WAS GREECE . 167
LXXVIII. HAIL AND FAREWELL . . . 171

CHARLES WOLFE (1791-1823).
LXXIX. AFTER CORUNNA 172

CONTENTS

FREDERICK MARRYAT (1792-1848).
LXXX. THE OLD NAVY 174

FELICIA HEMANS (1793-1825).
LXXXI. CASABIANCA 175
LXXXII. THE PILGRIM FATHERS 177

JOHN KEATS (1796-1821).
LXXXIII. TO THE ADVENTUROUS 179

THOMAS BABINGTON, LORD MACAULAY (1800-1859).
LXXXIV. HORATIUS
    The Trysting 179
    The Trouble in Rome 183
    The Keeping of the Bridge . . . 189
    Father Tiber 196
LXXXV. THE ARMADA 200
LXXXVI. THE LAST BUCCANEER 205
LXXXVII. A JACOBITE'S EPITAPH 206

ROBERT STEPHEN HAWKER (1803-1875).
LXXXVIII. THE SONG OF THE WESTERN MEN . . 207

HENRY WADSWORTH LONGFELLOW (1807-1882).
LXXXIX. THE BUILDING OF THE SHIP
    The Model 208
    The Builders 210
    In the Ship-Yard 214
    The Two Bridals 217
XC. THE DISCOVERER OF THE NORTH CAPE . 223
XCI. THE CUMBERLAND 227
XCII. A DUTCH PICTURE 228

JOHN GREENLEAF WHITTIER (b. 1807).
XCIII. BARBARA FRIETCHIE 230

CONTENTS

ALFRED, LORD TENNYSON (*b.* 1809).
XCIV. A BALLAD OF THE FLEET 232
XCV. THE HEAVY BRIGADE 239

SIR FRANCIS HASTINGS DOYLE (1810–1888).
XCVI. THE PRIVATE OF THE BUFFS . . . 242
XCVII. THE RED THREAD OF HONOUR . . . 244

ROBERT BROWNING (1812–1890).
XCVIII. HOME THOUGHTS FROM THE SEA . . 248
XCIX. HERVÉ RIEL 248

WALT WHITMAN (*b.* 1819).
C. THE DYING FIREMAN 254
CI. A SEA-FIGHT 255
CII. BEAT! BEAT! DRUMS! 257
CIII. TWO VETERANS 258

CHARLES KINGSLEY (1819–1875).
CIV. THE PLEASANT ISLE OF AVÈS . . . 260
CV. A WELCOME 262

SIR HENRY YULE (1820–1889).
CVI. THE BIRKENHEAD 264

MATTHEW ARNOLD (1822–1888).
CVII. APOLLO 265
CVIII. THE DEATH OF SOHRAB
    The Duel 267
    Sohrab 269
    The Recognition 272
    Ruksh the Horse 275
    Rustum 277
    Night 280
CIX. FLEE FRO' THE PRESS **282**

CONTENTS

WILLIAM CORY (*b.* 1823).
    CX. SCHOOL FENCIBLES 284
    CXI. THE TWO CAPTAINS 285

GEORGE MEREDITH (*b.* 1828).
    CXII. THE HEAD OF BRAN 290

WILLIAM MORRIS (*b.* 1834).
    CXIII. THE SLAYING OF THE NIBLUNGS
        Hogni 293
        Gunnar 297
        Gudrun 301
        The Sons of Giuki 304

ALFRED AUSTIN (*b.* 1835).
    CXIV. IS LIFE WORTH LIVING? 308

SIR ALFRED LYALL (*b.* 1835).
    CXV. THEOLOGY IN EXTREMIS 311

ALGERNON CHARLES SWINBURNE (*b.* 1837).
    CXVI. THE OBLATION 316
    CXVII. ENGLAND 317
    CXVIII. THE JACOBITE IN EXILE 319

BRET HARTE (*b.* 1839).
    CXIX. THE REVEILLÉ 322
    CXX. WHAT THE BULLET SANG 323

AUSTIN DOBSON (*b.* 1840).
    CXXI. A BALLAD OF THE ARMADA . . . 324

ANDREW LANG (*b.* 1844).
    CXXII. THE WHITE PACHA . . . 325

CONTENTS

ROBERT LOUIS STEVENSON (*b.* 1850).
 CXXIII. MOTHER AND SON 326

HENRY CHARLES BEECHING (*b.* 1859).
 CXXIV. PRAYERS 328

RUDYARD KIPLING (*b.* 1865).
 CXXV. A BALLAD OF EAST AND WEST . . . 329
 CXXVI. THE FLAG OF ENGLAND 335

NOTES 341

INDEX 359

*For I trust, if an enemy's fleet came yonder round by
    the hill,
And the rushing battle-bolt sang from the three-decker
    out of the foam,
That the smooth-faced snub-nosed rogue would leap from
    his counter and till,
And strike, if he could, were it but with his cheating
    yard-wand, home.*
                                    TENNYSON.

LYRA HEROICA

I

AGINCOURT

INTROIT

O FOR a Muse of fire, that would ascend
The brightest heaven of invention,
A kingdom for a stage, princes to act
And monarchs to behold the swelling scene!
Then should the warlike Harry, like himself,
Assume the port of Mars; and at his heels,
Leashed in like hounds, should Famine, Sword and Fire
Crouch for employment. But pardon, gentles all,
The flat unraisèd spirits that have dared
On this unworthy scaffold to bring forth
So great an object. Can this cockpit hold
The vasty fields of France? or may we cram
Within this wooden O the very casques
That did affright the air at Agincourt?
O pardon! since a crookèd figure may
Attest in little place a million,
And let us, ciphers to this great accompt,
On your imaginary forces work.
Suppose within the girdle of these walls
Are now confined two mighty monarchies,

Whose high upreare̒d and abutting fronts
The perilous narrow ocean parts asunder:
Piece out our imperfections with your thoughts;
Into a thousand parts divide one man,
And make imaginary puissance;
Think, when we talk of horses, that you see them
Printing their proud hoofs i' the receiving earth;
For 'tis your thoughts that now must deck our kings,
Carry them here and there, jumping o'er times,
Turning the accomplishment of many years
Into an hour-glass.

INTERLUDE

Now all the youth of England are on fire,
And silken dalliance in the wardrobe lies:
Now thrive the armourers, and honour's thought
Reigns solely in the breast of every man:
They sell the pasture now to buy the horse,
Following the mirror of all Christian kings,
With winge̒d heels, as English Mercuries:
For now sits Expectation in the air,
And hides a sword from hilts unto the point
With crowns imperial, crowns and coronets,
Promised to Harry and his followers.
The French, advised by good intelligence
Of this most dreadful preparation,
Shake in their fear, and with pale policy
Seek to divert the English purposes.
O England! model to thy inward greatness,
Like little body with a mighty heart,

What mightst thou do, that honour would thee do,
Were all thy children kind and natural!
But see thy fault: France hath in thee found out
A nest of hollow bosoms, which he fills
With treacherous crowns; and three corrupted men,
One, Richard Earl of Cambridge, and the second,
Henry Lord Scroop of Masham, and the third,
Sir Thomas Grey, knight, of Northumberland,
Have for the gilt of France—O guilt indeed!—
Confirmed conspiracy with fearful France;
And by their hands this grace of kings must die,
If hell and treason hold their promises,
Ere he take ship for France, and in Southampton!—

HARFLEUR

THUS with imagined wing our swift scene flies
In motion of no less celerity
Than that of thought. Suppose that you have seen
The well-appointed king at Hampton Pier
Embark his royalty, and his brave fleet
With silken streamers the young Phœbus fanning:
Play with your fancies, and in them behold
Upon the hempen tackle ship-boys climbing;
Hear the shrill whistle which doth order give
To sounds confused; behold the threaden sails,
Borne with the invisible and creeping wind
Draw the huge bottoms through the furrowed sea
Breasting the lofty surge. O, do but think
You stand upon the rivage and behold
A city on the inconstant billows dancing!

For so appears this fleet majestical,
Holding due course to Harfleur. Follow, follow:
Grapple your minds to sternage of this navy,
And leave your England, as dead midnight still,
Guarded with grandsires, babies and old women,
Or passed or not arrived to pith and puissance;
For who is he, whose chin is but enriched
With one appearing hair, that will not follow
These culled and choice-drawn cavaliers to France?
Work, work your thoughts, and therein see a siege:
Behold the ordnance on their carriages,
With fatal mouths gaping on girded Harfleur.
Suppose the ambassador from the French comes back;
Tells Harry that the king doth offer him
Katharine his daughter, and with her to dowry
Some petty and unprofitable dukedoms.
The offer likes not: and the nimble gunner
With linstock now the devilish cannon touches,
And down goes all before them!

THE EVE

Now entertain conjecture of a time
When creeping murmur and the poring dark
Fills the wide vessel of the universe.
From camp to camp through the foul womb of night
The hum of either army stilly sounds,
That the fixed sentinels almost receive
The secret whispers of each other's watch:
Fire answers fire, and through their paly flames
Each battle sees the other's umbered face;

SHAKESPEARE

Steed threatens steed, in high and boastful neighs
Piercing the night's dull ear, and from the tents
The armourers, accomplishing the knights,
With busy hammers closing rivets up,
Give dreadful note of preparation.
The country cocks do crow, the clocks do toll,
And the third hour of drowsy morning name.
Proud of their numbers and secure in soul,
The confident and over-lusty French
Do the low-rated English play at dice,
And chide the cripple, tardy-gaited night
Who like a foul and ugly witch doth limp
So tediously away. The poor condemnèd English,
Like sacrifices, by their watchful fires
Sit patiently and inly ruminate
The morning's danger, and their gesture sad,
Investing lank-lean cheeks and war-worn coats,
Presenteth them unto the gazing moon
So many horrid ghosts. O now, who will behold
The royal captain of this ruined band
Walking from watch to watch, from tent to tent,
Let him cry 'Praise and glory on his head!'
For forth he goes and visits all his host,
Bids them good-morrow with a modest smile,
And calls them brothers, friends, and countrymen.
Upon his royal face there is no note
How dread an army hath enrounded him;
Nor doth he dedicate one jot of colour
Unto the weary and all-watchèd night,
But freshly looks and over-bears attaint
With cheerful semblance and sweet majesty,

That every wretch, pining and pale before,
Beholding him, plucks comfort from his looks.
A largess universal like the sun
His liberal eye doth give to every one,
Thawing cold fear, that mean and gentle all,
Behold, as may unworthiness define,
A little touch of Harry in the night—
And so our scene must to the battle fly.
Shakespeare.

THE BATTLE

FAIR stood the wind for France,
When we our sails advance,
Nor now to prove our chance
    Longer will tarry;
But putting to the main,
At Caux, the mouth of Seine,
With all his martial train,
    Landed King Harry.

And taking many a fort,
Furnished in warlike sort,
Marched towards Agincourt
    In happy hour,
Skirmishing day by day
With those that stopped his way,
Where the French gen'ral lay
    With all his power:

Which, in his height of pride,
King Henry to deride,
His ransom to provide
    To the king sending;

Which he neglects the while
As from a nation vile,
Yet with an angry smile
    Their fall portending.

And turning to his men,
Quoth our brave Henry then,
' Though they to one be ten,
    Be not amazèd.
Yet have we well begun,
Battles so bravely won
Have ever to the sun
    By fame been raisèd.

And for myself, quoth he,
This my full rest shall be:
England ne'er mourn for me,
    Nor more esteem me;
Victor I will remain
Or on this earth lie slain;
Never shall she sustain
    Loss to redeem me.

Poitiers and Cressy tell,
When most their pride did swell,
Under our swords they fell;
    No less our skill is
Than when our grandsire great,
Claiming the regal seat,
By many a warlike feat
    Lopped the French lilies.'

The Duke of York so dread
The eager vaward led;
With the main Henry sped,
    Amongst his henchmen;
Excester had the rear,
A braver man not there:
O Lord, how hot they were
    On the false Frenchmen!

They now to fight are gone,
Armour on armour shone,
Drum now to drum did groan,
    To hear was wonder;
That with the cries they make
The very earth did shake,
Trumpet to trumpet spake,
    Thunder to thunder.

Well it thine age became,
O noble Erpingham,
Which did the signal aim
    To our hid forces!
When from the meadow by,
Like a storm suddenly,
The English archery
    Struck the French horses.

With Spanish yew so strong,
Arrows a cloth-yard long,
That like to serpents stung,
    Piercing the weather;

None from his fellow starts,
But playing manly parts,
And like true English hearts
    Stuck close together.

When down their bows they threw,
And forth their bilbos drew,
And on the French they flew,
    Not one was tardy;
Arms were from shoulders sent,
Scalps to the teeth were rent,
Down the French peasants went;
    Our men were hardy.

This while our noble king,
His broadsword brandishing,
Down the French host did ding
    As to o'erwhelm it,
And many a deep wound lent,
His arms with blood besprent,
And many a cruel dent
    Bruisèd his helmet.

Glo'ster, that duke so good,
Next of the royal blood,
For famous England stood,
    With his brave brother;
Clarence, in steel so bright,
Though but a maiden knight,
Yet in that furious fight
    Scarce such another!

  Warwick in blood did wade,
  Oxford the foe invade,
  And cruel slaughter made,
   Still as they ran up;
  Suffolk his axe did ply,
  Beaumont and Willoughby
  Bare them right doughtily,
   Ferrers and Fanhope.

  Upon Saint Crispin's Day
  Fought was this noble fray,
  Which fame did not delay,
   To England to carry.
  O, when shall Englishmen
  With such acts fill a pen,
  Or England breed again
   Such a King Harry?
       Drayton.

AFTER

   Now we bear the king
Toward Calais: grant him there; there seen,
Heave him away upon your wingèd thoughts
Athwart the sea. Behold, the English beach
Pales in the flood with men, with wives and boys,
Whose shouts and claps out-voice the deep-mouthed sea,
Which like a mighty whiffler 'fore the king
Seems to prepare his way: so let him land,
And solemnly see him set on to London.
So swift a pace hath thought that even now

You may imagine him upon Blackheath;
Where that his lords desire him to have borne
His bruisèd helmet and his bended sword
Before him through the city: he forbids it,
Being free from vainness and self-glorious pride,
Giving full trophy, signal and ostent,
Quite from himself to God.   But now behold,
In the quick forge and working-house of thought,
How London doth pour out her citizens!
The mayor and all his brethren in best sort,
Like to the senators of the antique Rome,
With the plebeians swarming at their heels,
Go forth and fetch their conquering Cæsar in!
Shakespeare.

II

LORD OF HIMSELF

How happy is he born or taught
   Who serveth not another's will;
Whose armour is his honest thought,
   And simple truth his highest skill;

Whose passions not his masters are;
   Whose soul is still prepared for death—
Not tied unto the world with care
   Of prince's ear or vulgar breath;

Who hath his ear from rumours freed;
   Whose conscience is his strong retreat;
Whose state can neither flatterers feed,
   Nor ruin make oppressors great;

Who envies none whom chance doth raise,
   Or vice; who never understood
How deepest wounds are given with praise,
   Nor rules of state but rules of good;

Who God doth late and early pray
   More of his grace than gifts to lend,
And entertains the harmless day
   With a well-chosen book or friend—

This man is free from servile bands
   Of hope to rise or fear to fall:
Lord of himself, though not of lands,
   And, having nothing, yet hath all.
                              Wotton.

III

TRUE BALM

High-spirited friend,
I send nor balms nor corsives to your wound;
   Your faith hath found
A gentler and more agile hand to tend
The cure of that which is but corporal,
And doubtful days, which were named critical,
   Have made their fairest flight
   And now are out of sight.
Yet doth some wholesome physic for the mind,
   Wrapped in this paper lie,
Which in the taking if you misapply
   You are unkind.

Your covetous hand,
Happy in that fair honour it hath gained,
    Must now be reined.
True valour doth her own renown commend
In one full action; nor have you now more
To do than be a husband of that store.
    Think but how dear you bought
    This same which you have caught—
Such thoughts will make you more in love with truth.
        'Tis wisdom, and that high,
For men to use their fortune reverently,
        Even in youth.

IV

HONOUR IN BUD

It is not growing like a tree
In bulk doth make man better be:
    A lily of a day
    Is fairer far in May:
Although it fall and die that night,
It was the plant and flower of light.

Jonson.

V

THE JOY OF BATTLE

Arm, arm, arm, arm! the scouts are all come in;
Keep your ranks close, and now your honours win.
Behold from yonder hill the foe appears;
Bows, bills, glaives, arrows, shields, and spears!

Like a dark wood he comes, or tempest pouring;
O view the wings of horse the meadows scouring!
The vanguard marches bravely.   Hark, the drums!
                    Dub, dub!

They meet, they meet, and now the battle comes:
            See how the arrows fly
            That darken all the sky!
            Hark how the trumpets sound!
            Hark how the hills rebound—
                    Tara, tara, tara, tara, tara!

Hark how the horses charge! in, boys! boys, in!
The battle totters; now the wounds begin:
            O how they cry!
            O how they die!
Room for the valiant Memnon, armed with thunder!
    See how he breaks the ranks asunder!
They fly! they fly! Eumenes has the chase,
And brave Polybius makes good his place:
            To the plains, to the woods,
            To the rocks, to the floods,
They fly for succour.   Follow, follow, follow!
Hark how the soldiers hollow!
                    Hey, hey!

            Brave Diocles is dead,
            And all his soldiers fled ;
            The battle's won, and lost,
            That many a life hath cost.

VI

IN WESTMINSTER ABBEY

MORTALITY, behold and fear!
What a change of flesh is here!
Think how many royal bones
Sleep beneath this heap of stones!
Here they lie had realms and lands,
Who now want strength to stir their hands.
Here from their pulpits sealed with dust
They preach, 'In greatness is no trust.'
Here is an acre sown indeed
With the richest, royall'st seed
That the earth did e'er suck in,
Since the first man died for sin.
Here the bones of birth have cried,
'Though gods they were, as men they died.'
Here are sands, ignoble things,
Dropt from the ruined sides of kings.
Here's a world of pomp and state,
Buried in dust, once dead by fate.

Beaumont.

VII

GOING A-MAYING

GET up, get up for shame! The blooming morn
Upon her wings presents the god unshorn:
    See how Aurora throws her fair
    Fresh-quilted colours through the air:

Get up, sweet slug-a-bed, and see
The dew-bespangled herb and tree!
Each flower has wept and bowed toward the east,
Above an hour since, yet you not drest,
    Nay, not so much as out of bed?
    When all the birds have matins said,
    And sung their thankful hymns, 'tis sin,
    Nay, profanation, to keep in,
Whenas a thousand virgins on this day
Spring sooner than the lark to fetch in May.

Rise, and put on your foliage, and be seen
To come forth like the spring-time fresh and green,
    And sweet as Flora. Take no care
    For jewels for your gown or hair:
    Fear not; the leaves will strew
    Gems in abundance upon you:
Besides, the childhood of the day has kept,
Against you come, some orient pearls unwept.
    Come, and receive them while the light
    Hangs on the dew-locks of the night,
    And Titan on the eastern hill
    Retires himself, or else stands still
Till you come forth! Wash, dress, be brief in praying:
Few beads are best when once we go a-Maying.

Come, my Corinna, come; and coming, mark
How each field turns a street, each street a park,
    Made green and trimmed with trees! see how
    Devotion gives each house a bough

Or branch! each porch, each door, ere this,
    An ark, a tabernacle is,
Made up of white-thorn neatly interwove,
As if here were those cooler shades of love.
    Can such delights be in the street
    And open fields, and we not see 't?
    Come, we'll abroad: and let's obey
    The proclamation made for May,
And sin no more, as we have done, by staying,
But, my Corinna, come, let's go a-Maying.

There's not a budding boy or girl this day,
But is got up and gone to bring in May.
    A deal of youth ere this is come
    Back and with white-thorn laden home.
    Some have despatched their cakes and cream,
    Before that we have left to dream:
And some have wept and wooed, and plighted troth,
And chose their priest, ere we can cast off sloth:
    Many a green-gown has been given,
    Many a kiss, both odd and even:
    Many a glance too has been sent
    From out the eye, love's firmament:
Many a jest told of the keys betraying
This night, and locks picked: yet we're not a-Maying.

Come, let us go, while we are in our prime,
And take the harmless folly of the time!
    We shall grow old apace, and die
    Before we know our liberty.

    Our life is short, and our days run
    As fast away as does the sun.
And, as a vapour or a drop of rain,
Once lost can ne'er be found again,
    So when or you or I are made
    A fable, song, or fleeting shade,
    All love, all liking, all delight,
    Lies drowned with us in endless night.
Then, while time serves, and we are but decaying,
Come, my Corinna, come, let's go a-Maying.

VIII

TO ANTHEA

WHO MAY COMMAND HIM ANYTHING

Bid me to live, and I will live
    Thy Protestant to be;
Or bid me love and I will give
    A loving heart to thee.

A heart as soft, a heart as kind,
    A heart as sound and free,
As in the whole world thou canst find,
    That heart I'll give to thee.

Bid that heart stay, and it will stay
    To honour thy decree;
Or bid it languish quite away,
    And 't shall do so for thee.

Bid me to weep, and I will weep
    While I have eyes to see;
And, having none, yet I will keep
    A heart to weep for thee.

Bid me despair, and I'll despair
   Under that cypress-tree;
Or bid me die, and I will dare
   E'en death to die for thee.

Thou art my life, my love, my heart,
   The very eyes of me,
And hast command of every part,
   To live and die for thee.
                    Herrick.

IX

MEMENTO MORI

Sweet day, so cool, so calm, so bright—
The bridal of the earth and sky—
The dew shall weep thy fall to-night,
   For thou must die.

Sweet rose, whose hue, angry and brave,
Bids the rash gazer wipe his eye,
Thy root is ever in its grave,
   And thou must die.

Sweet spring, full of sweet days and roses,
A box where sweets compacted lie,
My music shows ye have your closes,
   And all must die.

Only a sweet and virtuous soul
Like seasoned timber never gives,
But, though the whole world turn to coal,
   Then chiefly lives.

X

THE KING OF KINGS

The glories of our birth and state
   Are shadows, not substantial things:
There is no armour against fate:
   Death lays his icy hand on kings:
      Sceptre and crown
      Must tumble down,
And in the dust be equal made
With the poor crookèd scythe and spade.

Some men with swords may reap the field,
   And plant fresh laurels when they kill,
But their strong nerves at last must yield:
   They tame but one another still.
      Early or late
      They stoop to fate,
And must give up their murmuring breath
When they, pale captives, creep to death.

The garlands wither on their brow—
   Then boast no more your mighty deeds!
Upon Death's purple altar now
   See where the victor-victim bleeds!
      All heads must come
      To the cold tomb:
Only the actions of the just
Smell sweet, and blossom in their dust.

XI
LYCIDAS

YET once more, O ye laurels, and once more,
Ye myrtles brown, with ivy never sere,
I come to pluck your berries harsh and crude,
And with forced fingers rude
Shatter your leaves before the mellowing year.
Bitter constraint, and sad occasion dear,
Compels me to disturb your season due:
For Lycidas is dead, dead ere his prime,
Young Lycidas, and hath not left his peer:
Who would not sing for Lycidas? he knew
Himself to sing and build the lofty rhyme.
He must not float upon his watery bier
Unwept, and welter to the parching wind,
Without the meed of some melodious tear.

   Begin, then, sisters of the sacred well,
That from beneath the seat of Jove doth spring;
Begin, and somewhat loudly sweep the string;
Hence with denial vain, and coy excuse:
So may some gentle Muse
With lucky words favour my destined urn,
And, as he passes, turn
And bid fair peace be to my sable shroud!

   For we were nursed upon the selfsame hill,
Fed the same flock by fountain, shade, and rill.
Together both, ere the high lawns appeared
Under the opening eyelids of the morn,
We drove afield, and both together heard
What time the grey-fly winds her sultry horn

Battening our flocks with the fresh dews of night,
Oft till the star that rose at evening bright
Towards heaven's descent had sloped his westering wheel.
Meanwhile the rural ditties were not mute,
Tempered to the oaten flute;
Rough satyrs danced, and fauns with cloven heel
From the glad sound would not be absent long;
And old Damœtas loved to hear our song.

  But O the heavy change, now thou art gone,
Now thou art gone, and never must return!
Thee, Shepherd, thee the woods, and desert caves
With wild thyme and the gadding vine o'ergrown,
And all their echoes, mourn.
The willows and the hazel copses green
Shall now no more be seen
Fanning their joyous leaves to thy soft lays.
As killing as the canker to the rose,
Or taint-worm to the weanling herds that graze,
Or frost to flowers that their gay wardrobe wear
When first the white-thorn blows,
Such, Lycidas, thy loss to Shepherds' ear.

  Where were ye, Nymphs, when the remorseless deep
Closed o'er the head of your loved Lycidas?
For neither were ye playing on the steep
Where your old bards, the famous Druids, lie,
Nor on the shaggy top of Mona high,
Nor yet where Deva spreads her wizard stream:
Ay me! I fondly dream
'Had ye been there,' . . . for what could that have done?

What could the Muse herself that Orpheus bore,
The Muse herself, for her enchanting son
Whom universal nature did lament,
When by the rout that made the hideous roar
His gory visage down the stream was sent,
Down the swift Hebrus to the Lesbian shore?

  Alas! what boots it with incessant care
To tend the homely slighted shepherd's trade,
And strictly meditate the thankless Muse?
Were it not better done, as others use,
To sport with Amaryllis in the shade
Or with the tangles of Neæra's hair?
Fame is the spur that the clear spirit doth raise
(That last infirmity of noble mind)
To scorn delights and live laborious days;
But the fair guerdon when we hope to find,
And think to burst out into sudden blaze,
Comes the blind Fury with the abhorrèd shears,
And slits the thin-spun life. 'But not the praise,'
Phœbus replied, and touched my trembling ears:
'Fame is no plant that grows on mortal soil,
Nor in the glistering foil
Set off to the world nor in broad rumour lies,
But lives and spreads aloft by those pure eyes
And perfect witness of all-judging Jove;
As he pronounces lastly on each deed,
Of so much fame in heaven expect thy meed.'

  O fountain Arethuse, and thou honoured flood,
Smooth-sliding Mincius, crowned with vocal reeds,
That strain I heard was of a higher mood!
But now my oat proceeds,

And listens to the Herald of the Sea
That came in Neptune's plea.
He asked the waves, and asked the felon winds,
What hard mishap hath doomed this gentle swain?
And questioned every gust of rugged wings
That blows from off each beakèd promontory:
They knew not of his story,
And sage Hippotades their answer brings,
That not a blast was from his dungeon strayed:
The air was calm, and on the level brine
Sleek Panope with all her sisters played.
It was that fatal and perfidious bark,
Built in the eclipse and rigged with curses dark,
That sunk so low that sacred head of thine.

Next, Camus, reverend sire, went footing slow,
His mantle hairy, and his bonnet sedge,
Inwrought with figures dim, and on the edge
Like to that sanguine flower inscribed with woe.
'Ah! who hath reft,' quoth he, 'my dearest pledge?'
Last came, and last did go,
The Pilot of the Galilean Lake;
Two massy keys he bore of metals twain
(The golden opes, the iron shuts amain).
He shook his mitred locks, and stern bespake:
'How well could I have spared for thee, young swain,
Enow of such as for their bellies' sake
Creep, and intrude, and climb into the fold!
Of other care they little reckoning make
Than how to scramble at the shearers' feast,
And shove away the worthy bidden guest;

Blind mouths! that scarce themselves know how to hold
A sheep-hook, or have learnt aught else the least
That to the faithful herdman's art belongs!
What recks it them? What need they? They are sped;
And, when they list, their lean and flashy songs
Grate on their scrannel pipes of wretched straw;
The hungry sheep look up, and are not fed,
But, swoln with wind and the rank mist they draw,
Rot inwardly, and foul contagion spread:
Besides what the grim wolf with privy paw
Daily devours apace, and nothing said:
But that two-handed engine at the door
Stands ready to smite once, and smite no more.'
  Return, Alpheus, the dread voice is past
That shrunk thy streams; return, Sicilian Muse,
And call the vales, and bid them hither cast
Their bells and flowerets of a thousand hues.
Ye valleys low, where the mild whispers use
Of shades, and wanton winds, and gushing brooks,
On whose fresh lap the swart star sparely looks;
Throw hither all your quaint enamelled eyes
That on the green turf suck the honeyed showers,
And purple all the ground with vernal flowers.
Bring the rathe primrose that forsaken dies,
The tufted crow-toe and pale jessamine,
The white pink and the pansy freaked with jet,
The glowing violet,
The musk-rose and the well-attired woodbine,
With cowslips wan that hang the pensive head,

And every flower that sad embroidery wears:
Bid Amaranthus all his beauty shed,
And daffadillies fill their cups with tears,
To strew the laureate hearse where Lycid lies.
For, so to interpose a little ease,
Let our frail thoughts dally with false surmise;
Ay me! whilst thee the shores and sounding seas
Wash far away, where'er thy bones are hurled;
Whether beyond the stormy Hebrides,
Where thou perhaps under the whelming tide
Visit'st the bottom of the monstrous world;
Or whether thou, to our moist vows denied,
Sleep'st by the fable of Bellerus old,
Where the great vision of the guarded mount
Looks toward Namancos and Bayona's hold;
Look homeward, Angel, now, and melt with ruth:
And, O ye dolphins, waft the hapless youth.

   Weep no more, woeful shepherds, weep no more,
For Lycidas, your sorrow, is not dead,
Sunk though he be beneath the watery floor.
So sinks the day-star in the ocean bed,
And yet anon repairs his drooping head,
And tricks his beams, and with new spangled ore
Flames in the forehead of the morning sky:
So Lycidas sunk low, but mounted high,
Through the dear might of Him that walked the waves,
Where, other groves and other streams along,
With nectar pure his oozy locks he laves,
And hears the unexpressive nuptial song,
In the blest kingdoms meek of joy and love

There entertain him all the Saints above,
In solemn troops and sweet societies
That sing, and singing in their glory move,
And wipe the tears for ever from his eyes.
Now, Lycidas, the shepherds weep no more;
Henceforth thou art the genius of the shore
In thy large recompense, and shalt be good
To all that wander in that perilous flood.

   Thus sang the uncouth swain to the oaks and rills,
While the still morn went out with sandals grey;
He touched the tender stops of various quills,
With eager thought warbling his Doric lay:
And now the sun had stretched out all the hills,
And now was dropt into the western bay:
At last he rose, and twitched his mantle blue;
To-morrow to fresh woods and pastures new.

XII

ARMS AND THE MUSE

WHEN THE ASSAULT WAS INTENDED ON THE CITY

Captain, or Colonel, or Knight in Arms,
Whose chance on these defenceless doors may seize,
If deed of honour did thee ever please,
Guard them, and him within protect from harms.
He can requite thee; for he knows the charms
That call fame on such gentle acts as these,
And he can spread thy name o'er land and seas,
Whatever clime the sun's bright circle warms.
Lift not thy spear against the Muses' bower:

The great Emanthian conqueror bid spare
The house of Pindarus, when temple and tower
Went to the ground; and the repeated air
Of sad Electra's poet had the power
To save the Athenian walls from ruin bare.

XIII

TO THE LORD GENERAL

CROMWELL, our chief of men, who through a cloud
Not of war only, but detractions rude,
Guided by faith and matchless fortitude,
To peace and truth thy glorious way hast ploughed,
And on the neck of crownèd Fortune proud
Hast reared God's trophies, and his work pursued,
While Darwen stream, with blood of Scots imbrued,
And Dunbar field, resounds thy praises loud,
And Worcester's laureate wreath: yet much remains
To conquer still; peace hath her victories
No less renowned than war: new foes arise,
Threatening to bind our souls with secular chains.
Help us to save free conscience from the paw
Of hireling wolves whose gospel is their maw.

XIV

THE LATE MASSACRE IN PIEDMONT

AVENGE, O Lord, thy slaughtered saints, whose bones
Lie scattered on the Alpine mountains cold;
Even them who kept thy truth so pure of old,

When all our fathers worshipped stocks and stones,
Forget not: in thy book record their groans
Who were thy sheep, and in their ancient fold
Slain by the bloody Piedmontese that rolled
Mother with infant down the rocks. Their moans
The vales redoubled to the hills, and they
To heaven. Their martyred blood and ashes sow
O'er all the Italian fields, where still doth sway
The triple Tyrant; that from these may grow
A hundredfold, who, having learnt thy way,
Early may fly the Babylonian woe.

XV

ON HIS BLINDNESS

When I consider how my light is spent
Ere half my days in this dark world and wide,
And that one talent which is death to hide
Lodged with me useless, though my soul more bent
To serve therewith my Maker, and present
My true account, lest He, returning, chide;
'Doth God exact day-labour, light denied?'
I fondly ask: but patience, to prevent
That murmur soon replies: 'God doth not need
Either man's work or his own gifts. Who best
Bear his mild yoke, they serve him best. His state
Is kingly: thousands at his bidding speed,
And post o'er land and ocean without rest;
They also serve who only stand and wait.'

XVI

EYELESS AT GAZA

This, this is he; softly a while;
Let us not break in upon him.
O change beyond report, thought, or belief!
See how he lies at random, carelessly diffused
With languished head unpropt,
As one past hope, abandonèd,
And by himself given over,
In slavish habit, ill-fitted weeds
O'er-worn and soiled.
Or do my eyes misrepresent? Can this be he,
That heroic, that renowned,
Irresistible Samson? whom unarmed
No strength of man or fiercest wild beast could withstand;
Who tore the lion, as the lion tears the kid;
Ran on embattled armies clad in iron,
And, weaponless himself,
Made arms ridiculous, useless the forgery
Of brazen shield and spear, the hammered cuirass,
Chalybean-tempered steel, and frock of mail
Adamantéan proof: But safest he who stood aloof,
When insupportably his foot advanced,
In scorn of their proud arms and warlike tools,
Spurned them to death by troops. The bold Ascalonite
Fled from his lion ramp; old warriors turned
Their plated backs under his heel,
Or grovelling soiled their crested helmets in the dust.

XVII

OUT OF ADVERSITY

O how comely it is, and how reviving
To the spirits of just men long oppressed,
When God into the hands of their deliverer
Puts invincible might
To quell the mighty of the earth, the oppressor,
The brute and boisterous force of violent men,
Hardy and industrious to support
Tyrannic power, but raging to pursue
The righteous and all such as honour truth!
He all their ammunition
And feats of war defeats,
With plain heroic magnitude of mind
And celestial vigour armed;
Their armouries and magazines contemns,
Renders them useless, while
With wingèd expedition
Swift as the lightning glance he executes
His errand on the wicked, who, surprised,
Lose their defence, distracted and amazed.

Milton.

XVIII

HEROIC LOVE

My dear and only love, I pray
That little world of thee
Be governed by no other sway
But purest monarchy;

For if confusion have a part,
   Which virtuous souls abhor,
And hold a synod in thy heart,
   I'll never love thee more.

Like Alexander I will reign,
   And I will reign alone:
My thoughts did evermore disdain
   A rival on my throne.
He either fears his fate too much,
   Or his deserts are small,
Who dares not put it to the touch,
   To gain or lose it all.

But, if thou wilt prove faithful then
   And constant of thy word,
I'll make thee glorious by my pen,
   And famous by my sword;
I'll serve thee in such noble ways
   Was never heard before;
I'll crown and deck thee all with bays
   And love thee more and more.

Montrose.

XIX

GOING TO THE WARS

Tell me not, Sweet, I am unkind,
   That from the nunnery
Of thy chaste breast and quiet mind
   To war and arms I fly.

True, a new mistress now I chase,
   The first foe in the field,
And with a stronger faith embrace
   A sword, a horse, a shield.

Yet this inconstancy is such
   As you too shall adore:
I could not love thee, Dear, so much
   Loved I not Honour more.

XX

FROM PRISON

When Love with unconfinèd wings
   Hovers within my gates,
And my divine Althea brings
   To whisper at the grates;
When I lie tangled in her hair
   And fettered to her eye,
The Gods that wanton in the air
   Know no such liberty.

When flowing cups run swiftly round
   With no allaying Thames,
Our careless heads with roses crowned,
   Our hearts with loyal flames;
When thirsty grief in wine we steep,
   When healths and draughts go free,
Fishes that tipple in the deep
   Know no such liberty.

When, linnet-like confinèd, I
  With shriller throat shall sing
The sweetness, mercy, majesty,
  And glories of my King;
When I shall voice aloud how good
  He is, how great should be,
Enlargèd winds that curl the flood
  Know no such liberty.

Stone walls do not a prison make,
  Nor iron bars a cage;
Minds innocent and quiet take
  That for an hermitage:
If I have freedom in my love
  And in my soul am free,
Angels alone that soar above
  Enjoy such liberty.

Lovelace.

XXI

TWO KINGS

The forward youth that would appear
Must now forsake his Muses dear,
  Nor in the shadows sing
  His numbers languishing.

'Tis time to leave the books in dust,
And oil the unusèd armour's rust,
  Removing from the wall
  The corselet of the hall.

So restless Cromwell could not cease
In the inglorious arts of peace,
    But through adventurous war
    Urgèd his active star;

And, like the three-forked lightning, first
Breaking the clouds where it was nurst,
    Did thorough his own side
    His fiery way divide;

For 'tis all one to courage high,
The emulous or enemy,
    And with such to inclose
    Is more than to oppose;

Then burning through the air he went,
And palaces and temples rent;
    And Cæsar's head at last
    Did through his laurels blast.

'Tis madness to resist or blame
The face of angry Heaven's flame;
    And if we would speak true,
    Much to the man is due,

Who from his private gardens, where
He lived reservèd and austere,
    As if his highest plot
    To plant the bergamot,

Could by industrious valour climb
To ruin the great work of Time,
    And cast the kingdoms old
    Into another mould.

Though Justice against Fate complain,
And plead the ancient rights in vain
    (But those do hold or break,
    As men are strong or weak),

Nature, that hated emptiness,
Allows of penetration less,
    And therefore must make room
    Where greater spirits come.

What field of all the civil war,
Where his were not the deepest scar?
    And Hampton shows what part
    He had of wiser art,

Where, twining subtile fears with hope,
He wove a net of such a scope
    That Charles himself might chase
    To Carisbrook's narrow case,

That thence the royal actor borne
The tragic scaffold might adorn:
    While round the armèd bands,
    Did clap their bloody hands.

He nothing common did or mean
Upon that memorable scene,
    But with his keener eye
    The axe's edge did try;

Nor called the gods with vulgar spite
To vindicate his helpless right,
    But bowed his comely head
    Down, as upon a bed.

This was that memorable hour
Which first assured the forcèd power:
    So, when they did design
    The Capitol's first line,

A bleeding head, where they begun,
Did fright the architects to run;
    And yet in that the State
    Foresaw its happy fate!

And now the Irish are ashamed
To see themselves in one year tamed:
    So much one man can do
    That doth both act and know.

They can affirm his praises best,
And have, though overcome, confessed
    How good he is, how just,
    And fit for highest trust;

Nor yet grown stiffer with command,
But still in the Republic's hand
    (How fit he is to sway,
    That can so well obey!),

He to the Commons' feet presents
A kingdom for his first year's rents,
    And (what he may) forbears
    His fame to make it theirs:

And has his sword and spoils ungirt
To lay them at the public's skirt.
    So when the falcon high
    Falls heavy from the sky,

She, having killed, no more doth search
But on the next green bough to perch,
    Where, when he first does lure,
    The falconer has her sure.

What may not then our isle presume
While victory his crest does plume?
    What may not others fear
    If thus he crowns each year?

As Cæsar he, ere long, to Gaul,
To Italy an Hannibal,
    And to all states not free
    Shall climacteric be.

The Pict no shelter now shall find
Within his party-coloured mind,
    But from this valour sad
    Shrink underneath the plaid;

Happy if in the tufted brake
The English hunter him mistake,
    Nor lay his hounds in near
    The Caledonian deer.

But thou, the war's and fortune's son,
March indefatigably on,
    And for the last effect,
    Still keep the sword erect:

Besides the force it has to fright
The spirits of the shady night,
    The same arts that did gain,
    A power must it maintain.

XXII

IN EXILE

WHERE the remote Bermudas ride
In the Ocean's bosom unespied,
From a small boat that rowed along
The listening winds received this song.
  'What should we do but sing his praise
That led us through the watery maze,
Where he the huge sea-monsters wracks
That lift the deep upon their backs,
Unto an isle so long unknown,
And yet far kinder than our own?
He lands us on a grassy stage,
Safe from the storms and prelates' rage:
He gave us this eternal spring
Which here enamels everything,
And sends the fowls to us in care
On daily visits through the air.
He hangs in shades the orange bright
Like golden lamps in a green night,
And does in the pomegranates close
Jewels more rich than Ormus shows:
He makes the figs our mouths to meet,
And throws the melons at our feet;
But apples plants of such a price,
No tree could ever bear them twice.
With cedars chosen by his hand
From Lebanon he stores the land,
And makes the hollow seas that roar
Proclaim the ambergrease on shore.

He cast (of which we rather boast)
The Gospel's pearl upon our coast,
And in these rocks for us did frame
A temple where to sound his name.
O let our voice his praise exalt
'Till it arrive at heaven's vault,
Which thence (perhaps) rebounding may
Echo beyond the Mexique Bay!'
 Thus sang they in the English boat
A holy and a cheerful note:
And all the way, to guide their chime,
With falling oars they kept the time.

Marvell.

XXIII

ALEXANDER'S FEAST

'Twas at the royal feast for Persia won
  By Philip's warlike son:
   Aloft in awful state
   The godlike hero sate
   On his imperial throne;
 His valiant peers were placed around,
Their brows with roses and with myrtles bound
 (So should desert in arms be crowned);
The lovely Thais by his side
Sate like a blooming Eastern bride
In flower of youth and beauty's pride.
   Happy, happy, happy pair!
    None but the brave,
    None but the brave,
  None but the brave deserves the fair!

Timotheus, placed on high
    Amid the tuneful quire,
With flying fingers touched the lyre:
    The trembling notes ascend the sky
    And heavenly joys inspire.
  The song began from Jove
  Who left his blissful seats above,
  Such is the power of mighty love!
  A dragon's fiery form belied the god;
  Sublime on radiant spires he rode
  When he to fair Olympia pressed,
  And while he sought her snowy breast,
  Then round her slender waist he curled,
And stamped an image of himself, a sovereign of the world.
  The listening crowd admire the lofty sound;
  A present deity! they shout around:
  A present deity! the vaulted roofs rebound:
        With ravished ears
        The monarch hears,
        Assumes the god;
        Affects to nod
      And seems to shake the spheres.

The praise of Bacchus then the sweet musician sung,
  Of Bacchus ever fair and ever young:
    The jolly god in triumph comes;
    Sound the trumpets, beat the drums!
      Flushed with a purple grace
      He shows his honest face:

Now give the hautboys breath; he comes, he comes!
    Bacchus, ever fair and young,
      Drinking joys did first ordain;
    Bacchus' blessings are a treasure,
    Drinking is the soldier's pleasure:
        Rich the treasure,
        Sweet the pleasure,
      Sweet is pleasure after pain.

  Soothed with the sound the king grew vain;
    Fought all his battles o'er again,
And thrice he routed all his foes, and thrice he slew
    the slain!
    The master saw the madness rise,
    His glowing cheeks, his ardent eyes;
    And while he heaven and earth defied
    Changed his hand, and checked his pride.
      He chose a mournful Muse
      Soft pity to infuse:
    He sung Darius great and good,
      By too severe a fate
    Fallen, fallen, fallen, fallen,
      Fallen from his high estate,
    And weltering in his blood;
    Deserted at his utmost need
    By those his former bounty fed,
    On the bare earth exposed he lies
    With not a friend to close his eyes.
With downcast looks the joyless victor sate,
      Revolving in his altered soul
          The various turns of Chance below

And now and then a sigh he stole,
And tears began to flow.

The mighty master smiled to see
That love was in the next degree;
'Twas but a kindred-sound to move,
For pity melts the mind to love.
   Softly sweet, in Lydian measures
   Soon he soothed his soul to pleasures.
War, he sang, is toil and trouble,
Honour but an empty bubble;
   Never ending, still beginning,
Fighting still, and still destroying;
   If the world be worth thy winning,
Think, O think, it worth enjoying:
   Lovely Thais sits beside thee,
   Take the good the gods provide thee.
The many rend the skies with loud applause;
So love was crowned, but Music won the cause.
   The prince, unable to conceal his pain,
      Gazed on the fair
      Who caused his care,
   And sighed and looked, sighed and looked,
   Sighed and looked, and sighed again:
At length, with love and wine at once oppressed,
The vanquished victor sunk upon her breast.

Now strike the golden lyre again:
A louder yet, and yet a louder strain!
Break his bands of sleep asunder
And rouse him like a rattling peal of thunder.

Hark, hark! the horrid sound
  Has raised up his head:
  As awaked from the dead,
And amazed he stares around.
Revenge, revenge, Timotheus cries,
  See the Furies arise!
  See the snakes that they rear,
  How they hiss in their hair,
And the sparkles that flash from their eyes!
  Behold a ghastly band,
  Each a torch in his hand!
Those are Grecian ghosts, that in battle were slain
      And unburied remain
      Inglorious on the plain:
      Give the vengeance due
      To the valiant crew!
Behold how they toss their torches on high,
  How they point to the Persian abodes
And glittering temples of their hostile gods.
The princes applaud with a furious joy:
And the King seized a flambeau with zeal to destroy;
    Thais led the way
    To light him to his prey,
And like another Helen fired another Troy!

    Thus long ago,
  Ere heaving bellows learned to blow,
    While organs yet were mute,
    Timotheus, to his breathing flute
      And sounding lyre,
Could swell the soul to rage or kindle soft desire.

At last divine Cecilia came,
    Inventress of the vocal frame;
The sweet enthusiast from her sacred store
    Enlarged the former narrow bounds,
    And added length to solemn sounds,
With Nature's mother-wit and arts unknown before.
    Let old Timotheus yield the prize,
        Or both divide the crown:
    He raised a mortal to the skies;
        She drew an angel down.

Dryden.

XXIV

THE QUIET LIFE

CONDEMNED to Hope's delusive mine,
    As on we toil from day to day,
By sudden blast or slow decline
    Our social comforts drop away.

Well tried through many a varying year,
    See Levett to the grave descend:
Officious, innocent, sincere,
    Of every friendless name the friend.

Yet still he fills affection's eye,
    Obscurely wise and coarsely kind;
Nor, lettered arrogance, deny
    Thy praise to merit unrefined.

When fainting Nature called for aid,
   And hovering death prepared the blow,
His vigorous remedy displayed
   The power of art without the show.

In misery's darkest caverns known,
   His ready help was ever nigh,
Where hopeless anguish poured his groan,
   And lonely want retired to die.

No summons mocked by chill delay,
   No petty gains disdained by pride:
The modest wants of every day
   The toil of every day supplied.

His virtues walked their narrow round,
   Nor made a pause, nor left a void;
And sure the eternal Master found
   His single talent well employed.

The busy day, the peaceful night,
   Unfelt, uncounted, glided by;
His frame was firm, his powers were bright,
   Though now his eightieth year was nigh.

Then, with no throbs of fiery pain,
   No cold gradations of decay,
Death broke at once the vital chain,
   And freed his soul the nearest way.

XXV

CHEVY CHACE

THE HUNTING

God prosper long our noble king,
  Our lives and safeties all;
A woeful hunting once there did
  In Chevy-Chace befall;

To drive the deer with hound and horn
  Erle Percy took his way;
The child may rue that is unborn,
  The hunting of that day.

The stout Erle of Northumberland
  A vow to God did make,
His pleasure in the Scottish woods
  Three summer's days to take,

The chiefest harts in Chevy-Chace
  To kill and bear away.
These tydings to Erle Douglas came,
  In Scotland where he lay:

Who sent Erle Percy present word,
  He wold prevent his sport.
The English Erle, not fearing that,
  Did to the woods resort

With fifteen hundred bow-men bold,
    All chosen men of might,
Who knew full well in time of neede
    To ayme their shafts aright.

The gallant greyhounds swiftly ran,
    To chase the fallow deere:
On Monday they began to hunt,
    Ere daylight did appeare;

And long before high noone they had
    An hundred fat buckes slaine;
Then having dined, the drovyers went
    To rouse the deere againe.

The bow-men mustered on the hills,
    Well able to endure;
Their backsides all, with special care
    That day were guarded sure.

The hounds ran swiftly through the woods,
    The nimble deere to take,
And with their cryes the hills and dales
    An echo shrill did make.

Lord Percy to the quarry went,
    To view the slaughtered deere:
Quoth he, 'Erle Douglas promisèd
    This day to meet me here,

But if I thought he wold not come,
    No longer wold I stay.'
With that, a brave younge gentleman
    Thus to the Erle did say:

BALLADS

'Lo, yonder doth Erle Douglas come,
   His men in armour bright;
Full twenty hundred Scottish speares
   All marching in our sight;

All men of pleasant Tivydale,
   Fast by the river Tweede':
'O, cease your sports,' Erle Percy said,
   'And take your bowes with speede;

And now with me, my countrymen,
   Your courage forth advance,
For there was never champion yet,
   In Scotland or in France,

That ever did on horsebacke come,
   But if my hap it were,
I durst encounter man for man,
   And with him break a speare.'

THE CHALLENGE

Erle Douglas on his milke-white steede,
   Most like a baron bold,
Rode foremost of his company,
   Whose armour shone like gold.

'Show me,' said he, 'whose men ye be,
   That hunt so boldly here,
That, without my consent, do chase
   And kill my fallow-deere.'

The first man that did answer make,
   Was noble Percy he;

Who sayd, 'We list not to declare,
  Nor shew whose men we be,

Yet we will spend our dearest blood,
  Thy chiefest harts to slay.'
Then Douglas swore a solemn oath,
  And thus in rage did say:

'Ere thus I will out-bravèd be,
  One of us two shall dye:
I know thee well, an erle thou art;
  Lord Percy, so am I.

But trust me, Percy, pittye it were,
  And great offence to kill
Any of these our guiltlesse men,
  For they have done no ill.

Let thou and I the battell trye,
  And set our men aside.'
'Accurst be he,' Erle Percy said,
  'By whom this is denied.'

Then stept a gallant squier forth,
  Witherington was his name,
Who said, 'I wold not have it told
  To Henry our king for shame,

That ere my captaine fought on foote,
  And I stood looking on.
Ye be two erles,' said Witherington,
  'And I a squier alone:

Ile do the best that do I may,
  While I have power to stand:

While I have power to wield my sword,
  Ile fight with heart and hand.'

THE BATTLE

Our English archers bent their bowes,
  Their hearts were good and trew,
At the first flight of arrowes sent,
  Full fourscore Scots they slew.

Yet bides Erle Douglas on the bent,
  As Chieftain stout and good.
As valiant Captain, all unmoved
  The shock he firmly stood.

His host he parted had in three,
  As leader ware and try'd,
And soon his spearmen on their foes
  Bare down on every side.

Throughout the English archery
  They dealt full many a wound;
But still our valiant Englishmen
  All firmly kept their ground,

And, throwing strait their bowes away,
  They grasped their swords so bright,
And now sharp blows, a heavy shower,
  On shields and helmets light.

They closed full fast on every side,
  No slackness there was found;
And many a gallant gentleman
  Lay gasping on the ground.

O Christ! it was a griefe to see,
   And likewise for to heare,
The cries of men lying in their gore,
   And scattered here and there!

At last these two stout erles did meet,
   Like captaines of great might:
Like lions wode, they laid on lode,
   And made a cruel fight:

They fought untill they both did sweat
   With swords of tempered steele;
Until the blood like drops of rain
   They trickling downe did feele.

'Yield thee, Lord Percy,' Douglas said;
   'In faith I will thee bringe,
Where thou shalt high advancèd be
   By James our Scottish king:

Thy ransome I will freely give,
   And this report of thee,
Thou art the most courageous knight,
   That ever I did see.'

'No, Douglas,' quoth Erle Percy then,
   'Thy proffer I do scorne;
I will not yield to any Scot,
   That ever yet was borne.'

With that, there came an arrow keene
   Out of an English bow,
Which struck Erle Douglas to the heart,
   A deep and deadly blow:

Who never spake more words than these,
  'Fight on, my merry men all;
For why, my life is at an end;
  Lord Percy sees my fall.'

Then leaving life, Erle Percy tooke
  The dead man by the hand;
And said, 'Erle Douglas, for thy life
  Wold I had lost my land!

O Christ! my very heart doth bleed
  With sorrow for thy sake,
For sure, a more redoubted knight
  Mischance could never take.'

A knight amongst the Scots there was,
  Which saw Erle Douglas dye,
Who straight in wrath did vow revenge
  Upon the Lord Percye.

Sir Hugh Mountgomery was he called
  Who, with a speare most bright,
Well-mounted on a gallant steed,
  Ran fiercely through the fight,

And past the English archers all,
  Without or dread or feare,
And through Erle Percy's body then
  He thrust his hateful speare.

With such a vehement force and might
  He did his body gore,
The staff ran through the other side
  A large cloth-yard, and more.

So thus did both these nobles dye,
   Whose courage none could staine!
An English archer then perceived
   The noble Erle was slaine:

He had a bow bent in his hand,
   Made of a trusty tree;
An arrow of a cloth-yard long
   Up to the head drew he;

Against Sir Hugh Mountgomerye
   So right the shaft he set,
The grey goose-winge that was thereon
   In his heart's bloode was wet.

This fight did last from breake of day
   Till setting of the sun;
For when they rung the evening-bell,
   The battle scarce was done.

THE SLAIN

With stout Erle Percy, there was slaine
   Sir John of Egerton,
Sir Robert Ratcliff, and Sir John,
   Sir James, that bold baròn;

And with Sir George and stout Sir James,
   Both knights of good account,
Good Sir Ralph Raby there was slaine,
   Whose prowesse did surmount.

For Witherington needs must I wayle,
   As one in doleful dumpes;

For when his legs were smitten off,
  He fought upon his stumpes.

And with Erle Douglas, there was slaine
  Sir Hugh Mountgomerye,
Sir Charles Murray, that from the field
  One foote would never flee;

Sir Charles Murray, of Ratcliff, too,
  His sister's sonne was he;
Sir David Lamb, so well esteemed,
  Yet saved he could not be;

And the Lord Maxwell in like case
  Did with Erle Douglas dye:
Of twenty hundred Scottish speares,
  Scarce fifty-five did flye.

Of fifteen hundred Englishmen,
  Went home but fifty-three:
The rest were slaine in Chevy-Chace,
  Under the greene woode tree.

Next day did many widdowes come,
  Their husbands to bewayle;
They washt their wounds in brinish teares,
  But all wold not prevayle;

Their bodyes, bathed in purple gore,
  They bore with them away;
They kist them dead a thousand times,
  Ere they were clad in clay.

THE TIDINGS

The newes was brought to Eddenborrow,
  Where Scotland's king did raigne,
That brave Erle Douglas suddenlye
  Was with an arrow slaine:

'O heavy newes,' King James did say,
  'Scotland may witnesse be,
I have not any captaine more
  Of such account as he.'

Like tydings to King Henry came,
  Within as short a space,
That Percy of Northumberland
  Was slaine in Chevy-Chace:

'Now God be with him,' said our king,
  ' Sith it will no better be;
I trust I have, within my realme,
  Five hundred as good as he:

Yet shall not Scots nor Scotland say,
  But I will vengeance take:
I'll be revengèd on them all,
  For brave Erle Percy's sake.'

This vow full well the king performed
  After, at Humbledowne;
In one day, fifty knights were slayne,
  With lords of great renowne,

And of the rest, of small account,
  Did many thousands dye.

Thus endeth the hunting of Chevy-Chace,
  Made by the Erle Percye.

God save our king, and bless this land
  With plentye, joy, and peace,
And grant henceforth that foule debate
  'Twixt noblemen may cease!

XXVI

SIR PATRICK SPENS

The King sits in Dunfermline town,
  Drinking the blude-red wine:
'O whaur will I get a skeely skipper
  To sail this new ship o' mine?'

O up and spake an eldern knight,
  Sat at the King's right knee:
'Sir Patrick Spens is the best sailor
  That ever sailed the sea.'

Our King has written a braid letter
  And sealed it wi' his hand,
And sent it to Sir Patrick Spens,
  Was walking on the strand.

'To Noroway, to Noroway,
  To Noroway o'er the faem;
The King's daughter to Noroway,
  'Tis thou maun bring her hame.'

The first word that Sir Patrick read,
  Sae loud, loud lauchèd he;

The neist word that Sir Patrick read,
  The tear blinded his ee.

'O wha is this has done this deed,
  And tauld the King of me,
To send us out at this time o' year
  To sail upon the sea?

Be it wind, be it weet, be it hail, be it sleet,
  Our ship must sail the faem;
The King's daughter to Noroway,
  'Tis we must bring her hame.'

They hoysed their sails on Monday morn
  Wi' a' the speed they may;
They hae landed in Noroway
  Upon a Wodensday.

They hadna been a week, a week,
  In Noroway but twae,
When that the lords o' Noroway
  Began aloud to say:

'Ye Scottishmen spend a' our King's goud
  And a' our Queenis fee.'
'Ye lie, ye lie, ye liars loud,
  Fu' loud I hear ye lie!

For I brought as mickle white monie
  As gane my men and me,
And I brought a half-fou o' gude red goud
  Out-o'er the sea wi' me.

Mak' ready, mak' ready, my merry men a'!
  Our gude ship sails the morn.'

'Now, ever alake, my master dear,
  I fear a deadly storm.

I saw the new moon late yestreen
  Wi' the auld moon in her arm;
And, if we gang to sea, master,
  I fear we'll come to harm.'

They hadna sailed a league, a league,
  A league but barely three,
When the lift grew dark, and the wind blew loud,
  And gurly grew the sea.

'O where will I get a gude sailor
  To tak' my helm in hand,
Till I gae up to the tall topmast
  To see if I can spy land?'

'O here am I, a sailor gude,
  To tak' the helm in hand,
Till you gae up to the tall topmast;
  But I fear you'll ne'er spy land.'

He hadna gane a step, a step,
  A step but barely ane,
When a bolt flew out o' our goodly ship,
  And the salt sea it came in.

'Gae fetch a web o' the silken claith,
  Anither o' the twine,
And wap them into our ship's side,
  And letna the sea come in.'

They fetched a web o' the silken claith,
  Anither o' the twine,

And they wapped them round that gude ship's side,
  But still the sea cam' in.

O laith, laith were our gude Scots lords
  To weet their milk-white hands;
But lang ere a' the play was ower
  They wat their gowden bands.

O laith, laith were our gude Scots lords
  To weet their cork-heeled shoon;
But lang ere a' the play was played
  They wat their hats aboon.

O lang, lang may the ladies sit
  Wi' their fans intill their hand,
Before they see Sir Patrick Spens
  Come sailing to the strand!

And lang, lang may the maidens sit
  Wi' their goud kaims in their hair,
A' waiting for their ain dear loves!
  For them they'll see nae mair.

Half ower, half ower to Aberdour,
  It's fifty fathoms deep,
And there lies gude Sir Patrick Spens
  Wi' the Scots lords at his feet.

XXVII

BRAVE LORD WILLOUGHBY

The fifteenth day of July,
  With glistering spear and shield,
A famous fight in Flanders
  Was foughten in the field:

The most conspicuous officers
  Were English captains three,
But the bravest man in battel
  Was brave Lord Willoughby.

The next was Captain Norris,
  A valiant man was he:
The other, Captain Turner,
  From field would never flee.
With fifteen hundred fighting men,
  Alas! there were no more,
They fought with forty thousand then
  Upon the bloody shore.

'Stand to it, noble pikeman,
  And look you round about:
And shoot you right, you bow-men,
  And we will keep them out:
You musquet and cailiver men,
  Do you prove true to me,
I'll be the bravest man in fight,'
  Says brave Lord Willoughby.

And then the bloody enemy
  They fiercely did assail,
And fought it out most furiously,
  Not doubting to prevail:
The wounded men on both sides fell
  Most piteous for to see,
But nothing could the courage quell
  Of brave Lord Willoughby.

For seven hours to all men's view
　　This fight endurèd sore,
Until our men so feeble grew
　　That they could fight no more;
And then upon dead horses
　　Full savoury they eat,
And drank the puddle water,
　　That could no better get.

When they had fed so freely,
　　They kneelèd on the ground,
And praisèd God devoutly
　　For the favour they had found;
And bearing up their colours,
　　The fight they did renew,
And cutting tow'rds the Spaniard,
　　Five thousand more they slew.

The sharp steel-pointed arrows
　　And bullets thick did fly;
Then did our valiant soldiers
　　Charge on most furiously:
Which made the Spaniards waver,
　　They thought it best to flee:
They feared the stout behaviour
　　Of brave Lord Willoughby.

Then quoth the Spanish general,
　　'Come, let us march away,
I fear we shall be spoilèd all
　　If that we longer stay:

For yonder comes Lord Willoughby
　　With courage fierce and fell,
He will not give one inch of ground
　　For all the devils in hell.'

And when the fearful enemy
　　Was quickly put to flight,
Our men pursued courageously
　　To rout his forces quite;
And at last they gave a shout
　　Which echoed through the sky:
'God, and St. George for England!'
　　The conquerors did cry.

This news was brought to England
　　With all the speed might be,
And soon our gracious Queen was told
　　Of this same victory.
'O! this is brave Lord Willoughby,
　　My love that ever won:
Of all the lords of honour
　　'Tis he great deeds hath done!'

To the soldiers that were maimèd,
　　And wounded in the fray,
The queen allowed a pension
　　Of fifteen pence a day,
And from all costs and charges
　　She quit and set them free:
And this she did all for the sake
　　Of brave Lord Willoughby.

  Then courage, noble Englishmen,
   And never be dismayed!
  If that we be but one to ten,
   We will not be afraid
  To fight with foreign enemies,
   And set our country free.
  And thus I end the bloody bout
   Of brave Lord Willoughby.

XXVIII

HUGHIE THE GRÆME

Good Lord Scroope to the hills is gane,
 Hunting of the fallow deer;
And he has grippit Hughie the Græme
 For stealing of the Bishop's mare.

'Now, good Lord Scroope, this may not be!
 Here hangs a broadsword by my side;
And if that thou canst conquer me,
 The matter it may soon be tried.'

'I ne'er was afraid of a traitor thief;
 Although thy name be Hughie the Græme,
I'll make thee repent thee of thy deeds,
 If God but grant me life and time.'

But as they were dealing their blows so free,
 And both so bloody at the time,
Over the moss came ten yeomen so tall,
 All for to take bold Hughie the Græme.

O then they grippit Hughie the Græme,
   And brought him up through Carlisle town:
The lads and lasses stood on the walls,
   Crying, 'Hughie the Græme, thou'se ne'er gae down!'

'O loose my right hand free,' he says,
   'And gie me my sword o' the metal sae fine,
He's no in Carlisle town this day
   Daur tell the tale to Hughie the Græme.'

Up then and spake the brave Whitefoord,
   As he sat by the Bishop's knee,
'Twenty white owsen, my gude lord,
   If ye'll grant Hughie the Græme to me.'

'O haud your tongue,' the Bishop says,
   'And wi' your pleading let me be;
For tho' ten Grahams were in his coat,
   They suld be hangit a' for me.'

Up then and spake the fair Whitefoord,
   As she sat by the Bishop's knee,
'A peck o' white pennies, my good lord,
   If ye'll grant Hughie the Græme to me.'

'O haud your tongue now, lady fair,
   Forsooth, and so it sall na be;
Were he but the one Graham of the name,
   He suld be hangit high for me.'

They've ta'en him to the gallows knowe,
   He lookèd to the gallows tree,
Yet never colour left his cheek,
   Nor ever did he blink his e'e.

He lookèd over his left shoulder
  To try whatever he could see,
And he was aware of his auld father,
  Tearing his hair most piteouslie.

'O haud your tongue, my father dear,
  And see that ye dinna weep for me!
For they may ravish me o' my life,
  But they canna banish me fro' Heaven hie.

And ye may gie my brither John
  My sword that's bent in the middle clear,
And let him come at twelve o'clock,
  And see me pay the Bishop's mare.

And ye may gie my brither James
  My sword that's bent in the middle brown,
And bid him come at four o'clock,
  And see his brither Hugh cut down.

And ye may tell my kith and kin
  I never did disgrace their blood;
And when they meet the Bishop's cloak,
  To mak' it shorter by the hood.'

XXIX

KINMONT WILLIE

THE CAPTURE

O HAVE ye na heard o' the fause Sakelde?
  O have ye na heard o' the keen Lord Scroope?
How they hae ta'en bold Kinmont Willie,
  On Haribee to hang him up?

Had Willie had but twenty men,
   But twenty men as stout as he,
Fause Sakelde had never the Kinmont ta'en,
   Wi' eight score in his cumpanie.

They band his legs beneath the steed,
   They tied his hands behind his back;
They guarded him fivesome on each side,
   And they brought him ower the Liddel-rack.

They led him thro' the Liddel-rack,
   And also thro' the Carlisle sands;
They brought him on to Carlisle castle
   To be at my Lord Scroope's commands.

'My hands are tied, but my tongue is free,
   And wha will dare this deed avow?
Or answer by the Border law?
   Or answer to the bold Buccleuch?'

'Now haud thy tongue, thou rank reiver!
   There's never a Scot shall set thee free:
Before ye cross my castle yett,
   I trow ye shall take farewell o' me.'

'Fear na ye that, my lord,' quo' Willie:
   'By the faith o' my body, Lord Scroope,' he said,
'I never yet lodged in a hostelrie
   But I paid my lawing before I gaed.'

THE KEEPER'S WRATH

Now word is gane to the bold Keeper,
   In Branksome Ha' where that he lay,

That Lord Scroope has ta'en the Kinmont Willie,
  Between the hours of night and day.

He has ta'en the table wi' his hand,
  He garred the red wine spring on hie:
'Now a curse upon my head,' he said,
  'But avengèd of Lord Scroope I'll be!

O is my basnet a widow's curch?
  Or my lance a wand of the willow-tree?
Or my arm a lady's lily hand,
  That an English lord should lightly me!

And have they ta'en him, Kinmont Willie,
  Against the truce of Border tide?
And forgotten that the bold Buccleuch
  Is keeper here on the Scottish side?

And have they e'en ta'en him, Kinmont Willie,
  Withouten either dread or fear?
And forgotten that the bold Buccleuch
  Can back a steed or shake a spear?

O were there war between the lands,
  As well I wot that there is none,
I would slight Carlisle castle high,
  Though it were builded of marble stone.

I would set that castle in a lowe,
  And slocken it with English blood!
There's never a man in Cumberland
  Should ken where Carlisle castle stood.

But since nae war's between the lands,
  And there is peace, and peace should be,

I'll neither harm English lad or lass,
  And yet the Kinmont freed shall be!'

THE MARCH

He has called him forty Marchmen bold,
  I trow they were of his ain name,
Except Sir Gilbert Elliot, called
  The Laird of Stobs, I mean the same.

He has called him forty Marchmen bold,
  Were kinsmen to the bold Buccleuch;
With spur on heel, and splent on spauld,
  And gluves of green, and feathers blue.

There were five and five before them a',
  Wi' hunting-horns and bugles bright:
And five and five cam' wi' Buccleuch,
  Like warden's men, arrayed for fight.

And five and five like a mason gang
  That carried the ladders lang and hie;
And five and five like broken men;
  And so they reached the Woodhouselee.

And as we crossed the 'Bateable Land,
  When to the English side we held,
The first o' men that we met wi',
  Whae suld it be but fause Sakelde?

'Where be ye gaun, ye hunters keen?'
  Quo' fause Sakelde; 'come tell to me!'
'We go to hunt an English stag
  Has trespassed on the Scots countrie.'

'Where be ye gaun, ye marshal men?'
  Quo' fause Sakelde; 'come tell me true!'
'We go to catch a rank reiver
  Has broken faith wi' the bold Buccleuch.'

'Where are ye gaun, ye mason lads,
  Wi' a' your ladders lang and hie?'
'We gang to herry a corbie's nest
  That wons not far frae Woodhouselee.'

'Where be ye gaun, ye broken men?'
  Quo' fause Sakelde; 'come tell to me!'
Now Dickie of Dryhope led that band,
  And the never a word of lear had he.

'Why trespass ye on the English side?
  Row-footed outlaws, stand!' quo' he;
The never a word had Dickie to say,
  Sae he thrust the lance through his fause bodie.

Then on we held for Carlisle toun,
  And at Staneshaw-Bank the Eden we crossed;
The water was great and meikle of spait,
  But the never a horse nor man we lost.

And when we reached the Staneshaw-Bank,
  The wind was rising loud and hie;
And there the Laird garred leave our steeds,
  For fear that they should stamp and neigh.

And when we left the Staneshaw-Bank,
  The wind began full loud to blaw;
But 'twas wind and weet, and fire and sleet,
  When we came beneath the castle wa'.

We crept on knees, and held our breath,
   Till we placed the ladders against the wa';
And sae ready was Buccleuch himsell
   To mount the first before us a'.

He has ta'en the watchman by the throat,
   He flung him down upon the lead:
'Had there not been peace between our lands,
   Upon the other side thou'dst gaed!

Now sound out, trumpets!' quo' Buccleuch;
   'Let's waken Lord Scroope right merrilie!'
Then loud the warden's trumpet blew
   O wha dare meddle wi' me?

THE RESCUE

Then speedilie to wark we gaed,
   And raised the slogan ane and a',
And cut a hole through a sheet of lead,
   And so we wan to the castle ha'.

They thought King James and a' his men
   Had won the house wi' bow and spear;
It was but twenty Scots and ten
   That put a thousand in sic a stear!

Wi' coulters and wi' forehammers
   We garred the bars bang merrilie,
Until we came to the inner prison,
   Where Willie o' Kinmont he did lie.

And when we cam' to the lower prison,
   Where Willie o' Kinmont he did lie:

'O sleep ye, wake ye, Kinmont Willie,
  Upon the morn that thou's to die?'

'O I sleep saft, and I wake aft;
  It's lang since sleeping was fleyed frae me!
Gie my service back to my wife and bairns,
  And a' gude fellows that spier for me.'

Then Red Rowan has hente him up,
  The starkest man in Teviotdale:
'Abide, abide now, Red Rowan,
  Till of my Lord Scroope I take farewell.

Farewell, farewell, my gude Lord Scroope!
  My gude Lord Scroope, farewell!' he cried;
'I'll pay you for my lodging maill,
  When first we meet on the Border side.'

Then shoulder high with shout and cry
  We bore him down the ladder lang;
At every stride Red Rowan made,
  I wot the Kinmont's airns played clang.

'O mony a time,' quo' Kinmont Willie,
  'I have ridden horse baith wild and wood;
But a rougher beast than Red Rowan
  I ween my legs have ne'er bestrode.

And mony a time,' quo' Kinmont Willie,
  'I've pricked a horse out oure the furs;
But since the day I backed a steed,
  I never wore sic cumbrous spurs!'

We scarce had won the Staneshaw-Bank
  When a' the Carlisle bells were rung,

And a thousand men on horse and foot
   Cam' wi' the keen Lord Scroope along.

Buccleuch has turned to Eden Water,
   Even where it flowed frae bank to brim,
And he has plunged in wi' a' his band,
   And safely swam them through the stream.

He turned him on the other side,
   And at Lord Scroope his glove flung he:
'If ye like na my visit in merrie England,
   In fair Scotland come visit me!'

All sore astonished stood Lord Scroope,
   He stood as still as rock of stane;
He scarcely dared to trew his eyes,
   When through the water they had gane.

'He is either himsell a devil frae hell,
   Or else his mother a witch maun be;
I wadna have ridden that wan water
   For a' the gowd in Christentie.'

XXX

THE HONOUR OF BRISTOL

ATTEND you, and give ear awhile,
   And you shall understand
Of a battle fought upon the seas
   By a ship of brave command.
The fight it was so glorious
   Men's hearts it did ful-fill,
And it made them cry, 'To sea, to sea,
   With the Angel Gabriel!'

This lusty ship of Bristol
  Sailed out adventurously
Against the foes of England,
  Her strength with them to try:
Well victualled, rigged, and manned she was,
  With good provision still,
Which made men cry, 'To sea, to sea,
  With the Angel Gabriel!'

The Captain, famous Netherway
  (That was his noble name):
The Master—he was called John Mines—
  A mariner of fame:
The Gunner, Thomas Watson,
  A man of perfect skill:
With many another valiant heart
  In the Angel Gabriel.

They waving up and down the seas
  Upon the ocean main,
'It is not long ago,' quoth they,
  'That England fought with Spain:
O would the Spaniard we might meet
  Our stomachs to fulfil!
We would play him fair a noble bout
  With our Angel Gabriel!'

They had no sooner spoken
  But straight appeared in sight
Three lusty Spanish vessels
  Of warlike trim and might;

With bloody resolution
  They thought our men to spill,
And they vowed that they would make a prize
  Of our Angel Gabrìel.

Our gallant ship had in her
  Full forty fighting men:
With twenty piece of ordnance
  We played about them then,
With powder, shot, and bullets
  Right well we worked our will,
And hot and bloody grew the fight
  With our Angel Gabriel.

Our Captain to our Master said,
  'Take courage, Master bold!'
Our Master to the seamen said,
  'Stand fast, my hearts of gold!'
Our Gunner unto all the rest,
  'Brave hearts, be valiant still!
Fight on, fight on in the defence
  Of our Angel Gabriel!'

We gave them such a broadside,
  It smote their mast asunder,
And tore the bowsprit off their ship,
  Which made the Spaniards wonder,
And causèd them in fear to cry,
  With voices loud and shrill,
'Help, help, or sunken we shall be
  By the Angel Gabriel!'

So desperately they boarded us
  For all our valiant shot,
Threescore of their best fighting men
  Upon our decks were got;
And lo! at their first entrances
  Full thirty did we kill,
And thus we cleared with speed the deck
  Of our Angel Gabriel.

With that their three ships boarded us
  Again with might and main,
But still our noble Englishmen
  Cried out, 'A fig for Spain!'
Though seven times they boarded us
  At last we showed our skill,
And made them feel what men we were
  On the Angel Gabriel.

Seven hours this fight continued:
  So many men lay dead,
With Spanish blood for fathoms round
  The sea was coloured red.
Five hundred of their fighting men
  We there outright did kill,
And many more were hurt and maimed
  By our Angel Gabriel.

Then, seeing of these bloody spoils,
  The rest made haste away:
For why, they said, it was no boot
  The longer there to stay.

BALLADS

Then they fled into Calès,
   Where lie they must and will
For fear lest they should meet again
   With our Angel Gabriel.

We had within our English ship
   But only three men slain,
And five men hurt, the which I hope
   Will soon be well again.
At Bristol we were landed,
   And let us praise God still,
That thus hath blest our lusty hearts
   And our Angel Gabriel.

XXXI

HELEN OF KIRKCONNELL

I WISH I were where Helen lies,
Night and day on me she cries;
O that I were where Helen lies,
   On fair Kirkconnell lea!

Curst be the heart that thought the thought,
And curst the hand that fired the shot,
When in my arms burd Helen dropt,
   And died to succour me!

O thinkna ye my heart was sair
When my love dropt down, and spak' nae mair?
There did she swoon wi' meikle care,
   On fair Kirkconnell lea.

As I went down the water side,
None but my foe to be my guide,
None but my foe to be my guide
   On fair Kirkconnell lea;

I lighted down my sword to draw,
I hackèd him in pieces sma',
I hackèd him in pieces sma'
   For her sake that died for me.

O Helen fair beyond compare!
I'll mak' a garland o' thy hair,
Shall bind my heart for evermair,
   Until the day I dee!

O that I were where Helen lies!
Night and day on me she cries;
Out of my bed she bids me rise,
   Says, 'Haste, and come to me!'

O Helen fair! O Helen chaste!
If I were with thee I were blest,
Where thou lies low and takes thy rest,
   On fair Kirkconnell lea.

I wish my grave were growing green,
A winding-sheet drawn ower my e'en,
And I in Helen's arms lying
   On fair Kirkconnell lea.

I wish I were where Helen lies!
Night and day on me she cries,
And I am weary of the skies
   For her sake that died for me.

XXXII

THE TWA CORBIES

As I was walking all alane,
I heard twa corbies making a mane:
The tane unto the tither say,
'Where sall we gang and dine the day?'

'In behint yon auld fail dyke
I wot there lies a new-slain knight;
And naebody kens that he lies there
But his hawk, his hound, and his lady fair.

His hound is to the hunting gane,
His hawk to fetch the wild-fowl hame,
His lady's ta'en another mate,
Sae we may mak' our dinner sweet.

Ye'll sit on his white hause-bane,
And I'll pike out his bonny blue e'en:
Wi' ae lock o' his gowden hair
We'll theek our nest when it grows bare.

Mony a one for him makes mane,
But nane sall ken where he is gane:
O'er his white banes, when they are bare,
The wind sall blaw for evermair.'

XXXIII

THE BARD

'RUIN seize thee, ruthless King!
Confusion on thy banners wait!
Though fanned by Conquest's crimson wing
   They mock the air with idle state.
Helm, nor hauberk's twisted mail,
Nor e'en thy virtues, tyrant, shall avail
To save thy secret soul from nightly fears,
From Cambria's curse, from Cambria's tears!'
Such were the sounds that o'er the crested pride
   Of the first Edward scattered wild dismay,
As down the steep of Snowdon's shaggy side
   He wound with toilsome march his long array:
Stout Glo'ster stood aghast in speechless trance;
'To arms!' cried Mortimer, and couched his quivering lance.

On a rock, whose haughty brow
Frowns o'er old Conway's foaming flood,
   Robed in the sable garb of woe
With haggard eyes the Poet stood
(Loose his beard and hoary hair
Streamed like a meteor to the troubled air),
And with a master's hand and prophet's fire
Struck the deep sorrows of his lyre:
'Hark, how each giant oak and desert-cave
   Sighs to the torrent's awful voice beneath!
O'er thee, O King! their hundred arms they wave,
   Revenge on thee in hoarser murmurs breathe;

Vocal no more, since Cambria's fatal day,
To high-born Hoel's harp or soft Llewellyn's lay.

  'Cold is Cadwallo's tongue
    That hushed the stormy main:
Brave Urien sleeps upon his craggy bed:
    Mountains, ye mourn in vain
    Modred, whose magic song
Made huge Plinlimmon bow his cloud-topt head.
    On dreary Arvon's shore they lie
Smeared with gore and ghastly pale:
Far, far aloof the affrighted ravens sail;
    The famished eagle screams, and passes by.
Dear lost companions of my tuneful art,
    Dear as the light that visits these sad eyes,
Dear as the ruddy drops that warm my heart,
    Ye died amidst your dying country's cries!—
No more I weep. They do not sleep.
    On yonder cliffs, a grisly band,
I see them sit; they linger yet,
    Avengers of their native land:
With me in dreadful harmony they join,
And weave with bloody hands the tissue of thy line.

'Weave the warp and weave the woof
    The winding-sheet of Edward's race:
Give ample room and verge enough
    The characters of hell to trace.
Mark the year and mark the night
When Severn shall re-echo with affright

The shrieks of death through Berkeley's roof that ring,
Shrieks of an agonising king!

    She-wolf of France, with unrelenting fangs,
That tear'st the bowels of thy mangled mate,
    From thee be born, who o'er thy country hangs
The scourge of Heaven! What terrors round him wait!
Amazement in his van, with Flight combined,
And Sorrow's faded form, and Solitude behind.

'Mighty victor, mighty lord,
    Low on his funeral couch he lies!
No pitying heart, no eye, afford
    A tear to grace his obsequies.
Is the sable warrior fled?
Thy son is gone. He rests among the dead.
The swarm that in thy noontide beam were born?
Gone to salute the rising morn.
Fair laughs the Morn, and soft the zephyr blows,
    While proudly riding o'er the azure realm
In gallant trim the gilded vessel goes:
    Youth on the prow and Pleasure at the helm:
Regardless of the sweeping Whirlwind's sway,
That hushed in grim repose expects his evening
    prey.

  'Fill high the sparkling bowl.
The rich repast prepare;
    Reft of a crown, he yet may share the feast:
Close by the regal chair
    Fell Thirst and Famine scowl
    A baleful smile upon their baffled guest.

Heard ye the din of battle bray,
  Lance to lance and horse to horse?
  Long years of havoc urge their destined course,
And through the kindred squadrons mow their way.
  Ye towers of Julius, London's lasting shame,
With many a foul and midnight murder fed,
  Revere his consort's faith, his father's fame,
And spare the meek usurper's holy head!
Above, below, the rose of snow,
  Twined with her blushing foe, we spread:
The bristled boar in infant-gore
  Wallows beneath the thorny shade.
Now, brothers, bending o'er the accursed loom,
Stamp we our vengeance deep, and ratify his doom.

'Edward, lo! to sudden fate
  (Weave we the woof; the thread is spun;)
Half of thy heart we consecrate.
  (The web is wove; the work is done.)
Stay, O stay! nor thus forlorn
Leave me unblessed, unpitied, here to mourn:
In yon bright track that fires the western skies
They melt, they vanish from my eyes.
But O! what solemn scenes on Snowdon's height
  Descending slow their glittering skirts unroll?
Visions of glory, spare my aching sight,
  Ye unborn ages, crowd not on my soul!
No more our long-lost Arthur we bewail:
All hail, ye genuine kings! Britannia's issue, hail!

'Girt with many a baron bold
Sublime their starry fronts they rear;
   And gorgeous dames, and statesmen old
In bearded majesty, appear.
In the midst a form divine!
Her eye proclaims her of the Briton-line:
Her lion-port, her awe commanding face
Attempered sweet to virgin grace.
What strings symphonious tremble in the air,
   What strains of vocal transport round her play?
Hear from the grave, great Taliessin, hear;
   They breathe a soul to animate thy clay.
Bright Rapture calls and, soaring as she sings,
Waves in the eye of Heaven her many-coloured wings.

'The verse adorn again
   Fierce War and faithful Love
And Truth severe, by fairy fiction drest.
   In buskined measures move
Pale Grief and pleasing Pain,
With Horror, tyrant of the throbbing breast.
A voice as of the cherub-choir
   Gales from blooming Eden bear,
   And distant warblings lessen on my ear
That lost in long futurity expire.
Fond impious man, think'st thou yon sanguine cloud,
   Raised by thy breath, has quenched the orb of day?
To-morrow he repairs the golden flood
   And warms the nations with redoubled ray.
Enough for me: with joy I see

The different doom our fates assign:
Be thine Despair and sceptred Care,
  To triumph and to die are mine.'
He spoke, and headlong from the mountain's height
Deep in the roaring tide he plunged to endless night.
                                            Gray.

XXXIV

THE ROYAL GEORGE

Toll for the Brave!
The brave that are no more!
All sunk beneath the wave
Fast by their native shore!

Eight hundred of the brave,
Whose courage well was tried,
Had made the vessel heel
And laid her on her side.

A land-breeze shook the shrouds
And she was overset;
Down went the Royal George
With all her crew complete.

Toll for the brave!
Brave Kempenfelt is gone;
His last sea-fight is fought,
His work of glory done.

It was not in the battle;
No tempest gave the shock;
She sprang no fatal leak,
She ran upon no rock.

His sword was in its sheath,
His fingers held the pen,
When Kempenfelt went down
With twice four hundred men.

Weigh the vessel up
Once dreaded by our foes!
And mingle with our cup
The tear that England owes.

Her timbers yet are sound,
And she may float again
Full charged with England's thunder,
And plough the distant main:

But Kempenfelt is gone,
His victories are o'er;
And he and his eight hundred
Shall plough the wave no more.

XXXV

BOADICEA

When the British warrior queen,
  Bleeding from the Roman rods,
Sought with an indignant mien
  Counsel of her country's gods,

Sage beneath the spreading oak
  Sat the Druid, hoary chief,
Every burning word he spoke
  Full of rage, and full of grief:

'Princess! if our aged eyes
  Weep upon thy matchless wrongs,
'Tis because resentment ties
  All the terrors of our tongues.

Rome shall perish,—write that word
  In the blood that she has spilt;
Perish hopeless and abhorred,
  Deep in ruin as in guilt.

Rome, for empire far renowned,
  Tramples on a thousand states;
Soon her pride shall kiss the ground,
  Hark! the Gaul is at her gates!

Other Romans shall arise
  Heedless of a soldier's name;
Sounds, not arms, shall win the prize,
  Harmony the path to fame.

Then the progeny that springs
  From the forests of our land,
Armed with thunder, clad with wings,
  Shall a wider world command.

Regions Cæsar never knew
  Thy posterity shall sway;
Where his eagles never flew,
  None invincible as they.'

Such the bard's prophetic words,
  Pregnant with celestial fire,
Bending as he swept the chords
  Of his sweet but awful lyre.

She with all a monarch's pride
  Felt them in her bosom glow,
Rushed to battle, fought, and died,
  Dying, hurled them at the foe:

'Ruffians, pitiless as proud,
  Heaven awards the vengeance due;
Empire is on us bestowed,
  Shame and ruin wait for you.'

Cowper.

XXXVI

TO HIS LADY

If doughty deeds my lady please
  Right soon I'll mount my steed;
And strong his arm, and fast his seat
  That bears frae me the meed.
I'll wear thy colours in my cap
  Thy picture at my heart;
And he that bends not to thine eye
  Shall rue it to his smart!
    Then tell me how to woo thee, Love;
      O tell me how to woo thee!
    For thy dear sake, nae care I'll take,
      Tho' ne'er another trow me.

If gay attire delight thine eye
  I'll dight me in array;
I'll tend thy chamber door all night,
  And squire thee all the day.

If sweetest sounds can win thine ear
  These sounds I'll strive to catch;
Thy voice I'll steal to woo thysell,
  That voice that nane can match.

But if fond love thy heart can gain,
  I never broke a vow;
Nae maiden lays her skaith to me,
  I never loved but you.
For you alone I ride the ring,
  For you I wear the blue;
For you alone I strive to sing,
  O tell me how to woo!
    Then tell me how to woo thee, Love;
      O tell me how to woo thee!
    For thy dear sake, nae care I'll take,
      Tho' ne'er another trow me.
Graham of Gartmore.

XXXVII

CONSTANCY

Blow high, blow low, let tempests tear
  The mainmast by the board;
My heart, with thoughts of thee, my dear,
  And love well stored,
Shall brave all danger, scorn all fear,
  The roaring winds, the raging sea,
In hopes on shore to be once more
  Safe moored with thee!

Aloft while mountains high we go,
  The whistling winds that scud along,
And surges roaring from below,
  Shall my signal be to think on thee,
    And this shall be my song:
      Blow high, blow low—

And on that night, when all the crew,
  The memory of their former lives
O'er flowing cans of flip renew,
  And drink their sweethearts and their wives,
    I'll heave a sigh and think on thee,
    And, as the ship rolls through the sea,
    The burden of my song shall be:
      Blow high, blow low—

XXXVIII

THE PERFECT SAILOR

Here, a sheer hulk, lies poor Tom Bowling,
  The darling of our crew;
No more he'll hear the tempest howling,
  For death has broached him to.
His form was of the manliest beauty,
  His heart was kind and soft,
Faithful, below, he did his duty,
  But now he's gone aloft.

Tom never from his word departed,
  His virtues were so rare,
His friends were many and true-hearted,
  His Poll was kind and fair;

And then he'd sing so blithe and jolly,
  Ah, many's the time and oft!
But mirth is turned to melancholy,
  For Tom is gone aloft.

Yet shall poor Tom find pleasant weather,
  When He, who all commands,
Shall give, to call life's crew together,
  The word to pipe all hands.
Thus Death, who kings and tars despatches,
  In vain Tom's life has doffed,
For, though his body's under hatches,
  His soul has gone aloft.

Dibdin.

XXXIX

THE DESERTER

If sadly thinking,
With spirits sinking,
Could more than drinking
  My cares compose,
A cure for sorrow
From sighs I'd borrow,
And hope to-morrow
  Would end my woes.
But as in wailing
There's nought availing,
And Death unfailing
  Will strike the blow,

Then for that reason,
And for a season,
Let us be merry
   Before we go.

To joy a stranger,
A way-worn ranger,
In every danger
   My course I've run;
Now hope all ending,
And Death befriending,
His last aid lending,
   My cares are done:
No more a rover,
Or hapless lover,
My griefs are over,
   My glass runs low;
Then for that reason,
And for a season,
Let us be merry
   Before we go!

Curran.

XL

THE ARETHUSA

Come, all ye jolly sailors bold,
Whose hearts are cast in honour's mould,
While English glory I unfold,
   Huzza for the Arethusa!
She is a frigate tight and brave,
As ever stemmed the dashing wave;

PRINCE HOARE

    Her men are staunch
    To their fav'rite launch,
And when the foe shall meet our fire,
Sooner than strike, we'll all expire
    On board of the Arethusa.

'Twas with the spring fleet she went out
The English Channel to cruise about,
When four French sail, in show so stout
    Bore down on the Arethusa.
The famed Belle Poule straight ahead did lie,
The Arethusa seemed to fly,
    Not a sheet, or a tack,
    Or a brace, did she slack;
Though the Frenchman laughed and thought it stuff,
But they knew not the handful of men, how tough,
    On board of the Arethusa.

On deck five hundred men did dance,
The stoutest they could find in France;
We with two hundred did advance
    On board of the Arethusa.
Our captain hailed the Frenchman, 'Ho!'
The Frenchman then cried out 'Hallo!'
    'Bear down, d'ye see,
    To our Admiral's lee!'
'No, no,' says the Frenchman, 'that can't be!'
'Then I must lug you along with me,'
    Says the saucy Arethusa.

The fight was off the Frenchman's land,
We forced them back upon their strand,
For we fought till not a stick could stand
    Of the gallant Arethusa.
And now we've driven the foe ashore
Never to fight with Britons more,
    Let each fill his glass
    To his fav'rite lass;
A health to our captain and officers true,
And all that belong to the jovial crew
    On board of the Arethusa.

Prince Hoare.

XLI

THE BEAUTY OF TERROR

TIGER, tiger, burning bright
In the forests of the night,
What immortal hand or eye
Could frame thy fearful symmetry?

In what distant deeps or skies
Burnt the fire of thine eyes?
On what wings dare he aspire?
What the hand dare seize the fire?

And what shoulder, and what art,
Could twist the sinews of thy heart?
And when thy heart began to beat,
What dread hand? and what dread feet?

What the hammer? what the chain?
In what furnace was thy brain?
What the anvil? what dread grasp
Dare its deadly terrors clasp?

When the stars threw down their spears,
And watered heaven with their tears,
Did He smile His work to see?
Did He who made the lamb make thee?

Tiger, tiger, burning bright
In the forests of the night,
What immortal hand or eye
Dare frame thy fearful symmetry?

Blake.

XLII

DEFIANCE

Farewell, ye dungeons dark and strong,
   The wretch's destinie:
M'Pherson's time will not be long
   On yonder gallows tree.

> Sae rantingly, sae wantonly,
>   Sae dauntingly gaed he;
> He played a spring and danced it round,
>   Below the gallows tree.

Oh, what is death but parting breath?—
   On monie a bloody plain
I've dared his face, and in this place
   I scorn him yet again!

Untie these bands from off my hands,
  And bring to me my sword!
And there's no a man in all Scotland,
  But I'll brave him at a word.

I've lived a life of sturt and strife;
  I die by treacherie:
It burns my heart I must depart
  And not avengèd be.

Now farewell light, thou sunshine bright,
  And all beneath the sky!
May coward shame distain his name,
  The wretch that dares not die!

> Sae rantingly, sae wantonly,
>   Sae dauntingly gaed he;
> He played a spring and danced it round,
>   Below the gallows tree.

XLIII

THE GOAL OF LIFE

SHOULD auld acquaintance be forgot,
  And never brought to min'?
Should auld acquaintance be forgot,
  And days o' lang syne?

> For auld lang syne, my dear,
>   For auld lang syne,
> We'll tak a cup o' kindness yet
>   For auld lang syne.

And surely ye'll be your pint-stowp,
  And surely I'll be mine;
And we'll tak a cup o' kindness yet
  For auld lang syne.

We twa hae run about the braes,
  And pu'd the gowans fine;
But we've wandered mony a weary foot
  Sin' auld lang syne.

We twa hae paidled i' the burn
  From mornin' sun till dine;
But seas between us braid hae roared
  Sin' auld lang syne.

And here's a hand, my trusty fiere,
  And gie's a hand o' thine;
And we'll tak a right guid-willie waught
  For auld lang syne.

> For auld lang syne, my dear,
>   For auld lang syne,
> We'll tak a cup o' kindness yet
>   For auld lang syne.

XLIV

BEFORE PARTING

Go fetch to me a pint o' wine,
  An' fill it in a silver tassie;
That I may drink before I go
  A service to my bonnie lassie.

The boat rocks at the pier o' Leith,
    Fu' loud the wind blaws frae the ferry,
The ship rides by the Berwick-law,
    And I maun leave my bonnie Mary.

The trumpets sound, the banners fly,
    The glittering spears are rankèd ready,
The shouts o' war are heard afar,
    The battle closes thick and bloody;
But it's no the roar o' sea or shore
    Wad mak me langer wish to tarry,
Nor shout o' war that's heard afar,
    It's leaving thee, my bonnie Mary.

XLV

DEVOTION

O Mary, at thy window be,
    It is the wished, the trysted hour!
Those smiles and glances let me see,
    That mak the miser's treasure poor.
    How blythely wad I bide the stoure,
A weary slave frae sun to sun,
    Could I the rich reward secure,
The lovely Mary Morison!

Yestreen, when to the trembling string
    The dance gaed through the lighted ha',
To thee my fancy took its wing,
    I sat, but neither heard or saw:

Tho' this was fair, and that was braw,
And yon the toast of a' the toun,
  I sighed, and said amang them a',
'Ye are na Mary Morison.'

O Mary, canst thou wreck his peace,
  Wha for thy sake wad gladly die?
Or canst thou break that heart of his
  Whase only faut is loving thee?
  If love for love thou wilt na gie,
At least be pity to me shown!
  A thought ungentle canna be
The thought o' Mary Morison.

XLVI

TRUE UNTIL DEATH

It was a' for our rightfu' King,
  We left fair Scotland's strand;
It was a' for our rightfu' King
  We e'er saw Irish land,
      My dear,
  We e'er saw Irish land.

Now a' is done that men can do,
  And a' is done in vain;
My love and native land farewell,
  For I maun cross the main,
      My dear,
  For I maun cross the main.

He turned him right and round about
  Upon the Irish shore;
And gae his bridle-reins a shake,
  With adieu for evermore,
      My dear,
  Adieu for evermore.

The sodger from the wars returns,
  The sailor frae the main;
But I hae parted frae my love,
  Never to meet again,
      My dear,
  Never to meet again.

When day is gane, and night is come,
  And a' folk bound to sleep;
I think on him that's far awa,
  The lee-lang night, and weep,
      My dear,
  The lee-lang night, and weep.

Burns.

XLVII

VENICE

ONCE did She hold the gorgeous East in fee
And was the safeguard of the West: the worth
Of Venice did not fall below her birth,
Venice, the eldest Child of Liberty.
She was a maiden City, bright and free;
No guile seduced, no force could violate;
And, when she took unto herself a Mate,

She must espouse the everlasting Sea.
And what if she had seen those glories fade,
Those titles vanish, and that strength decay;
Yet shall some tribute of regret be paid
When her long life hath reached its final day:
Men are we, and must grieve when even the Shade
Of that which once was great is passed away.

XLVIII

DESTINY

It is not to be thought of that the Flood
Of British freedom, which, to the open sea
Of the world's praise, from dark antiquity
Hath flowed, 'with pomp of waters, unwithstood,'
Roused though it be full often to a mood
Which spurns the check of salutary bands,
That this most famous Stream in bogs and sands
Should perish; and to evil and to good
Be lost for ever. In our halls is hung
Armoury of the invincible Knights of old:
We must be free or die, who speak the tongue
That Shakespeare spake; the faith and morals hold
Which Milton held. In everything we are sprung
Of Earth's first blood, have titles manifold.

XLIX

THE MOTHERLAND

When I have borne in memory what has tamed
Great Nations, how ennobling thoughts depart

When men change swords for ledgers, and desert
The student's bower for gold, some fears unnamed
I had, my Country!—am I to be blamed?
But when I think of thee, and what thou art,
Verily, in the bottom of my heart,
Of those unfilial fears I am ashamed.
But dearly must we prize thee; we who find
In thee a bulwark for the cause of men;
And I by my affection was beguiled.
What wonder if a Poet now and then,
Among the many movements of his mind,
Felt for thee as a lover or a child!

L

IDEAL

Milton! thou shouldst be living at this hour:
England hath need of thee: she is a fen
Of stagnant waters: altar, sword, and pen,
Fireside, the heroic wealth of hall and bower,
Have forfeited their ancient English dower
Of inward happiness.   We are selfish men;
Oh! raise us up, return to us again;
And give us manners, virtue, freedom, power.
Thy soul was like a Star, and dwelt apart:
Thou hadst a voice whose sound was like the sea:
Pure as the naked heavens, majestic, free,
So didst thou travel on life's common way,
In cheerful godliness; and yet thy heart
The lowliest duties on itself did lay.

LI

TO DUTY

Stern Daughter of the Voice of God!
O Duty! if that name thou love
Who art a light to guide, a rod
To check the erring, and reprove;
Thou, who art victory and law
When empty terrors overawe;
From vain temptations dost set free;
And calm'st the weary strife of frail humanity!

There are who ask not if thine eye
Be on them; who, in love and truth,
Where no misgiving is, rely
Upon the genial sense of youth:
Glad Hearts! without reproach or blot;
Who do thy work, and know it not:
May joy be theirs while life shall last!
And Thou, if they should totter, teach them to stand fast!

Serene will be our days and bright,
And happy will our nature be,
When love is an unerring light,
And joy its own security.
And they a blissful course may hold
Even now, who, not unwisely bold,
Live in the spirit of this creed;
Yet find that other strength, according to their need.

I, loving freedom, and untried;
No sport of every random gust,
Yet being to myself a guide,
Too blindly have reposed my trust:
And oft, when in my heart was heard
Thy timely mandate, I deferred
The task, in smoother walks to stray;
But thee I now would serve more strictly, if I may.

Through no disturbance of my soul
Or strong compunction in me wrought,
I supplicate for thy control;
But in the quietness of thought:
Me this unchartered freedom tires;
I feel the weight of chance-desires:
My hopes no more must change their name,
I long for a repose that ever is the same.

Stern Lawgiver! yet thou dost wear
The Godhead's most benignant grace;
Nor know we anything so fair
As is the smile upon thy face:
Flowers laugh before thee on their beds
And fragrance in thy footing treads;
Thou dost preserve the stars from wrong;
And the most ancient heavens, through thee, are fresh and strong.

To humbler functions, awful Power!
I call thee: I myself commend
Unto thy guidance from this hour;
O let my weakness have an end!

Give unto me, made lowly wise,
The spirit of self-sacrifice;
The confidence of reason give;
And in the light of truth thy Bondman let me live!

LII

TWO VICTORIES

I SAID, when evil men are strong,
No life is good, no pleasure long,
A weak and cowardly untruth!
Our Clifford was a happy Youth,
And thankful through a weary time
That brought him up to manhood's prime.
Again he wanders forth at will,
And tends a flock from hill to hill:
His garb is humble; ne'er was seen
Such garb with such a noble mien;
Among the shepherd grooms no mate
Hath he, a Child of strength and state!
Yet lacks not friends for simple glee,
Nor yet for higher sympathy.
To his side the fallow-deer
Came, and rested without fear;
The eagle, lord of land and sea,
Stooped down to pay him fealty;
And both the undying fish that swim
Through Bowscale-Tarn did wait on him;
The pair were servants of his eye
In their immortality;

And glancing, gleaming, dark or bright,
Moved to and fro, for his delight.
He knew the rocks which Angels haunt
Upon the mountains visitant;
He hath kenned them taking wing:
And into caves where Faeries sing
He hath entered; and been told
By Voices how men lived of old.
Among the heavens his eye can see
The face of thing that is to be;
And, if that men report him right,
His tongue could whisper words of might.
Now another day is come,
Fitter hope, and nobler doom;
He hath thrown aside his crook,
And hath buried deep his book;
Armour rusting in his halls
On the blood of Clifford calls:
'Quell the Scot!' exclaims the Lance;
'Bear me to the heart of France,'
Is the longing of the Shield;
Tell thy name, thou trembling field;
Field of death, where'er thou be,
Groan thou with our victory!
Happy day, and mighty hour,
When our Shepherd in his power,
Mailed and horsed, with lance and sword,
To his ancestors restored
Like a reappearing Star,
Like a glory from afar,
First shall head the flock of war!

LIII

IN MEMORIAM

NELSON: PITT: FOX

To mute and to material things
New life revolving summer brings;
The genial call dead Nature hears,
And in her glory reappears.
But O my Country's wintry state
What second spring shall renovate?
What powerful call shall bid arise
The buried warlike and the wise;
The mind that thought for Britain's weal,
The hand that grasped the victor steel?
The vernal sun new life bestows
Even on the meanest flower that blows;
But vainly, vainly may he shine,
Where glory weeps o'er NELSON's shrine;
And vainly pierce the solemn gloom,
That shrouds, O PITT, thy hallowed tomb!

Deep graved in every British heart,
O never let those names depart!
Say to your sons,—Lo, here his grave,
Who victor died on Gadite wave;
To him, as to the burning levin,
Short, bright, resistless course was given.
Where'er his country's foes were found
Was heard the fated thunder's sound,
Till burst the bolt on yonder shore,
Rolled, blazed, destroyed,—and was no more.

Nor mourn ye less his perished worth,
Who bade the conqueror go forth,
And launched that thunderbolt of war
On Egypt, Hafnia, Trafalgar;
Who, born to guide such high emprise,
For Britain's weal was early wise;
Alas! to whom the Almighty gave,
For Britain's sins, an early grave!
His worth, who in his mightiest hour
A bauble held the pride of power,
Spurned at the sordid lust of pelf,
And served his Albion for herself;
Who, when the frantic crowd amain
Strained at subjection's bursting rein,
O'er their wild mood full conquest gained,
The pride he would not crush restrained,
Showed their fierce zeal a worthier cause,
And brought the freeman's arm to aid the freeman's laws.

Hadst thou but lived, though stripped of power,
A watchman on the lonely tower,
Thy thrilling trump had roused the land,
When fraud or danger were at hand;
By thee, as by the beacon-light,
Our pilots had kept course aright;
As some proud column, though alone,
Thy strength had propped the tottering throne:
Now is the stately column broke,
The beacon-light is quenched in smoke,

The trumpet's silver sound is still,
The warder silent on the hill!

O think, how to his latest day,
When death, just hovering, claimed his prey,
With Palinure's unaltered mood
Firm at his dangerous post he stood;
Each call for needful rest repelled,
With dying hand the rudder held,
Till in his fall with fateful sway,
The steerage of the realm gave way!
Then, while on Britain's thousand plains
One unpolluted church remains,
Whose peaceful bells ne'er sent around
The bloody tocsin's maddening sound,
But still, upon the hallowed day,
Convoke the swains to praise and pray;
While faith and civil peace are dear,
Grace this cold marble with a tear,—
He, who preserved them, PITT, lies here!

Nor yet suppress the generous sigh,
Because his rival slumbers nigh;
Nor be thy *requiescat* dumb,
Lest it be said o'er Fox's tomb.
For talents mourn, untimely lost,
When best employed, and wanted most;
Mourn genius high, and lore profound,
And wit that loved to play, not wound;
And all the reasoning powers divine,
To penetrate, resolve, combine;

And feelings keen, and fancy's glow,—
They sleep with him who sleeps below:
And, if thou mourn'st they could not save
From error him who owns this grave,
Be every harsher thought suppressed,
And sacred be the last long rest.
Here, where the end of earthly things
Lays heroes, patriots, bards, and kings;
Where stiff the hand, and still the tongue,
Of those who fought, and spoke, and sung;
Here, where the fretted aisles prolong
The distant notes of holy song,
As if some angel spoke agen,
'All peace on earth, good-will to men';
If ever from an English heart,
O, *here* let prejudice depart,
And, partial feeling cast aside,
Record, that Fox a Briton died!
When Europe crouched to France's yoke,
And Austria bent, and Prussia broke,
And the firm Russian's purpose brave
Was bartered by a timorous slave,
Even then dishonour's peace he spurned,
The sullied olive-branch returned,
Stood for his country's glory fast,
And nailed her colours to the mast!
Heaven, to reward his firmness, gave
A portion in this honoured grave,
And ne'er held marble in its trust
Of two such wondrous men the dust.

With more than mortal powers endowed,
How high they soared above the crowd!
Theirs was no common party race,
Jostling by dark intrigue for place;
Like fabled Gods, their mighty war
Shook realms and nations in its jar;
Beneath each banner proud to stand,
Looked up the noblest of the land,
Till through the British world were known
The names of Pitt and Fox alone.
Spells of such force no wizard grave
E'er framed in dark Thessalian cave,
Though his could drain the ocean dry,
And force the planets from the sky.
These spells are spent, and, spent with these
The wine of life is on the lees.
Genius, and taste, and talent gone,
For ever tombed beneath the stone,
Where—taming thought to human pride!—
The mighty chiefs sleep side by side.
Drop upon Fox's grave the tear,
'Twill trickle to his rival's bier;
O'er Pitt's the mournful requiem sound,
And Fox's shall the notes rebound.
The solemn echo seems to cry,—
'Here let their discord with them die.
Speak not for those a separate doom
Whom fate made Brothers in the tomb;
But search the land of living men,
Where wilt thou find their like agen?'

LIV

LOCHINVAR

O, YOUNG Lochinvar is come out of the west,
Through all the wide Border his steed was the best;
And save his good broadsword he weapons had none,
He rode all unarmed, and he rode all alone.
So faithful in love and so dauntless in war,
There never was knight like the young Lochinvar.

He staid not for brake, and he stopped not for stone,
He swam the Eske river where ford there was none;
But ere he alighted at Netherby gate,
The bride had consented, the gallant came late;
For a laggard in love, and a dastard in war,
Was to wed the fair Ellen of brave Lochinvar.

So boldly he entered the Netherby Hall,
Among bride's-men, and kinsmen, and brothers, and all:
Then spoke the bride's father, his hand on his sword,
(For the poor craven bridegroom said never a word,)
'O come ye in peace here, or come ye in war,
Or to dance at our bridal, young Lord Lochinvar?'

'I long wooed your daughter, my suit you denied;
Love swells like the Solway, but ebbs like its tide;
And now am I come with this lost love of mine
To lead but one measure, drink one cup of wine.
There are maidens in Scotland more lovely by far
That would gladly be bride to the young Lochinvar.'

The bride kissed the goblet: the knight took it up,
He quaffed off the wine, and he threw down the cup.
She looked down to blush, and she looked up to sigh,
With a smile on her lips and a tear in her eye.
He took her soft hand, ere her mother could bar,
'Now tread we a measure!' said young Lochinvar.

So stately his form, and so lovely her face,
That never a hall such a galliard did grace;
While her mother did fret, and her father did fume,
And the bridegroom stood dangling his bonnet and plume;
And the bride-maidens whispered, ''Twere better by far,
To have matched our fair cousin with young Lochinvar.'

One touch to her hand and one word in her ear,
When they reached the hall-door, and the charger stood near;
So light to the croup the fair lady he swung,
So light to the saddle before her he sprung!
'She is won! we are gone, over bank, bush, and scaur;
They'll have fleet steeds that follow,' quoth young Lochinvar.

There was mounting 'mong Græmes of the Netherby clan;
Forsters, Fenwicks, and Musgraves, they rode and they ran:

There was racing and chasing on Cannobie Lee,
But the lost bride of Netherby ne'er did they see.
So daring in love and so dauntless in war,
Have ye e'er heard of gallant like young Lochinvar?

LV

FLODDEN

THE MARCH

NEXT morn the Baron climbed the tower,
To view afar the Scottish power
　Encamped on Flodden edge:
The white pavilions made a show,
Like remnants of the winter snow,
　Along the dusky ridge.
Long Marmion looked: at length his eye
Unusual movement might descry
　Amid the shifting lines:
The Scottish host drawn out appears,
For flashing on the hedge of spears
　The eastern sunbeam shines.
Their front now deepening, now extending;
Their flank inclining, wheeling, bending,
Now drawing back, and now descending,
The skilful Marmion well could know,
They watched the motions of some foe
Who traversed on the plain below.

Even so it was. From Flodden ridge
　The Scots beheld the English host
　　Leave Barmore-wood, their evening post,

And heedful watched them as they crossed
The Till by Twisel bridge.
  High sight it is and haughty, while
  They dive into the deep defile;
  Beneath the caverned cliff they fall,
  Beneath the castle's airy wall.
By rock, by oak, by hawthorn-tree,
  Troop after troop are disappearing;
  Troop after troop their banners rearing
Upon the eastern bank you see.
Still pouring down the rocky den,
  Where flows the sullen Till,
And rising from the dim-wood glen,
Standards on standards, men on men,
  In slow succession still,
And sweeping o'er the Gothic arch,
And pressing on in ceaseless march,
  To gain the opposing hill.
That morn to many a trumpet clang,
Twisel! thy rocks deep echo rang;
And many a chief of birth and rank,
Saint Helen! at thy fountain drank.
Thy hawthorn glade, which now we see
In spring-tide bloom so lavishly,
Had then from many an axe its doom,
To give the marching columns room.

And why stands Scotland idly now,
Dark Flodden! on thy airy brow,
Since England gains the pass the while,
And struggles through the deep defile?

What checks the fiery soul of James?
Why sits that champion of the dames
   Inactive on his steed,
And sees between him and his land,
Between him and Tweed's southern strand,
   His host Lord Surrey lead?
What 'vails the vain knight-errant's brand?
O, Douglas, for thy leading wand!
   Fierce Randolph, for thy speed!
O for one hour of Wallace wight,
Or well-skilled Bruce, to rule the fight,
And cry 'Saint Andrew and our right!'
Another sight had seen that morn,
From Fate's dark book a leaf been torn,
And Flodden had been Bannockburn!
The precious hour has passed in vain,
And England's host has gained the plain;
Wheeling their march, and circling still,
Around the base of Flodden hill.

THE ATTACK

'But see! look up—on Flodden bent
The Scottish foe has fired his tent.'
   And sudden, as he spoke,
From the sharp ridges of the hill,
All downward to the banks of Till
   Was wreathed in sable smoke.
Volumed and fast, and rolling far,
The cloud enveloped Scotland's war,
   As down the hill they broke;

Nor martial shout nor minstrel tone
Announced their march; their tread alone,
At times one warning trumpet blown,
   At times a stifled hum,
Told England, from his mountain-throne
   King James did rushing come.
Scarce could they hear, or see their foes,
   Until at weapon-point they close.
They close in clouds of smoke and dust,
With sword-sway and with lance's thrust;
   And such a yell was there
Of sudden and portentous birth,
As if men fought upon the earth
And fiends in upper air;
O life and death were in the shout,
Recoil and rally, charge and rout,
   And triumph and despair.
Long looked the anxious squires; their eye
Could in the darkness nought descry.

At length the freshening western blast
Aside the shroud of battle cast;
And first the ridge of mingled spears
Above the brightening cloud appears;
And in the smoke the pennons flew,
As in the storm the white sea-mew.
Then marked they, dashing broad and far,
The broken billows of the war,
And plumèd crests of chieftains brave
Floating like foam upon the wave;
   But nought distinct they see:

Wide raged the battle on the plain;
Spears shook, and falchions flashed amain;
Fell England's arrow-flight like rain;
Crests rose, and stooped, and rose again,
   Wild and disorderly.
Amid the scene of tumult, high
They saw Lord Marmion's falcon fly:
And stainless Tunstall's banner white
And Edmund Howard's lion bright
Still bear them bravely in the fight:
   Although against them come
Of gallant Gordons many a one,
And many a stubborn Badenoch-man,
And many a rugged Border clan,
   With Huntly and with Home.

Far on the left, unseen the while,
Stanley broke Lennox and Argyle;
Though there the western mountaineer
Rushed with bare bosom on the spear,
And flung the feeble targe aside,
And with both hands the broadsword plied.
'Twas vain: but Fortune, on the right,
With fickle smile cheered Scotland's fight.
Then fell that spotless banner white,
   The Howard's lion fell;
Yet still Lord Marmion's falcon flew
With wavering flight, while fiercer grew
   Around the battle-yell.
The Border slogan rent the sky!
A Home! a Gordon! was the cry:

Loud were the clanging blows;
Advanced, forced back, now low, now high,
　　The pennon sank and rose;
As bends the bark's mast in the gale,
When rent are rigging, shrouds, and sail,
　　It wavered 'mid the foes.

THE LAST STAND

By this, though deep the evening fell,
Still rose the battle's deadly swell,
For still the Scots, around their King,
Unbroken, fought in desperate ring.
Where's now their victor vaward wing,
　　Where Huntly, and where Home?
O for a blast of that dread horn,
On Fontarabian echoes borne,
　　That to King Charles did come,
When Roland brave, and Olivier,
And every paladin and peer,
　　On Roncesvalles died!
Such blast might warn them, not in vain,
To quit the plunder of the slain,
And turn the doubtful day again,
　　While yet on Flodden side
Afar the Royal Standard flies,
And round it toils, and bleeds, and dies
　　Our Caledonian pride!

But as they left the dark'ning heath,
More desperate grew the strife of death.

The English shafts in volleys hailed,
In headlong charge their horse assailed;
Front, flank, and rear, the squadrons sweep
To break the Scottish circle deep
    That fought around their King.
But yet, though thick the shafts as snow,
Though charging knights like whirlwinds go,
Though bill-men ply the ghastly blow,
    Unbroken was the ring;
The stubborn spear-men still made good
Their dark impenetrable wood,
Each stepping where his comrade stood,
    The instant that he fell.
No thought was there of dastard flight;
Linked in the serried phalanx tight,
Groom fought like noble, squire like knight,
    As fearlessly and well;
Till utter darkness closed her wing
O'er their thin host and wounded King.
Then skilful Surrey's sage commands
Led back from strife his shattered bands;
And from the charge they drew,
As mountain waves from wasted lands
    Sweep back to ocean blue.
Then did their loss his foemen know;
Their King, their Lords, their mightiest low,
They melted from the field, as snow,
When streams are swoln and south winds blow,
    Dissolves in silent dew.
Tweed's echoes heard the ceaseless plash,
    While many a broken band

Disordered through her currents dash,
    To gain the Scottish land;
To town and tower, to town and dale,
To tell red Flodden's dismal tale,
And raise the universal wail.
Tradition, legend, tune, and song
Shall many an age that wail prolong:
Still from the sire the son shall hear
Of the stern strife and carnage drear
    Of Flodden's fatal field,
Where shivered was fair Scotland's spear,
    And broken was her shield!

LVI

THE CHASE

THE stag at eve had drunk his fill,
Where danced the moon on Monan's rill,
And deep his midnight lair had made
In lone Glenartney's hazel shade;
But, when the sun his beacon red
Had kindled on Benvoirlich's head,
The deep-mouthed bloodhound's heavy bay
Resounded up the rocky way,
And faint from farther distance borne
Were heard the clanging hoof and horn.

As Chief, who hears his warder call,
'To arms! the foemen storm the wall,'
The antlered monarch of the waste
Sprang from his heathery couch in haste.

But, ere his fleet career he took,
The dew-drops from his flanks he shook;
Like crested leader proud and high,
Tossed his beamed frontlet to the sky;
A moment gazed adown the dale,
A moment snuffed the tainted gale,
A moment listened to the cry
That thickened as the chase drew nigh;
Then, as the headmost foes appeared,
With one brave bound the copse he cleared,
And, stretching forward free and far,
Sought the wild heaths of Uam-Var.

Yelled on the view the opening pack;
Rock, glen, and cavern paid them back:
To many a mingled sound at once
The awakened mountain gave response.
A hundred dogs bayed deep and strong,
Clattered a hundred steeds along,
Their peal the merry horns rang out,
A hundred voices joined the shout;
With hark and whoop and wild halloo
No rest Benvoirlich's echoes knew.
Far from the tumult fled the roe,
Close in her covert cowered the doe,
The falcon from her cairn on high
Cast on the rout a wondering eye,
Till far beyond her piercing ken
The hurricane had swept the glen.
Faint and more faint, its failing din
Returned from cavern, cliff, and linn,

And silence settled wide and still
On the lone wood and mighty hill.

Less loud the sounds of silvan war
Disturbed the heights of Uam-Var,
And roused the cavern where, 'tis told,
A giant made his den of old;
For ere that steep ascent was won,
High in his pathway hung the sun,
And many a gallant, stayed perforce,
Was fain to breathe his faltering horse,
And of the trackers of the deer
Scarce half the lessening pack was near;
So shrewdly on the mountain-side
Had the bold burst their mettle tried.

The noble stag was pausing now
Upon the mountain's southern brow,
Where broad extended, far beneath,
The varied realms of fair Menteith.
With anxious eye he wandered o'er
Mountain and meadow, moss and moor,
And pondered refuge from his toil
By far Lochard or Aberfoyle.
But nearer was the copsewood grey
That waved and wept on Loch-Achray,
And mingled with the pine-trees blue
On the bold cliffs of Benvenue.
Fresh vigour with the hope returned,
With flying foot the heath he spurned,
Held westward with unwearied race,
And left behind the panting chase.

'Twere long to tell what steeds gave o'er,
As swept the hunt through Cambus-more;
What reins were tightened in despair,
When rose Benledi's ridge in air;
Who flagged upon Bochastle's heath,
Who shunned to stem the flooded Teith,
For twice that day from shore to shore
The gallant stag swam stoutly o'er.
Few were the stragglers, following far,
That reached the lake of Vennachar;
And when the Brigg of Turk was won,
The headmost horseman rode alone.

Alone, but with unbated zeal,
That horseman plied the scourge and steel;
For jaded now and spent with toil,
Embossed with foam and dark with soil,
While every gasp with sobs he drew,
The labouring stag strained full in view.
Two dogs of black Saint Hubert's breed,
Unmatched for courage, breath, and speed,
Fast on his flying traces came
And all but won that desperate game;
For scarce a spear's length from his haunch
Vindictive toiled the bloodhounds staunch;
Nor nearer might the dogs attain,
Nor farther might the quarry strain.
Thus up the margin of the lake,
Between the precipice and brake,
O'er stock and rock their race they take.

The Hunter marked that mountain high,
The lone lake's western boundary,
And deemed the stag must turn to bay
Where that huge rampart barred the way;
Already glorying in the prize,
Measured his antlers with his eyes;
For the death-wound and death-halloo
Mustered his breath, his whinyard drew;
But thundering as he came prepared,
With ready arm and weapon bared,
The wily quarry shunned the shock,
And turned him from the opposing rock;
Then, dashing down a darksome glen,
Soon lost to hound and hunter's ken,
In the deep Trosach's wildest nook
His solitary refuge took.
There, while close couched, the thicket shed
Cold dews and wild-flowers on his head,
He heard the baffled dogs in vain
Rave through the hollow pass amain,
Chiding the rocks that yelled again.

Close on the hounds the hunter came,
To cheer them on the vanished game;
But, stumbling in the rugged dell,
The gallant horse exhausted fell.
The impatient rider strove in vain
To rouse him with the spur and rein,
For the good steed, his labours o'er,
Stretched his stiff limbs, to rise no more;
Then touched with pity and remorse
He sorrowed o'er the expiring horse.

'I little thought, when first thy rein
I slacked upon the banks of Seine,
That Highland eagle e'er should feed
On thy fleet limbs, my matchless steed!
Woe worth the chase, woe worth the day,
That costs thy life, my gallant grey!'

Then through the dell his horn resounds,
From vain pursuit to call the hounds.
Back limped with slow and crippled pace
The sulky leaders of the chase;
Close to their master's side they pressed,
With drooping tail and humbled crest;
But still the dingle's hollow throat
Prolonged the swelling bugle-note.
The owlets started from their dream,
The eagles answered with their scream,
Round and around the sounds were cast,
Till echoes seemed an answering blast;
And on the hunter hied his way,
To join some comrades of the day.

LVII

THE OUTLAW

O, BRIGNALL banks are wild and fair,
  And Greta woods are green,
And you may gather garlands there
  Would grace a summer queen.

And as I rode by Dalton-hall,
　　Beneath the turrets high,
A Maiden on the castle wall
　　Was singing merrily:

'O, Brignall banks are fresh and fair,
　　And Greta woods are green;
I'd rather rove with Edmund there
　　Than reign our English queen.'

'If, Maiden, thou wouldst wend with me,
　　To leave both tower and town,
Thou first must guess what life lead we
　　That dwell by dale and down.
And if thou canst that riddle read,
　　As read full well you may,
Then to the greenwood shalt thou speed,
　　As blythe as Queen of May.'

Yet sang she, 'Brignall banks are fair,
　　And Greta woods are green;
I'd rather rove with Edmund there
　　Than reign our English queen.

I read you, by your bugle-horn
　　And by your palfrey good,
I read you for a Ranger sworn
　　To keep the king's greenwood.'
'A Ranger, lady, winds his horn,
　　And 'tis at peep of light;
His blast is heard at merry morn,
　　And mine at dead of night.'

Yet sang she 'Brignall banks are fair,
  And Greta woods are gay;
I would I were with Edmund there,
  To reign his Queen of May!

With burnished brand and musketoon
  So gallantly you come,
I read you for a bold Dragoon
  That lists the tuck of drum.'
'I list no more the tuck of drum,
  No more the trumpet hear;
But when the beetle sounds his hum,
  My comrades take the spear.

And O! though Brignall banks be fair,
  And Greta woods be gay,
Yet mickle must the maiden dare
  Would reign my Queen of May!

Maiden! a nameless life I lead,
  A nameless death I'll die!
The fiend, whose lantern lights the mead,
  Were better mate than I!
And when I'm with my comrades met,
  Beneath the Greenwood bough,
What once we were we all forget,
  Nor think what we are now.

Yet Brignall banks are fresh and fair,
  And Greta woods are green,
And you may gather garlands there
  Would grace a summer queen.'

LVIII

PIBROCH

Pibroch of Donuil Dhu,
   Pibroch of Donuil,
Wake thy wild voice anew,
   Summon Clan-Conuil.
Come away, come away,
   Hark to the summons!
Come in your war array,
   Gentles and commons.

Come from deep glen and
   From mountains so rocky,
The war-pipe and pennon
   Are at Inverlocky.
Come every hill-plaid and
   True heart that wears one,
Come every steel blade and
   Strong hand that bears one.

Leave untended the herd,
   The flock without shelter;
Leave the corpse uninterred,
   The bride at the altar;
Leave the deer, leave the steer,
   Leave nets and barges:
Come with your fighting gear,
   Broadswords and targes.

Come as the winds come when
  Forests are rended,
Come as the waves come when
  Navies are stranded:
Faster come, faster come,
  Faster and faster,
Chief, vassal, page and groom,
  Tenant and master.

Fast they come, fast they come;
  See how they gather!
Wide waves the eagle plume
  Blended with heather.
Cast your plaids, draw your blades,
  Forward each man set!
Pibroch of Donuil Dhu,
  Knell for the onset!

LIX

THE OMNIPOTENT

'Why sitt'st thou by that ruined hall,
  Thou agèd carle so stern and grey?
Dost thou its former pride recall,
  Or ponder how it passed away?'

'Know'st thou not me?' the Deep Voice cried;
  'So long enjoyed, so often misused,
Alternate, in thy fickle pride,
  Desired, neglected, and accused!

Before my breath, like blazing flax,
   Man and his marvels pass away!
And changing empires wane and wax,
   Are founded, flourish, and decay.

Redeem mine hours—the space is brief—
   While in my glass the sand-grains shiver,
And measureless thy joy or grief,
   When TIME and thou shalt part for ever!'

LX

THE RED HARLAW

THE herring loves the merry moonlight,
   The mackerel loves the wind,
But the oyster loves the dredging sang,
   For they come of a gentle kind.

Now haud your tongue, baith wife and carle,
   And listen, great and sma',
And I will sing of Glenallan's Earl
   That fought on the red Harlaw.

The cronach's cried on Bennachie,
   And doun the Don and a',
And hieland and lawland may mournfu' be
   For the sair field of Harlaw.

They saddled a hundred milk-white steeds,
   They hae bridled a hundred black,
With a chafron of steel on each horse's head
   And a good knight upon his back.

They hadna ridden a mile, a mile,
    A mile, but barely ten,
When Donald came branking down the brae
    Wi' twenty thousand men.

Their tartans they were waving wide,
    Their glaives were glancing clear,
The pibrochs rang frae side to side,
    Would deafen ye to hear.

The great Earl in his stirrups stood,
    That Highland host to see:
'Now here a knight that's stout and good
    May prove a jeopardie:

What wouldst thou do, my squire so gay,
    That rides beside my reyne,
Were ye Glenallan's Earl the day,
    And I were Roland Cheyne?

To turn the rein were sin and shame,
    To fight were wondrous peril:
What would ye do now, Roland Cheyne,
    Were ye Glenallan's Earl?'

'Were I Glenallan's Earl this tide,
    And ye were Roland Cheyne,
The spur should be in my horse's side,
    And the bridle upon his mane.

If they hae twenty thousand blades,
    And we twice ten times ten,
Yet they hae but their tartan plaids,
    And we are mail-clad men.

My horse shall ride through ranks sae rude,
   As through the moorland fern,
Then ne'er let the gentle Norman blude
   Grow cauld for Highland kerne.'

LXI

FAREWELL

Farewell! Farewell! the voice you hear
   Has left its last soft tone with you;
Its next must join the seaward cheer,
   And shout among the shouting crew.

The accents which I scarce could form
   Beneath your frown's controlling check,
Must give the word, above the storm,
   To cut the mast and clear the wreck.

The timid eye I dared not raise,
   The hand that shook when pressed to thine,
Must point the guns upon the chase,
   Must bid the deadly cutlass shine.

To all I love, or hope, or fear,
   Honour or own, a long adieu!
To all that life has soft and dear,
   Farewell! save memory of you!

LXII

BONNY DUNDEE

To the Lords of Convention 'twas Claver'se who spoke,
'Ere the King's crown shall fall there are crowns to be broke;
So let each Cavalier who loves honour and me,
Come follow the bonnet of Bonny Dundee.

   Come fill up my cup, come fill up my can,
   Come saddle your horses, and call up your men;
   Come open the West Port, and let me gang free,
   And it's room for the bonnets of Bonny Dundee!'

Dundee he is mounted, he rides up the street,
The bells are rung backward, the drums they are beat;
But the Provost, douce man, said, 'Just e'en let him be,
The Gude Town is weel quit of that Deil of Dundee.'

As he rode down the sanctified bends of the Bow,
Ilk carline was flyting and shaking her pow;
But the young plants of grace they looked couthie and slee,
Thinking, luck to thy bonnet, thou Bonny Dundee!

With sour-featured Whigs the Grassmarket was crammed,
As if half the West had set tryst to be hanged;
There was spite in each look, there was fear in each e'e,
As they watched for the bonnets of Bonny Dundee.

These cowls of Kilmarnock had spits and had spears,
And lang-hafted gullies to kill Cavaliers;
But they shrunk to close-heads, and the causeway was free,
At the toss of the bonnet of Bonny Dundee.

He spurred to the foot of the proud Castle rock,
And with the gay Gordon he gallantly spoke;
'Let Mons Meg and her marrows speak twa words or three
For the love of the bonnet of Bonny Dundee.'

The Gordon demands of him which way he goes:
'Where'er shall direct me the shade of Montrose!
Your Grace in short space shall hear tidings of me,
Or that low lies the bonnet of Bonny Dundee.

'There are hills beyond Pentland, and lands beyond Forth,
If there's lords in the Lowlands, there's chiefs in the North;
There are wild Duniewassals three thousand times three,
Will cry *hoigh!* for the bonnet of Bonny Dundee.

There's brass on the target of barkened bull-hide;
There's steel in the scabbard that dangles beside;
The brass shall be burnished, the steel shall flash free
At a toss of the bonnet of Bonny Dundee.

Away to the hills, to the caves, to the rocks,
Ere I owe an usurper, I'll couch with the fox;
And tremble, false Whigs, in the midst of your glee,
You have not seen the last of my bonnet and me!'

He waved his proud hand, and the trumpets were
    blown,
The kettle-drums clashed, and the horsemen rode on,
Till on Ravelston's cliffs and on Clermiston's lee
Died away the wild war-notes of Bonny Dundee.

> Come fill up my cup, come fill up my can,
> Come saddle the horses and call up the men,
> Come open your gates, and let me gae free,
> For it's up with the bonnets of Bonny Dundee!
> *Sir Walter Scott.*

LXIII

ROMANCE

IN Xanadu did Kubla Khan
A stately pleasure-dome decree:
Where Alph, the sacred river, ran
Through caverns measureless to man
Down to a sunless sea.
So twice five miles of fertile ground
With walls and towers were girdled round:
And there were gardens bright with sinuous rills
Where blossomed many an incense-bearing tree;
And here were forests ancient as the hills,
Enfolding sunny spots of greenery.

But O! that deep romantic chasm which slanted
Down the green hill athwart a cedarn cover!
A savage place! as holy and enchanted
As e'er beneath a waning moon was haunted
By woman wailing for her demon-lover!

And from this chasm, with ceaseless turmoil seething,
As if this earth in fast thick pants were breathing,
A mighty fountain momently was forced:
Amid whose swift half-intermitted burst
Huge fragments vaulted like rebounding hail,
Or chaffy grain beneath the thresher's flail:
And 'mid these dancing rocks at once and ever
It flung up momently the sacred river.
Five miles meandering with a mazy motion
Through wood and dale the sacred river ran,
Then reached the caverns measureless to man,
And sank in tumult to a lifeless ocean:
And 'mid this tumult Kubla heard from far
Ancestral voices prophesying war!

The shadow of the dome of pleasure
Floated midway on the waves;
Where was heard the mingled measure
From the fountain and the caves.
It was a miracle of rare device,
A sunny pleasure-dome with caves of ice!
A damsel with a dulcimer
In a vision once I saw:
It was an Abyssinian maid,
And on her dulcimer she played,
Singing of Mount Abora.
Could I revive within me
Her symphony and song,
To such a deep delight 'twould win me,
That with music loud and long,
I would build that dome in air,

That sunny dome! those caves of ice!
And all who heard should see them there,
And all should cry, Beware! Beware!
His flashing eyes, his floating hair!
Weave a circle round him thrice,
And close your eyes with holy dread,
For he on honey-dew hath fed,
And drunk the milk of Paradise.

Coleridge.

LXIV

SACRIFICE

IPHIGENEIA, when she heard her doom
At Aulis, and when all beside the King
Had gone away, took his right hand, and said,
'O father! I am young and very happy.
I do not think the pious Calchas heard
Distinctly what the Goddess spake. Old-age
Obscures the senses. If my nurse, who knew
My voice so well, sometimes misunderstood
While I was resting on her knee both arms
And hitting it to make her mind my words,
And looking in her face, and she in mine,
Might he not also hear one word amiss,
Spoken from so far off, even from Olympus?'
The father placed his cheek upon her head,
And tears dropt down it, but the king of men
Replied not. Then the maiden spake once more.
'O father! say'st thou nothing? Hear'st thou not
Me, whom thou ever hast, until this hour,

Listened to fondly, and awakened me
To hear my voice amid the voice of birds,
When it was inarticulate as theirs,
And the down deadened it within the nest?'
He moved her gently from him, silent still,
And this, and this alone, brought tears from her,
Although she saw fate nearer: then with sighs,
'I thought to have laid down my hair before
Benignant Artemis, and not have dimmed
Her polisht altar with my virgin blood;
I thought to have selected the white flowers
To please the Nymphs, and to have asked of each
By name, and with no sorrowful regret,
Whether, since both my parents willed the change,
I might at Hymen's feet bend my clipt brow;
And (after those who mind us girls the most)
Adore our own Athena, that she would
Regard me mildly with her azure eyes.
But, father! to see you no more, and see
Your love, O father! go ere I am gone.' . . .
Gently he moved her off, and drew her back,
Bending his lofty head far over hers,
And the dark depths of nature heaved and burst.
He turned away; not far, but silent still.
She now first shuddered; for in him, so nigh,
So long a silence seemed the approach of death,
And like it. Once again she raised her voice.
'O father! if the ships are now detained,
And all your vows move not the Gods above,
When the knife strikes me there will be one **prayer**
The less to them: and purer can there be

Any, or more fervent than the daughter's prayer
For her dear father's safety and success?'
A groan that shook him shook not his resolve.
An aged man now entered, and without
One word, stept slowly on, and took the wrist
Of the pale maiden. She looked up, and saw
The fillet of the priest and calm cold eyes.
Then turned she where her parent stood, and cried,
'O father! grieve no more: the ships can sail.'
Landor.

LXV

SOLDIER AND SAILOR

I LOVE contemplating, apart
   From all his homicidal glory,
The traits that soften to our heart
   Napoleon's story!

'Twas when his banners at Boulogne
   Armed in our island every freeman,
His navy chanced to capture one
   Poor British seaman.

They suffered him, I know not how,
   Unprisoned on the shore to roam;
And aye was bent his longing brow
   On England's home.

His eye, methinks, pursued the flight
   Of birds to Britain half-way over
With envy; *they* could reach the white
   Dear cliffs of Dover.

A stormy midnight watch, he thought,
  Than this sojourn would have been dearer,
If but the storm his vessel brought
  To England nearer.

At last, when care had banished sleep,
  He saw one morning—dreaming—doating,
An empty hogshead from the deep
  Come shoreward floating;

He hid it in a cave, and wrought
  The live-long day laborious; lurking
Until he launched a tiny boat
  By mighty working.

Heaven help us! 'twas a thing beyond
  Description, wretched: such a wherry
Perhaps ne'er ventured on a pond,
  Or crossed a ferry.

For ploughing in the salt-sea field,
  It would have made the boldest shudder;
Untarred, uncompassed, and unkeeled,
  No sail—no rudder.

From neighb'ring woods he interlaced
  His sorry skiff with wattled willows;
And thus equipped he would have passed
  The foaming billows—

But Frenchmen caught him on the beach,
  His little Argo sorely jeering;
Till tidings of him chanced to reach
  Napoleon's hearing.

With folded arms Napoleon stood,
   Serene alike in peace and danger;
And, in his wonted attitude,
   Addressed the stranger:—

'Rash man, that wouldst yon Channel pass
   On twigs and staves so rudely fashioned;
Thy heart with some sweet British lass
   Must be impassioned.'

'I have no sweetheart,' said the lad;
   'But—absent long from one another—
Great was the longing that I had
   To see my mother.'

'And so thou shalt,' Napoleon said,
   'Ye've both my favour fairly won;
A noble mother must have bred
   So brave a son.'

He gave the tar a piece of gold,
   And, with a flag of truce, commanded
He should be shipped to England Old,
   And safely landed.

Our sailor oft could scantly shift
   To find a dinner, plain and hearty;
But *never* changed the coin and gift
   Of Bonaparté.

LXVI

'YE MARINERS'

Ye Mariners of England!
That guard our native seas;
Whose flag has braved a thousand years
The battle and the breeze!
Your glorious standard launch again
To match another foe!
And sweep through the deep,
While the stormy winds do blow;
While the battle rages loud and long,
And the stormy winds do blow.

The spirits of your fathers
Shall start from every wave!
For the deck it was their field of fame,
And Ocean was their grave:
Where Blake and mighty Nelson fell
Your manly hearts shall glow,
As ye sweep through the deep,
While the stormy winds do blow;
While the battle rages loud and long,
And the stormy winds do blow.

Britannia needs no bulwarks,
No towers along the steep;
Her march is o'er the mountain-waves,
Her home is on the deep.
With thunders from her native oak
She quells the floods below,

As they roar on the shore,
When the stormy winds do blow;
When the battle rages loud and long,
And the stormy winds do blow.

The meteor flag of England
Shall yet terrific burn;
Till danger's troubled night depart,
And the star of peace return.
Then, then, ye ocean warriors!
Our song and feast shall flow
To the fame of your name,
When the storm has ceased to blow;
When the fiery fight is heard no more,
And the storm has ceased to blow.

LXVII

THE BATTLE OF THE BALTIC

Of Nelson and the North
Sing the glorious day's renown,
When to battle fierce came forth
All the might of Denmark's crown,
And her arms along the deep proudly shone;
By each gun the lighted brand
In a bold determined hand,
And the Prince of all the land
Led them on.

Like leviathans afloat,
Lay their bulwarks on the brine;

While the sign of battle flew
On the lofty British line:
It was ten of April morn by the chime:
As they drifted on their path,
There was silence deep as death;
And the boldest held his breath,
For a time.

But the might of England flushed
To anticipate the scene;
And her van the fleeter rushed
O'er the deadly space between.
'Hearts of oak!' our captains cried; when each gun
From its adamantine lips
Spread a death-shade round the ships,
Like the hurricane eclipse
Of the sun.

Again! again! again!
And the havoc did not slack,
Till a feeble cheer the Dane,
To our cheering sent us back;—
Their shots along the deep slowly boom:—
Then cease—and all is wail,
As they strike the shattered sail;
Or, in conflagration pale
Light the gloom.

Now joy, Old England, raise
For the tidings of thy might,
By the festal cities' blaze,
Whilst the wine-cup shines in light;

And yet amidst that joy and uproar,
    Let us think of them that sleep
    Full many a fathom deep
    By thy wild and stormy steep,
Elsinore!

Campbell.

LXVIII

BATTLE SONG

DAY, like our souls, is fiercely dark;
    What then? 'Tis day!
We sleep no more; the cock crows—hark!
    To arms! away!
They come! they come! the knell is rung
    Of us or them;
Wide o'er their march the pomp is flung
    Of gold and gem.
What collared hound of lawless sway,
    To famine dear,
What pensioned slave of Attila,
    Leads in the rear?
Come they from Scythian wilds afar
    Our blood to spill?
Wear they the livery of the Czar?
    They do his will.
Nor tasselled silk, nor epaulette,
    Nor plume, nor torse—
No splendour gilds, all sternly met,
    Our foot and horse.

But, dark and still, we inly glow,
    Condensed in ire!
Strike, tawdry slaves, and ye shall know
    Our gloom is fire.
In vain your pomp, ye evil powers,
    Insults the land;
Wrongs, vengeance, and *the cause* are ours,
    And God's right hand!
Madmen! they trample into snakes
    The wormy clod!
Like fire, beneath their feet awakes
    The sword of God!
Behind, before, above, below,
    They rouse the brave;
Where'er they go, they make a foe,
    Or find a grave.

Elliott.

LXIX

LOYALTY

Hame, hame, hame, hame fain wad I be,
O hame, hame, hame, to my ain countrie!
When the flower is i' the bud and the leaf is on the tree,
The lark shall sing me hame in my ain countrie;
Hame, hame, hame, hame fain wad I be,
O hame, hame, hame, to my ain countrie!

The green leaf o' loyaltie's begun for to fa',
The bonnie white rose it is withering an' a';
But I'll water 't wi' the blude of usurping tyrannie,
An' green it will grow in my ain countrie.

Hame, hame, hame, hame fain wad I be,
O hame, hame, hame, to my ain countrie!

The great are now gane, a' wha ventured to save;
The new grass is springing on the tap o' their grave:
But the sun thro' the mirk blinks blythe in my e'e,
'I'll shine on ye yet in yere ain countrie.'
Hame, hame, hame, hame fain wad I be,
Hame, hame, hame, to my ain countrie!

LXX

A SEA-SONG

A WET sheet and a flowing sea,
   A wind that follows fast
And fills the white and rustling sail
   And bends the gallant mast;
And bends the gallant mast, my boys,
   While like the eagle free
Away the good ship flies, and leaves
   Old England on the lee.

O for a soft and gentle wind!
   I heard a fair one cry;
But give to me the snoring breeze
   And white waves heaving high;
And white waves heaving high, my lads,
   The good ship tight and free—
The world of waters is our home,
   And merry men are we.

There's tempest in yon hornèd moon,
    And lightning in yon cloud;
But hark the music, mariners!
    The wind is piping loud;
The wind is piping loud, my boys,
    The lightning flashes free—
While the hollow oak our palace is,
    Our heritage the sea.

Cunningham.

LXXI

A SONG OF THE SEA

The Sea! the Sea! the open Sea!
The blue, the fresh, the ever free!
Without a mark, without a bound,
It runneth the earth's wide regions 'round;
It plays with the clouds; it mocks the skies;
Or like a cradled creature lies.

I'm on the Sea! I'm on the Sea!
I am where I would ever be;
With the blue above, and the blue below,
And silence wheresoe'er I go;
If a storm should come and awake the deep,
What matter? *I* shall ride and sleep.

I love (O! *how* I love) to ride
On the fierce foaming bursting tide,
When every mad wave drowns the moon,
Or whistles aloft his tempest tune,
And tells how goeth the world below,
And why the south-west blasts do blow.

I never was on the dull, tame shore,
But I loved the great Sea more and more,
And backwards flew to her billowy breast,
Like a bird that seeketh its mother's nest;
And a mother she *was*, and *is* to me;
For I was born on the open Sea!

The waves were white, and red the morn,
In the noisy hour when I was born;
And the whale it whistled, the porpoise rolled,
And the dolphins bared their backs of gold;
And never was heard such an outcry wild
As welcomed to life the Ocean-child!

I've lived since then, in calm and strife,
Full fifty summers a sailor's life,
With wealth to spend, and a power to range,
But never have sought, nor sighed for change;
And Death, whenever he come to me,
Shall come on the wide unbounded Sea!

Procter.

LXXII

SENNACHERIB

The Assyrian came down like the wolf on the fold,
And his cohorts were gleaming in purple and gold;
And the sheen of their spears was like stars on the sea,
When the blue wave rolls nightly on deep Galilee.

Like the leaves of the forest when Summer is green,
That host with their banners at sunset were seen:

Like the leaves of the forest when Autumn hath blown,
That host on the morrow lay withered and strown.

For the Angel of Death spread his wings on the blast,
And breathed in the face of the foe as he passed;
And the eyes of the sleepers waxed deadly and chill,
And their hearts but once heaved, and for ever grew still!

And there lay the steed with his nostril all wide,
But through it there rolled not the breath of his pride:
And the foam of his gasping lay white on the turf,
And cold as the spray of the rock-beating surf.

And there lay the rider distorted and pale,
With the dew on his brow and the rust on his mail;
And the tents were all silent, the banners alone,
The lances unlifted, the trumpet unblown.

And the widows of Ashur are loud in their wail,
And the idols are broke in the temple of Baal;
And the might of the Gentile, unsmote by the sword,
Hath melted like snow in the glance of the Lord!

LXXIII

THE STORMING OF CORINTH

THE SIGNAL

The night is past, and shines the sun
As if that morn were a jocund one.
Lightly and brightly breaks away
The Morning from her mantle grey,
And the noon will look on a sultry day.

Hark to the trump, and the drum,
And the mournful sound of the barbarous horn,
And the flap of the banners that flit as they're borne,
And the neigh of the steed, and the multitude's hum,
And the clash, and the shout, 'They come! they come!'
The horsetails are plucked from the ground, and the sword
From its sheath; and they form, and but wait for the word.
Tartar, and Spahi, and Turcoman,
Strike your tents, and throng to the van;
Mount ye, spur ye, skirr the plain,
That the fugitive may flee in vain,
When he breaks from the town; and none escape,
Aged or young, in the Christian shape;
While your fellows on foot, in a fiery mass,
Bloodstain the breach through which they pass.
The steeds are all bridled, and snort to the rein;
Curved is each neck, and flowing each mane;
White is the foam of their champ on the bit:
The spears are uplifted; the matches are lit;
The cannon are pointed, and ready to roar,
And crush the wall they have crumbled before:
Forms in his phalanx each janizar;
Alp at their head; his right arm is bare,
So is the blade of his scimitar;
The khan and the pachas are all at their post;
The vizier himself at the head of the host.
When the culverin's signal is fired, then on;
Leave not in Corinth a living one—

A priest at her altars, a chief in her halls,
A hearth in her mansions, a stone on her walls.
God and the prophet—Alla Hu!
Up to the skies with that wild halloo!
'There the breach lies for passage, the ladder to scale;
And your hands on your sabres, and how should ye fail?
He who first downs with the red cross may crave
His heart's dearest wish; let him ask it, and have!'
Thus uttered Coumourgi, the dauntless vizier;
The reply was the brandish of sabre and spear,
And the shout of fierce thousands in joyous ire:—
Silence—hark to the signal—fire!

THE ASSAULT

As the spring-tides, with heavy plash,
From the cliffs invading dash
Huge fragments, sapped by the ceaseless flow,
Till white and thundering down they go,
Like the avalanche's snow
On the Alpine vales below;
Thus at length, outbreathed and worn,
Corinth's sons were downward borne
By the long and oft renewed
Charge of the Moslem multitude.
In firmness they stood, and in masses they fell,
Heaped by the host of the infidel,
Hand to hand, and foot to foot:
Nothing there, save death, was mute:
Stroke, and thrust, and flash, and cry
For quarter or for victory,

Mingle there with the volleying thunder,
Which makes the distant cities wonder
How the sounding battle goes,
If with them, or for their foes;
If they must mourn, or may rejoice
In that annihilating voice,
Which pierces the deep hills through and through
With an echo dread and new:
You might have heard it, on that day,
O'er Salamis and Megara;
(We have heard the hearers say,)
Even unto Piræus' bay.

From the point of encountering blades to the hilt,
Sabres and swords with blood were gilt;
But the rampart is won, and the spoil begun,
And all but the after carnage done.
Shriller shrieks now mingling come
From within the plundered dome:
Hark to the haste of flying feet
That splash in the blood of the slippery street;
But here and there, where 'vantage ground
Against the foe may still be found,
Desperate groups, of twelve or ten,
Make a pause, and turn again—
With banded backs against the wall,
Fiercely stand, or fighting fall.

There stood an old man—his hairs were white,
But his veteran arm was full of might:
So gallantly bore he the brunt of the fray,

The dead before him, on that day,
In a semicircle lay;
Still he combated unwounded,
Though retreating, unsurrounded.
Many a scar of former fight
Lurked beneath his corselet bright;
But of every wound his body bore,
Each and all had been ta'en before:
Though aged, he was so iron of limb,
Few of our youth could cope with him,
And the foes, whom he singly kept at bay,
Outnumbered his thin hairs of silver grey.
From right to left his sabre swept;
Many an Othman mother wept
Sons that were unborn, when dipped
His weapon first in Moslem gore,
Ere his years could count a score.
Of all he might have been the sire
Who fell that day beneath his ire:
For, sonless left long years ago,
His wrath made many a childless foe;
And since the day, when in the strait
His only boy had met his fate,
His parent's iron hand did doom
More than a human hecatomb.
If shades by carnage be appeased,
Patroclus' spirit less was pleased
Than his, Minotti's son, who died
Where Asia's bounds and ours divide.
Buried he lay, where thousands before
For thousands of years were inhumed on the shore;

What of them is left, to tell
Where they lie, and how they fell?
Not a stone on their turf, nor a bone in their graves;
But they live in the verse that immortally saves.

THE MAGAZINE

Darkly, sternly, and all alone,
Minotti stood o'er the altar-stone:
Madonna's face upon him shone,
Painted in heavenly hues above,
With eyes of light and looks of love;
And placed upon that holy shrine
To fix our thoughts on things divine,
When pictured there, we kneeling see
Her, and the boy-God on her knee,
Smiling sweetly on each prayer
To heaven, as if to waft it there.
Still she smiled; even now she smiles,
Though slaughter streams along her aisles:
Minotti lifted his aged eye,
And made the sign of a cross with a sigh,
Then seized a torch which blazed thereby;
And still he stood, while with steel and flame
Inward and onward the Mussulman came.

The vaults beneath the mosaic stone
Contained the dead of ages gone;
Their names were on the graven floor,
But now illegible with gore;
The carvèd crests, and curious hues
The varied marble's veins diffuse,

Were smeared, and slippery, stained, and strown
With broken swords and helms o'erthrown:
There were dead above, and the dead below
Lay cold in many a coffined row;
You might see them piled in sable state,
By a pale light through a gloomy grate;
But War had entered their dark caves,
And stored along the vaulted graves
Her sulphurous treasures, thickly spread
In masses by the fleshless dead:
   Here, throughout the siege, had been
   The Christians' chiefest magazine;
To these a late formed train now led,
Minotti's last and stern resource
Against the foe's o'erwhelming force.

The foe came on, and few remain
To strive, and those must strive in vain:
For lack of further lives, to slake
The thirst of vengeance now awake,
With barbarous blows they gash the dead,
And lop the already lifeless head,
And fell the statues from their niche,
And spoil the shrines of offerings rich,
And from each other's rude hands wrest
The silver vessels saints had blessed.
To the high altar on they go;
O, but it made a glorious show!
On its table still behold
The cup of consecrated gold;
Massy and deep, a glittering prize,
Brightly it sparkles to plunderers' eyes:

That morn it held the holy wine,
Converted by Christ to his blood so divine,
Which his worshippers drank at the break of day,
To shrive their souls ere they joined in the fray.
Still a few drops within it lay;
And round the sacred table glow
Twelve lofty lamps, in splendid row,
From the purest metal cast;
A spoil—the richest, and the last.

So near they came, the nearest stretched
To grasp the spoil he almost reached,
   When old Minotti's hand
Touched with the torch the train—
   'Tis fired!
Spire, vaults, the shrine, the spoil, the slain,
   The turbaned victors, the Christian band,
All that of living or dead remain,
Hurl'd on high with the shivered fane,
   In one wild roar expired!
The shattered town—the walls thrown down—
The waves a moment backward bent—
The hills that shake, although unrent,
   As if an earthquake passed—
The thousand shapeless things all driven
In cloud and flame athwart the heaven
   By that tremendous blast—
Proclaimed the desperate conflict o'er
On that too long afflicted shore:
Up to the sky like rockets go
All that mingled there below:

Many a tall and goodly man,
Scorched and shrivelled to a span,
When he fell to earth again
Like a cinder strewed the plain:
Down the ashes shower like rain;
Some fell in the gulf, which received the sprinkles
With a thousand circling wrinkles;
Some fell on the shore, but far away
Scattered o'er the isthmus lay;
Christian or Moslem, which be they?
Let their mother say and say!
When in cradled rest they lay,
And each nursing mother smiled
On the sweet sleep of her child,
Little deemed she such a day
Would rend those tender limbs away.
Not the matrons that them bore
Could discern their offspring more;
That one moment left no trace
More of human form or face
Save a scattered scalp or bone:
And down came blazing rafters, strown
Around, and many a falling stone,
Deeply dinted in the clay,
All blackened there and reeking lay.
All the living things that heard
That deadly earth-shock disappeared:
The wild birds flew; the wild dogs fled,
And howling left the unburied dead;
The camels from their keepers broke;
The distant steer forsook the yoke—

The nearer steed plunged o'er the plain,
And burst his girth, and tore his rein;
The bull-frog's note from out the marsh
Deep-mouthed arose, and doubly harsh;
The wolves yelled on the caverned hill
Where echo rolled in thunder still;
The jackals' troop in gathered cry
Bayed from afar complainingly,
With a mixed and mournful sound,
Like crying babe, and beaten hound:
With sudden wing and ruffled breast
The eagle left his rocky nest,
And mounted nearer to the sun,
The clouds beneath him seemed so dun;
Their smoke assailed his startled beak,
And made him higher soar and shriek—
  Thus was Corinth lost and won!

LXXIV

ALHAMA

The Moorish King rides up and down,
Through Granada's royal town;
From Elvira's gates to those
Of Bivarambla on he goes.
                Woe is me, Alhama!

Letters to the monarch tell
How Alhama's city fell:
In the fire the scroll he threw,
And the messenger he slew.
                Woe is me, Alhama!

He quits his mule, and mounts his horse,
And through the street directs his course;
Through the street of Zacatin
To the Alhambra spurring in.
    Woe is me, Alhama!

When the Alhambra walls he gained,
On the moment he ordained
That the trumpet straight should sound
With the silver clarion round.
    Woe is me, Alhama!

And when the hollow drums of war
Beat the loud alarm afar,
That the Moors of town and plain
Might answer to the martial strain—
    Woe is me, Alhama!—

Then the Moors, by this aware,
That bloody Mars recalled them there
One by one, and two by two,
To a mighty squadron grew.
    Woe is me, Alhama!

Out then spake an aged Moor
In these words the king before,
'Wherefore call on us, O King?
What may mean this gathering?'
    Woe is me, Alhama!

'Friends! ye have, alas! to know
Of a most disastrous blow;

That the Christians, stern and bold,
Have obtained Alhama's hold.'
    Woe is me, Alhama!

Out then spake old Alfaqui,
With his beard so white to see,
'Good King! thou art justly served,
Good King! this thou hast deserved.
    Woe is me, Alhama!

By thee were slain, in evil hour,
The Abencerrage, Granada's flower;
And strangers were received by thee
Of Cordova the Chivalry.
    Woe is me, Alhama!

And for this, O King! is sent
On thee a double chastisement:
Thee and thine, thy crown and realm,
One last wreck shall overwhelm.
    Woe is me, Alhama!

He who holds no laws in awe,
He must perish by the law;
And Granada must be won,
And thyself with her undone.'
    Woe is me, Alhama!

Fire flashed from out the old Moor's eyes,
The monarch's wrath began to rise,
Because he answered, and because
He spake exceeding well of laws.
    Woe is me, Alhama!

'There is no law to say such things
As may disgust the ear of kings:'
Thus, snorting with his choler, said
The Moorish King, and doomed him dead.
          Woe is me, Alhama!

Moor Alfaqui! Moor Alfaqui!
Though thy beard so hoary be,
The King hath sent to have thee seized,
For Alhama's loss displeased.
          Woe is me, Alhama!

And to fix thy head upon
High Alhambra's loftiest stone;
That this for thee should be the law,
And others tremble when they saw.
          Woe is me, Alhama!

'Cavalier, and man of worth!
Let these words of mine go forth!
Let the Moorish Monarch know,
That to him I nothing owe.
          Woe is me, Alhama!

But on my soul Alhama weighs,
And on my inmost spirit preys;
And if the King his land hath lost,
Yet others may have lost the most.
          Woe is me, Alhama!

Sires have lost their children, wives
Their lords, and valiant men their lives!

One what best his love might claim
Hath lost, another wealth, or fame.
>Woe is me, Alhama!

I lost a damsel in that hour,
Of all the land the loveliest flower;
Doubloons a hundred I would pay,
And think her ransom cheap that day.'
>Woe is me, Alhama!

And as these things the old Moor said,
They severed from the trunk his head;
And to the Alhambra's wall with speed
'Twas carried, as the King decreed.
>Woe is me, Alhama!

And men and infants therein weep
Their loss, so heavy and so deep;
Granada's ladies, all she rears
Within her walls, burst into tears.
>Woe is me, Alhama!

And from the windows o'er the walls
The sable web of mourning falls;
The King weeps as a woman o'er
His loss, for it is much and sore.
>Woe is me, Alhama!

LXXV

FRIENDSHIP

My boat is on the shore,
   And my bark is on the sea;
But, before I go, Tom Moore,
   Here's a double health to thee!

Here's a sigh to those who love me,
    And a smile to those who hate;
And, whatever sky's above me,
    Here's a heart for every fate.

Though the ocean roar around me,
    Yet it still shall bear me on;
Though a desert should surround me,
    It hath springs that may be won.

Were 't the last drop in the well,
    As I gasped upon the brink,
Ere my fainting spirit fell,
    'Tis to thee that I would drink.

With that water, as this wine,
    The libation I would pour
Should be, 'Peace with thine and mine,
    And a health to thee, Tom Moore!'

LXXVI

THE RACE WITH DEATH

O VENICE! Venice! when thy marble walls
    Are level with the waters, there shall be
A cry of nations o'er thy sunken halls,
    A loud lament along the sweeping sea!
If I, a northern wanderer, weep for thee,
What should thy sons do?—anything but weep:
And yet they only murmur in their sleep.
In contrast with their fathers—as the slime,
The dull green ooze of the receding deep.

Is with the dashing of the spring-tide foam
That drives the sailor shipless to his home,
Are they to those that were; and thus they creep,
Crouching and crab-like, through their sapping streets.
O agony! that centuries should reap
No mellower harvest! Thirteen hundred years
Of wealth and glory turned to dust and tears,
And every monument the stranger meets,
Church, palace, pillar, as a mourner greets;
And even the Lion all subdued appears,
And the harsh sound of the barbarian drum
With dull and daily dissonance repeats
The echo of thy tyrant's voice along
The soft waves, once all musical to song,
That heaved beneath the moonlight with the throng
Of gondolas and to the busy hum
Of cheerful creatures, whose most sinful deeds
Were but the overbeating of the heart,
And flow of too much happiness, which needs
The aid of age to turn its course apart
From the luxuriant and voluptuous flood
Of sweet sensations, battling with the blood.
But these are better than the gloomy errors,
The weeds of nations in their last decay,
When Vice walks forth with her unsoftened terrors,
And Mirth is madness, and but smiles to slay;
And Hope is nothing but a false delay,
The sick man's lightening half an hour ere death,
When Faintness, the last mortal birth of Pain,
And apathy of limb, the dull beginning

Of the cold staggering race which Death is winning,
Steals vein by vein and pulse by pulse away;
Yet so relieving the o'er-tortured clay,
To him appears renewal of his breath,
And freedom the mere numbness of his chain;
And then he talks of life, and how again
He feels his spirits soaring—albeit weak,
And of the fresher air, which he would seek:
And as he whispers knows not that he gasps,
That his thin finger feels not what it clasps;
And so the film comes o'er him, and the dizzy
Chamber swims round and round, and shadows busy,
At which he vainly catches, flit and gleam,
Till the last rattle chokes the strangled scream,
And all is ice and blackness, and the earth
That which it was the moment ere our birth.

LXXVII

THE GLORY THAT WAS GREECE

The isles of Greece, the isles of Greece!
　Where burning Sappho loved and sung,
Where grew the arts of war and peace,
　Where Delos rose, and Phœbus sprung!
Eternal summer gilds them yet,
But all except their sun is set.

The Scian and the Teian muse,
　The hero's harp, the lover's lute,
Have found the fame your shores refuse:
　Their place of birth alone is mute

To sounds which echo further west
Than your sires' 'Islands of the Blest.'

The mountains look on Marathon—
   And Marathon looks on the sea;
And, musing there an hour alone,
   I dreamed that Greece might still be free;
For, standing on the Persians' grave,
I could not deem myself a slave.

A king sate on the rocky brow
   Which looks o'er sea-born Salamis;
And ships by thousands lay below,
   And men in nations;—all were his!
He counted them at break of day,
And when the sun set, where were they?

And where are they? and where art thou,
   My country? On thy voiceless shore
The heroic lay is tuneless now,
   The heroic bosom beats no more!
And must thy lyre, so long divine,
Degenerate into hands like mine?

'Tis something in the dearth of fame,
   Though linked among a fettered race,
To feel at least a patriot's shame,
   Even as I sing, suffuse my face;
For what is left the poet here?
For Greeks a blush, for Greece a tear!

Must *we* but weep o'er days more blest?
   Must *we* but blush? Our fathers bled.
Earth! render back from out thy breast
   A remnant of our Spartan dead!

Of the three hundred grant but three,
To make a new Thermopylæ!

What, silent still? and silent all?
　Ah! no: the voices of the dead
Sound like a distant torrent's fall,
　And answer, 'Let one living head,
But one arise,—we come, we come!'
'Tis but the living who are dumb.

In vain—in vain: strike other chords;
　Fill high the cup with Samian wine!
Leave battles to the Turkish hordes,
　And shed the blood of Scio's vine!
Hark! rising to the ignoble call,
How answers each bold Bacchanal!

You have the Pyrrhic dance as yet;
　Where is the Pyrrhic phalanx gone?
Of two such lessons, why forget
　The nobler and the manlier one?
You have the letters Cadmus gave;
Think ye he meant them for a slave?

Fill high the bowl with Samian wine!
　We will not think of themes like these!
It made Anacreon's song divine:
　He served—but served Polycrates:
A tyrant; but our masters then
Were still, at least, our countrymen.

The tyrant of the Chersonese
　Was freedom's best and bravest friend;
That tyrant was Miltiades!
　Oh! that the present hour would lend

Another despot of the kind!
Such chains as his were sure to bind.

Fill high the bowl with Samian wine!
　On Suli's rock and Parga's shore
Exists the remnant of a line
　Such as the Doric mothers bore;
And there, perhaps, some seed is sown
The Heracleidan blood might own.

Trust not for freedom to the Franks—
　They have a king who buys and sells;
In native swords and native ranks
　The only hope of courage dwells:
But Turkish force and Latin fraud
Would break your shield, however broad.

Fill high the bowl with Samian wine!
　Our virgins dance beneath the shade—
I see their glorious black eyes shine;
　But, gazing on each glowing maid,
My own the burning tear-drop laves,
To think such breasts must suckle slaves.

Place me on Sunium's marbled steep,
　Where nothing save the waves and I
May hear our mutual murmurs sweep;
　There, swan-like, let me sing and die:
A land of slaves shall ne'er be mine—
Dash down yon cup of Samian wine!

LXXVIII

HAIL AND FAREWELL

'Tis time this heart should be unmoved,
  Since others it hath ceased to move:
Yet, though I cannot be beloved,
    Still let me love!

My days are in the yellow leaf;
  The flowers and fruits of love are gone;
The worm, the canker, and the grief
    Are mine alone!

The fire that on my bosom preys
  Is lone as some volcanic isle;
No torch is kindled at its blaze—
    A funeral pile.

The hope, the fear, the jealous care,
  The exalted portion of the pain
And power of love, I cannot share,
    But wear the chain.

But 'tis not thus, and 'tis not here,
  Such thoughts should shake my soul, nor *now*
Where glory decks the hero's bier,
    Or binds his brow.

The sword, the banner, and the field,
  Glory and Greece, around me see!
The Spartan borne upon his shield
    Was not more free.

Awake! (not Greece—she *is* awake!)
　　Awake, my spirit! Think through *whom*
Thy life-blood tracks its parent lake,
　　And then strike home!

Tread those reviving passions down,
　　Unworthy manhood! unto thee
Indifferent should the smile or frown
　　Of beauty be.

If thou regrett'st thy youth, *why live?*
　　The lad of honourable death
Is here: up to the field, and give
　　Away thy breath!

Seek out—less often sought than found—
　　A soldier's grave, for thee the best;
Then look around, and choose thy ground,
　　And take thy rest.
　　　　　　　　　　　　　Byron.

LXXIX

AFTER CORUNNA

Not a drum was heard, not a funeral note,
　　As his corse to the rampart we hurried;
Not a soldier discharged his farewell shot
　　O'er the grave where our hero we buried.

We buried him darkly at dead of night,
　　The sods with our bayonets turning,
By the struggling moonbeam's misty light,
　　And the lantern dimly burning.

No useless coffin enclosed his breast,
  Nor in sheet nor in shroud we wound him;
But he lay like a warrior taking his rest
  With his martial cloak around him.

Few and short were the prayers we said,
  And we spoke not a word of sorrow;
But we steadfastly gazed on the face that was dead,
  And we bitterly thought of the morrow.

We thought, as we hollowed his narrow bed
  And smoothed down his lonely pillow,
How the foe and the stranger would tread o'er his head,
  And we far away on the billow!

Lightly they'll talk of the spirit that's gone,
  And o'er his cold ashes upbraid him;
But little he'll reck, if they let him sleep on
  In the grave where a Briton has laid him.

But half of our heavy task was done,
  When the clock struck the hour for retiring;
And we heard the distant and random gun
  That the foe was sullenly firing.

Slowly and sadly we laid him down,
  From the field of his fame fresh and gory;
We carved not a line, and we raised not a stone—
  But we left him alone with his glory.

LXXX

THE OLD NAVY

The captain stood on the carronade: 'First lieutenant,' says he,
'Send all my merry men aft here, for they must list to me;
I haven't the gift of the gab, my sons—because I'm bred to the sea;
That ship there is a Frenchman, who means to fight with we.
    And odds bobs, hammer and tongs, long as I've been to sea,
    I've fought 'gainst every odds—but I've gained the victory!

That ship there is a Frenchman, and if we don't take *she*,
'Tis a thousand bullets to one, that she will capture *we;*
I haven't the gift of the gab, my boys; so each man to his gun;
If she's not mine in half an hour, I'll flog each mother's son.
    For odds bobs, hammer and tongs, long as I've been to sea,
    I've fought 'gainst every odds—and I've gained the victory!'

We fought for twenty minutes, when the Frenchman had enough;
'I little thought,' said he, 'that your men were of such stuff';

Our captain took the Frenchman's sword, a low bow
    made to *he;*
'I haven't the gift of the gab, monsieur, but polite
    I wish to be.
        And odds bobs, hammer and tongs, long as
            I've been to seà,
        I've fought 'gainst every odds—and I've
            gained the victory!'

Our captain sent for all of us: 'My merry men,' said
    he,
'I haven't the gift of the gab, my lads, but yet I
    thankful be:
You've done your duty handsomely, each man stood
    to his gun;
If you hadn't, you villains, as sure as day, I'd have
    flogged each mother's son.
        For odds bobs, hammer and tongs, as long as
            I'm at sea,
        I'll fight 'gainst every odds—and I'll gain
            the victory!'

Marryat.

LXXXI

CASABIANCA

THE boy stood on the burning deck
    Whence all but he had fled;
The flame that lit the battle's wreck
    Shone round him o'er the dead.

Yet beautiful and bright he stood,
  As born to rule the storm:
A creature of heroic blood,
  A proud though child-like form.

The flames rolled on—he would not go
  Without his father's word;
That father, faint in death below,
  His voice no longer heard.

He called aloud: 'Say, father! say
  If yet my task is done!'
He knew not that the chieftain lay
  Unconscious of his son.

'Speak, father!' once again he cried,
  'If I may yet be gone!'
And but the booming shots replied,
  And fast the flames rolled on.

Upon his brow he felt their breath,
  And in his waving hair;
He looked from that lone post of death
  In still yet brave despair,

And shouted but once more aloud,
  'My father! must I stay?'
While o'er him fast, through sail and shroud,
  The wreathing fires made way.

They wrapt the ship in splendour wild,
  They caught the flag on high,
And streamed above the gallant child
  Like banners in the sky.

There came a burst of thunder-sound—
  The boy—O! where was he?
Ask of the winds that far around
  With fragments strewed the sea:

With mast, and helm, and pennon fair,
  That well had borne their part!
But the noblest thing which perished there
  Was that young faithful heart.

LXXXII

THE PILGRIM FATHERS

The breaking waves dashed high
  On a stern and rock-bound coast,
And the woods against a stormy sky
  Their giant branches tossed;

And the heavy night hung dark
  The hills and waters o'er,
When a band of exiles moored their bark
  On the wild New England shore.

Not as the conqueror comes,
  They, the true-hearted, came;
Not with the roll of the stirring drums,
  And the trumpet that sings of fame;

Not as the flying come,
  In silence and in fear;—

They shook the depths of the desert gloom
   With their hymns of lofty cheer.

Amidst the storm they sang,
   And the stars heard and the sea;
And the sounding aisles of the dim woods rang
   To the anthem of the free!

The ocean eagle soared
   From his nest by the white wave's foam;
And the rocking pines of the forest roared—
   This was their welcome home!

There were men with hoary hair
   Amidst that pilgrim band;
Why had *they* come to wither there,
   Away from their childhood's land?

There was woman's fearless eye,
   Lit by her deep love's truth;
There was manhood's brow serenely high,
   And the fiery heart of youth.

What sought they thus afar?
   Bright jewels of the mine?
The wealth of seas, the spoils of war?
   They sought a faith's pure shrine!

Ay, call it holy ground,
   The soil where first they trod.
They have left unstained what there they found—
   Freedom to worship God.

LXXXIII

TO THE ADVENTUROUS

Much have I travelled in the realms of gold,
And many goodly states and kingdoms seen;
Round many western islands have I been
Which bards in fealty to Apollo hold.
Oft of one wide expanse had I been told
That deep-browed Homer ruled as his demesne:
Yet did I never breathe its pure serene
Till I heard Chapman speak out loud and bold:
Then felt I like some watcher of the skies
When a new planet swims into his ken;
Or like stout Cortez when with eagle eyes
He stared at the Pacific—and all his men
Looked at each other with a wild surmise—
Silent, upon a peak in Darien.

Keats.

LXXXIV

HORATIUS

THE TRYSTING

Lars Porsena of Clusium
  By the Nine Gods he swore
That the great house of Tarquin
  Should suffer wrong no more.
By the Nine Gods he swore it,
  And named a trysting day,
And bade his messengers ride forth
East and west and south and north
  To summon his array.

East and west and south and north
    The messengers ride fast,
And tower and town and cottage
    Have heard the trumpet's blast.
Shame on the false Etruscan
    Who lingers in his home,
When Porsena of Clusium
    Is on the march for Rome.

The horsemen and the footmen
    Are pouring in amain
From many a stately market-place,
    From many a fruitful plain;
From many a lonely hamlet
    Which, hid by beech and pine,
Like an eagle's nest hangs on the crest
    Of purple Apennine;

From lordly Volaterræ,
    Where scowls the far-famed hold
Piled by the hands of giants
    For godlike kings of old;
From sea-girt Populonia
    Whose sentinels descry
Sardinia's snowy mountain-tops
    Fringing the southern sky;

From the proud mart of Pisæ,
    Queen of the western waves,
Where ride Massilia's triremes
    Heavy with fair-haired slaves;

From where sweet Clanis wanders
　　Through corn and vines and flowers;
From where Cortona lifts to heaven
　　Her diadem of towers.

Tall are the oaks whose acorns
　　Drop in dark Auser's rill;
Fat are the stags that champ the boughs
　　Of the Ciminian hill;
Beyond all streams Clitumnus
　　Is to the herdsman dear;
Best of all pools the fowler loves
　　The great Volsinian mere.

But now no stroke of woodman
　　Is heard by Auser's rill;
No hunter tracks the stag's green path
　　Up the Ciminian hill;
Unwatched along Clitumnus
　　Grazes the milk-white steer;
Unharmed the water-fowl may dip
　　In the Volsinian mere.

The harvests of Arretium
　　This year old men shall reap;
This year young boys in Umbro
　　Shall plunge the struggling sheep;
And in the vats of Luna
　　This year the must shall foam
Round the white feet of laughing girls
　　Whose sires have marched to Rome.

There be thirty chosen prophets,
   The wisest of the land,
Who alway by Lars Porsena
   Both morn and evening stand:
Evening and morn the Thirty
   Have turned the verses o'er,
Traced from the right on linen white
   By mighty seers of yore.

And with one voice the Thirty
   Have their glad answer given:
'Go forth, go forth, Lars Porsena;
   Go forth, beloved of Heaven;
Go, and return in glory
   To Clusium's royal dome,
And hang round Nurscia's altars
   The golden shields of Rome.'

And now hath every city
   Sent up her tale of men;
The foot are fourscore thousand,
   The horse are thousands ten.
Before the gates of Sutrium
   Is met the great array.
A proud man was Lars Porsena
   Upon the trysting day!

For all the Etruscan armies
   Were ranged beneath his eye,
And many a banished Roman,
   And many a stout ally;

And with a mighty following
　　To join the muster came
The Tusculan Mamilius,
　　Prince of the Latian name.

THE TROUBLE IN ROME

But by the yellow Tiber
　　Was tumult and affright:
From all the spacious champaign
　　To Rome men took their flight.
A mile around the city
　　The throng stopped up the ways;
A fearful sight it was to see
　　Through two long nights and days.

For aged folk on crutches,
　　And women great with child,
And mothers sobbing over babes
　　That clung to them and smiled,
And sick men borne in litters
　　High on the necks of slaves,
And troops of sun-burned husbandmen
　　With reaping-hooks and staves,

And droves of mules and asses
　　Laden with skins of wine,
And endless flocks of goats and sheep,
　　And endless herds of kine,
And endless trains of waggons
　　That creaked beneath the weight
Of corn-sacks and of household goods,
　　Choked every roaring gate.

Now from the rock Tarpeian
  Could the wan burghers spy
The line of blazing villages
  Red in the midnight sky.
The Fathers of the City,
  They sat all night and day,
For every hour some horseman came
  With tidings of dismay.

To eastward and to westward
  Have spread the Tuscan bands;
Nor house, nor fence, nor dovecote
  In Crustumerium stands.
Verbenna down to Ostia
  Hath wasted all the plain;
Astur hath stormed Janiculum,
  And the stout guards are slain.

I wis, in all the Senate
  There was no heart so bold
But sore it ached, and fast it beat,
  When that ill news was told.
Forthwith up rose the Consul,
  Up rose the Fathers all;
In haste they girded up their gowns,
  And hied them to the wall.

They held a council standing
  Before the River-Gate;
Short time was there, ye well may guess,
  For musing or debate.

Out spake the Consul roundly:
  'The bridge must straight go down;
For, since Janiculum is lost,
  Nought else can save the town.'

Just then a scout came flying,
  All wild with haste and fear:
'To arms! to arms! Sir Consul:
  Lars Porsena is here.'
On the low hills to westward
  The Consul fixed his eye,
And saw the swarthy storm of dust
  Rise fast along the sky.

And nearer fast and nearer
  Doth the red whirlwind come;
And louder still and still more loud,
From underneath that rolling cloud
Is heard the trumpet's war-note proud,
  The trampling, and the hum.
And plainly and more plainly
  Now through the gloom appears,
Far to left and far to right,
In broken gleams of dark-blue light,
The long array of helmets bright,
  The long array of spears.

And plainly and more plainly
  Above that glimmering line
Now might ye see the banners
  Of twelve fair cities shine;

But the banner of proud Clusium
  Was highest of them all,
The terror of the Umbrian,
  The terror of the Gaul.

And plainly and more plainly
  Now might the burghers know,
By port and vest, by horse and crest,
  Each warlike Lucumo.
There Cilnius of Arretium
  On his fleet roan was seen;
And Astur of the fourfold shield,
Girt with the brand none else may wield,
Tolumnius with the belt of gold,
And dark Verbenna from the hold
  By reedy Thrasymene.

Fast by the royal standard
  O'erlooking all the war,
Lars Porsena of Clusium
  Sate in his ivory car.
By the right wheel rode Mamilius,
  Prince of the Latian name;
And by the left false Sextus,
  That wrought the deed of shame.

But when the face of Sextus
  Was seen among the foes,
A yell that rent the firmament
  From all the town arose.

On the house-tops was no woman
    But spat towards him, and hissed;
No child but screamed out curses,
    And shook its little fist.

But the Consul's brow was sad,
    And the Consul's speech was low,
And darkly looked he at the wall,
    And darkly at the foe.
'Their van will be upon us
    Before the bridge goes down;
And if they once may win the bridge,
    What hope to save the town?'

Then out spake brave Horatius,
    The Captain of the gate:
'To every man upon this earth
    Death cometh soon or late;
And how can man die better
    Than facing fearful odds,
For the ashes of his fathers
    And the temples of his Gods,

And for the tender mother
    Who dandled him to rest,
And for the wife who nurses
    His baby at her breast,
And for the holy maidens
    Who feed the eternal flame,
To save them from false Sextus
    That wrought the deed of shame?

Hew down the bridge, Sir Consul,
  With all the speed ye may;
I, with two more to help me,
  Will hold the foe in play.
In yon strait path a thousand
  May well be stopped by three.
Now who will stand on either hand,
  And keep the bridge with me?'

Then out spake Spurius Lartius,
  A Ramnian proud was he:
'Lo, I will stand at thy right hand,
  And keep the bridge with thee.'
And out spake strong Heminius,
  Of Titian blood was he:
'I will abide on thy left side,
  And keep the bridge with thee.'

'Horatius,' quoth the Consul,
  'As thou sayest, so let it be.'
And straight against that great array
  Forth went the dauntless Three.
For Romans in Rome's quarrel
  Spared neither land nor gold,
Nor son nor wife, nor limb nor life,
  In the brave days of old.

Then none was for a party;
  Then all were for the state;
Then the great man helped the poor,
  And the poor man loved the great:

Then lands were fairly portioned;
  Then spoils were fairly sold:
The Romans were like brothers
  In the brave days of old.

Now Roman is to Roman
  More hateful than a foe,
And the Tribunes beard the high,
  And the Fathers grind the low.
As we wax hot in faction,
  In battle we wax cold:
Wherefore men fight not as they fought
  In the brave days of old.

THE KEEPING OF THE BRIDGE

Now while the Three were tightening
  Their harness on their backs,
The Consul was the foremost man
  To take in hand an axe:
And Fathers mixed with Commons
  Seized hatchet, bar, and crow,
And smote upon the planks above,
  And loosed the props below.

Meanwhile the Tuscan army,
  Right glorious to behold,
Came flashing back the noonday light,
Rank behind rank, like surges bright
  Of a broad sea of gold.
Four hundred trumpets sounded
  A peal of warlike glee,

As that great host, with measured tread,
　And spears advanced, and ensigns spread,
Rolled slowly towards the bridge's head,
　　Where stood the dauntless Three.

The Three stood calm and silent,
　And looked upon the foes,
And a great shout of laughter
　From all the vanguard rose:
And forth three chiefs came spurring
　Before that deep array;
To earth they sprang, their swords they drew,
And lifted high their shields, and flew
　To win the narrow way;

Aunus from green Tifernum,
　Lord of the Hill of Vines;
And Seius, whose eight hundred slaves
　Sicken in Ilva's mines;
And Picus, long to Clusium
　Vassal in peace and war,
Who led to fight his Umbrian powers
From that grey crag where, girt with towers,
The fortress of Nequinum lowers
　O'er the pale waves of Nar.

Stout Lartius hurled down Aunus
　Into the stream beneath:
Herminius struck at Seius,
　And clove him to the teeth:

At Picus brave Horatius
   Darted one fiery thrust,
And the proud Umbrian's gilded arms
   Clashed in the bloody dust.

Then Ocnus of Falerii
   Rushed on the Roman Three;
And Lausulus of Urgo,
   The rover of the sea;
And Aruns of Volsinium,
   Who slew the great wild boar,
The great wild boar that had his den
Amidst the reeds of Cosa's fen,
And wasted fields, and slaughtered men,
   Along Albinia's shore.

Herminius smote down Aruns:
   Lartius laid Ocnus low:
Right to the heart of Lausulus
   Horatius sent a blow.
'Lie there,' he cried, 'fell pirate!
   No more, aghast and pale,
From Ostia's walls the crowd shall mark
The track of thy destroying bark.
No more Campania's hinds shall fly
To woods and caverns when they spy
   Thy thrice-accursed sail.'

But now no sound of laughter
   Was heard amongst the foes.
A wild and wrathful clamour
   From all the vanguard rose.

Six spears' lengths from the entrance
  Halted that deep array,
And for a space no man came forth
  To win the narrow way.

But hark! the cry is Astur:
  And lo! the ranks divide;
And the great Lord of Luna
  Comes with his stately stride.
Upon his ample shoulders
Clangs loud the fourfold shield,
And in his hand he shakes the brand
  Which none but he can wield.

He smiled on those bold Romans
  A smile serene and high;
He eyed the flinching Tuscans,
  And scorn was in his eye.
Quoth he, 'The she-wolf's litter
  Stands savagely at bay:
But will ye dare to follow,
  If Astur clears the way?'

Then, whirling up his broadsword
  With both hands to the height,
He rushed against Horatius,
  And smote with all his might.
With shield and blade Horatius
  Right deftly turned the blow.
The blow, though turned, came yet too nigh;
  It missed his helm, but gashed his thigh:
The Tuscans raised a joyful cry
  To see the red blood flow.

He reeled, and on Herminius
  He leaned one breathing-space;
Then, like a wild cat mad with wounds,
  Sprang right at Astur's face.
Through teeth, and skull, and helmet,
  So fierce a thrust he sped
The good sword stood a handbreadth out
  Behind the Tuscan's head.

And the great Lord of Luna
  Fell at that deadly stroke,
As falls on Mount Alvernus
  A thunder-smitten oak:
Far o'er the crashing forest
  The giant arms lie spread;
And the pale augurs, muttering low,
  Gaze on the blasted head.

On Astur's throat Horatius
  Right firmly pressed his heel,
And thrice and four times tugged amain,
  Ere he wrenched out the steel.
'And see,' he cried, 'the welcome,
  Fair guests, that waits you here!
What noble Lucumo comes next
  To taste our Roman cheer?'

But at his haughty challenge
  A sullen murmur ran,
Mingled of wrath and shame and dread,
  Along that glittering van.

There lacked not men of prowess,
  Nor men of lordly race;
For all Etruria's noblest
  Were round the fatal place.

But all Etruria's noblest
  Felt their hearts sink to see
On the earth the bloody corpses,
  In the path the dauntless Three:
And, from the ghastly entrance
  Where those bold Romans stood,
All shrank, like boys who unaware,
Ranging the woods to start a hare,
Come to the mouth of the dark lair
Where, growling low, a fierce old bear
  Lies amidst bones and blood.

Was none who would be foremost
  To lead such dire attack;
But those behind cried 'Forward!'
  And those before cried 'Back!'
And backward now and forward
  Wavers the deep array;
And on the tossing sea of steel,
  To and fro the standards reel;
And the victorious trumpet-peal
  Dies fitfully away.

Yet one man for one moment
  Strode out before the crowd;
Well known was he to all the Three,
  And they gave him greeting loud.

'Now welcome, welcome, Sextus!
  Now welcome to thy home!
Why dost thou stay, and turn away?
  Here lies the road to Rome.'

Thrice looked he at the city;
  Thrice looked he at the dead;
And thrice came on in fury,
  And thrice turned back in dread:
And, white with fear and hatred,
  Scowled at the narrow way
Where, wallowing in a pool of blood,
  The bravest Tuscans lay.

But meanwhile axe and lever
  Have manfully been plied;
And now the bridge hangs tottering
  Above the boiling tide.
'Come back, come back, Horatius!'
  Loud cried the Fathers all.
'Back, Lartius! back, Herminius!
  Back, ere the ruin fall!'

Back darted Spurius Lartius;
  Herminius darted back:
And, as they passed, beneath their feet
  They felt the timbers crack.
But, when they turned their faces,
  And on the farther shore
Saw brave Horatius stand alone,
  They would have crossed once more.

But with a crash like thunder
  Fell every loosened beam,
And, like a dam, the mighty wreck
  Lay right athwart the stream:
And a long shout of triumph
  Rose from the walls of Rome,
As to the highest turret-tops
  Was splashed the yellow foam.

And, like a horse unbroken
  When first he feels the rein,
The furious river struggled hard,
  And tossed his tawny mane;
And burst the curb, and bounded,
  Rejoicing to be free;
And whirling down, in fierce career,
Battlement, and plank, and pier,
  Rushed headlong to the sea.

FATHER TIBER

Alone stood brave Horatius,
  But constant still in mind;
Thrice thirty thousand foes before,
  And the broad flood behind.
'Down with him!' cried false Sextus,
  With a smile on his pale face.
'Now yield thee,' cried Lars Porsena,
  'Now yield thee to our grace.'

Round turned he, as not deigning
  Those craven ranks to see;

Nought spake he to Lars Porsena,
  To Sextus nought spake he;
But he saw on Palatinus
  The white porch of his home;
And he spake to the noble river
  That rolls by the towers of Rome.

'O Tiber! father Tiber!
  To whom the Romans pray,
A Roman's life, a Roman's arms,
  Take thou in charge this day!'
So he spake, and speaking sheathed
  The good sword by his side,
And with his harness on his back
  Plunged headlong in the tide.

No sound of joy or sorrow
  Was heard from either bank;
But friends and foes in dumb surprise,
With parted lips and straining eyes,
  Stood gazing where he sank;
And when above the surges
  They saw his crest appear,
All Rome sent forth a rapturous cry,
And even the ranks of Tuscany
  Could scarce forbear to cheer.

But fiercely ran the current,
  Swollen high by months of rain:
And fast his blood was flowing;
  And he was sore in pain,

And heavy with his armour,
   And spent with changing blows:
And oft they thought him sinking,
   But still again he rose.

Never, I ween, did swimmer,
   In such an evil case,
Struggle through such a raging flood
   Safe to the landing-place:
But his limbs were borne up bravely
   By the brave heart within,
And our good father Tiber
   Bare bravely up his chin.

'Curse on him!' quoth false Sextus;
   'Will not the villain drown?
But for this stay ere close of day
   We should have sacked the town!'
'Heaven help him!' quoth Lars Porsena,
   'And bring him safe to shore;
For such a gallant feat of arms
   Was never seen before.'

And now he feels the bottom;
   Now on dry earth he stands;
Now round him throng the Fathers
   To press his gory hands;
And now with shouts and clapping,
   And noise of weeping loud,
He enters through the River-Gate,
   Borne by the joyous crowd.

They gave him of the corn-land,
  That was of public right,
As much as two strong oxen
  Could plough from morn till night;
And they made a molten image,
  And set it up on high,
And there it stands unto this day
  To witness if I lie.

It stands in the Comitium
  Plain for all folk to see;
Horatius in his harness,
  Halting upon one knee:
And underneath is written,
  In letters all of gold,
How valiantly he kept the bridge
  In the brave days of old.

And still his name sounds stirring
  Unto the men of Rome,
As the trumpet-blast that cries to them
  To charge the Volscian home;
And wives still pray to Juno
  For boys with hearts as bold
As his who kept the bridge so well
  In the brave days of old.

And in the nights of winter,
  When the cold north winds blow,
And the long howling of the wolves
  Is heard amidst the snow;

When round the lonely cottage
  Roars loud the tempest's din,
And the good logs of Algidus
  Roar louder yet within;

When the oldest cask is opened,
  And the largest lamp is lit;
When the chestnuts glow in the embers,
  And the kid turns on the spit;
When young and old in circle
  Around the firebrands close;
When the girls are weaving baskets,
  And the lads are shaping bows;

When the goodman mends his armour
  And trims his helmet's plume;
When the goodwife's shuttle merrily
  Goes flashing through the loom;
With weeping and with laughter
  Still is the story told,
How well Horatius kept the bridge
  In the brave days of old.

LXXXV

THE ARMADA

Attend, all ye who list to hear our noble England's praise;
I tell of the thrice famous deeds she wrought in ancient days,

When that great fleet invincible against her bore in vain
The richest spoils of Mexico, the stoutest hearts of Spain.
It was about the lovely close of a warm summer day,
There came a gallant merchant-ship full sail to Plymouth Bay;
Her crew hath seen Castile's black fleet, beyond Aurigny's isle,
At earliest twilight, on the waves lie heaving many a mile.
At sunrise she escaped their van, by God's especial grace;
And the tall Pinta, till the noon, had held her close in chase.
Forthwith a guard at every gun was placed along the wall;
The beacon blazed upon the roof of Edgecumbe's lofty hall;
Many a light fishing-bark put out to pry along the coast,
And with loose rein and bloody spur rode inland many a post.
With his white hair unbonneted, the stout old sheriff comes;
Behind him march the halberdiers; before him sound the drums;
His yeomen round the market cross make clear an ample space;
For there behoves him to set up the standard of Her Grace.

And haughtily the trumpets peal, and gaily dance
 the bells,
As slow upon the labouring wind the royal blazon
 swells.
Look how the Lion of the sea lifts up his ancient crown,
And underneath his deadly paw treads the gay lilies
 down!
So stalked he when he turned to flight, on that
 famed Picard field,
Bohemia's plume, and Genoa's bow, and Cæsar's
 eagle shield.
So glared he when at Agincourt in wrath he turned
 to bay,
And crushed and torn beneath his claws the princely
 hunters lay.
Ho! strike the flagstaff deep, Sir Knight: ho! scatter
 flowers, fair maids:
Ho! gunners, fire a loud salute: ho! gallants, draw
 your blades:
Thou sun, shine on her joyously: ye breezes, waft
 her wide;
Our glorious SEMPER EADEM, the banner of our pride.

The freshening breeze of eve unfurled that banner's
 massy fold;
The parting gleam of sunshine kissed that haughty
 scroll of gold;
Night sank upon the dusky beach and on the
 purple sea,
Such night in England ne'er had been, nor e'er
 again shall be.

From Eddystone to Berwick bounds, from Lynn to Milford Bay,
That time of slumber was as bright and busy as the day;
For swift to east and swift to west the ghastly war-flame spread,
High on St. Michael's Mount it shone: it shone on Beachy Head.
Far on the deep the Spaniard saw, along each southern shire,
Cape beyond cape, in endless range, those twinkling points of fire.
The fisher left his skiff to rock on Tamar's glittering waves:
The rugged miners poured to war from Mendip's sunless caves!
O'er Longleat's towers, o'er Cranbourne's oaks, the fiery herald flew:
He roused the shepherds of Stonehenge, the rangers of Beaulieu.
Right sharp and quick the bells all night rang out from Bristol town,
And ere the day three hundred horse had met on Clifton down;
The sentinel on Whitehall gate looked forth into the night,
And saw o'erhanging Richmond Hill the streak of blood-red light:
Then bugle's note and cannon's roar the death-like silence broke,
And with one start, and with one cry, the royal city woke.

At once on all her stately gates arose the answering fires;
At once the wild alarum clashed from all her reeling spires;
From all the batteries of the Tower pealed loud the voice of fear;
And all the thousand masts of Thames sent back a louder cheer;
And from the furthest wards was heard the rush of hurrying feet,
And the broad streams of pikes and flags rushed down each roaring street;
And broader still became the blaze, and louder still the din,
As fast from every village round the horse came spurring in.
And eastward straight from wild Blackheath the warlike errand went,
And roused in many an ancient hall the gallant squires of Kent.
Southward from Surrey's pleasant hills flew those bright couriers forth;
High on bleak Hampstead's swarthy moor they started for the north;
And on, and on, without a pause, untired they bounded still:
All night from tower to tower they sprang; they sprang from hill to hill:
Till the proud Peak unfurled the flag o'er Darwin's rocky dales,
Till like volcanoes flared to heaven the stormy hills of Wales,

Till twelve fair counties saw the blaze on Malvern's
    lonely height,
Till streamed in crimson on the wind the Wrekin's
    crest of light,
Till broad and fierce the star came forth on Ely's
    stately fane,
And tower and hamlet rose in arms o'er all the
    boundless plain;
Till Belvoir's lordly terraces the sign to Lincoln
    sent,
And Lincoln sped the message on o'er the wide vale
    of Trent;
Till Skiddaw saw the fire that burned on Gaunt's
    embattled pile,
And the red glare on Skiddaw roused the burghers
    of Carlisle.

LXXXVI

THE LAST BUCCANEER

The winds were yelling, the waves were swelling,
    The sky was black and drear,
When the crew with eyes of flame brought the ship
        without a name
    Alongside the last Buccaneer.

'Whence flies your sloop full sail before so fierce a
    gale,
    When all others drive bare on the seas?
Say, come ye from the shore of the holy Salvador,
    Or the gulf of the rich Caribbees?'

'From a shore no search hath found, from a gulf no
     line can sound,
  Without rudder or needle we steer;
Above, below, our bark dies the sea-fowl and the
     shark,
  As we fly by the last Buccaneer.

To-night there shall be heard on the rocks of
     Cape de Verde
  A loud crash and a louder roar;
And to-morrow shall the deep with a heavy moaning sweep
  The corpses and wreck to the shore.'

The stately ship of Clyde securely now may ride
  In the breath of the citron shades;
And Severn's towering mast securely now hies fast,
  Through the seas of the balmy Trades.

From St. Jago's wealthy port, from Havannah's royal
     fort,
  The seaman goes forth without fear;
For since that stormy night not a mortal hath had sight
  Of the flag of the last Buccaneer.

LXXXVII

A JACOBITE'S EPITAPH

To my true king I offered free from stain
Courage and faith; vain faith, and courage vain.
For him, I threw lands, honours, wealth, away,
And one dear hope, that was more prized than they.

For him I languished in a foreign clime,
Grey-haired with sorrow in my manhood's prime;
Heard on Lavernia Scargill's whispering trees,
And pined by Arno for my lovelier Tees;
Beheld each night my home in fevered sleep,
Each morning started from the dream to weep;
Till God, who saw me tried too sorely, gave
The resting-place I asked—an early grave.
Oh thou, whom chance leads to this nameless stone,
From that proud country which was once mine own,
By those white cliffs I never more must see,
By that dear language which I speak like thee,
Forget all feuds, and shed one English tear
O'er English dust.   A broken heart lies here.

Macaulay.

LXXXVIII

THE SONG OF THE WESTERN MEN

A GOOD sword and a trusty hand!
   A merry heart and true!
King James's men shall understand
   What Cornish lads can do.

And have they fixed the where and when?
   And shall Trelawny die?
Here's twenty thousand Cornish men
   Will know the reason why!

Out spake their captain brave and bold,
   A merry wight was he:
'If London Tower were Michael's hold,
   We'll set Trelawny free!

We'll cross the Tamar, land to land,
    The Severn is no stay,
With "one and all," and hand in hand,
    And who shall bid us nay?

And when we come to London Wall,
    A pleasant sight to view,
Come forth! come forth! ye cowards all,
    Here's men as good as you.

Trelawny he's in keep and hold,
    Trelawny he may die;
But here's twenty thousand Cornish bold
    Will know the reason why!'

Hawker.

LXXXIX

THE BUILDING OF THE SHIP

THE MODEL

'BUILD me straight, O worthy Master!
    Staunch and strong, a goodly vessel,
That shall laugh at all disaster,
    And with wave and whirlwind wrestle!'

The merchant's word
Delighted the Master heard;
For his heart was in his work, and the heart
Giveth grace unto every Art.
A quiet smile played round his lips,
As the eddies and dimples of the tide
Play round the bows of ships,
That steadily at anchor ride.

And with a voice that was full of glee,
He answered, 'Ere long we will launch
A vessel as goodly, and strong, and staunch,
As ever weathered a wintry sea!'

And first with nicest skill and art,
Perfect and finished in every part,
A little model the Master wrought,
Which should be to the larger plan
What the child is to the man,
Its counterpart in miniature;
That with a hand more swift and sure
The greater labour might be brought
To answer to his inward thought.
And as he laboured, his mind ran o'er
The various ships that were built of yore,
And above them all, and strangest of all,
Towered the Great Harry, crank and tall,
Whose picture was hanging on the wall,
With bows and stern raised high in air,
And balconies hanging here and there,
And signal lanterns and flags afloat,
And eight round towers, like those that frown
From some old castle, looking down
Upon the drawbridge and the moat.
And he said with a smile, 'Our ship, I wis,
Shall be of another form than this!'

It was of another form, indeed;
Built for freight, and yet for speed,
A beautiful and gallant craft;

Broad in the beam, that the stress of the blast,
Pressing down upon sail and mast,
Might not the sharp bows overwhelm;
Broad in the beam, but sloping aft
With graceful curve and slow degrees,
That she might be docile to the helm,
And that the currents of parted seas,
Closing behind, with mighty force,
Might aid and not impede her course.

THE BUILDERS

In the ship-yard stood the Master,
  With the model of the vessel,
That should laugh at all disaster,
  And with wave and whirlwind wrestle!

Covering many a rood of ground,
Lay the timber piled around;
Timber of chestnut, and elm, and oak,
And scattered here and there, with these,
The knarred and crooked cedar knees;
Brought from regions far away,
From Pascagoula's sunny bay,
And the banks of the roaring Roanoke!
Ah! what a wondrous thing it is
To note how many wheels of toil
One thought, one word, can set in motion!
There's not a ship that sails the ocean,
But every climate, every soil,
Must bring its tribute, great or small,
And help to build the wooden wall!

The sun was rising o'er the sea,
And long the level shadows lay,
As if they, too, the beams would be
Of some great, airy argosy,
Framed and launched in a single day.
That silent architect, the sun,
Had hewn and laid them every one,
Ere the work of man was yet begun.
Beside the Master, when he spoke,
A youth, against an anchor leaning,
Listened to catch his slightest meaning.
Only the long waves, as they broke
In ripples on the pebbly beach,
Interrupted the old man's speech.

Beautiful they were, in sooth,
The old man and the fiery youth!
The old man, in whose busy brain
Many a ship that sailed the main
Was modelled o'er and o'er again;—
The fiery youth, who was to be
The heir of his dexterity,
The heir of his house, and his daughter's hand,
When he had built and launched from land
What the elder head had planned.

'Thus,' said he, 'will we build this ship!
Lay square the blocks upon the slip,
And follow well this plan of mine.
Choose the timbers with greatest care;
Of all that is unsound beware;

For only what is sound and strong
To this vessel shall belong.
Cedar of Maine and Georgia pine
Here together shall combine.
A goodly frame, and a goodly fame,
And the UNION be her name!
For the day that gives her to the sea
Shall give my daughter unto thee!'

The Master's word
Enrapturèd the young man heard;
And as he turned his face aside,
With a look of joy and a thrill of pride,
Standing before
Her father's door,
He saw the form of his promised bride.
The sun shone on her golden hair,
And her cheek was glowing fresh and fair,
With the breath of morn and the soft sea air.
Like a beauteous barge was she,
Still at rest on the sandy beach,
Just beyond the billow's reach;
But he
Was the restless, seething, stormy sea!

Ah! how skilful grows the hand
That obeyeth Love's command!
It is the heart, and not the brain,
That to the highest doth attain,
And he who followeth Love's behest
Far exceedeth all the rest!

Thus with the rising of the sun
Was the noble task begun,
And soon throughout the ship-yard's bounds
Were heard the intermingled sounds
Of axes and of mallets, plied
With vigourous arms on every side;
Plied so deftly and so well,
That ere the shadows of evening fell,
The keel of oak for a noble ship,
Scarfed and bolted, straight and strong,
Was lying ready, and stretched along
The blocks, well placed upon the slip.
Happy, thrice happy, every one
Who sees his labour well begun,
And not perplexed and multiplied,
By idly waiting for time and tide!

And when the hot, long day was o'er,
The young man at the Master's door
Sat with the maiden calm and still.
And within the porch, a little more
Removed beyond the evening chill,
The father sat, and told them tales
Of wrecks in the great September gales,
Of pirates upon the Spanish Main,
And ships that never came back again;
The chance and change of a sailor's life,
Want and plenty, rest and strife,
His roving fancy, like the wind,
That nothing can stay and nothing can bind;
And the magic charm of foreign lands,
With shadows of palms and shining sands,

Where the tumbling surf,
O'er the coral reefs of Madagascar,
Washes the feet of the swarthy Lascar,
As he lies alone and asleep on the turf.

And the trembling maiden held her breath
At the tales of that awful, pitiless sea,
With all its terror and mystery,
The dim, dark sea, so like unto Death,
That divides and yet unites mankind!
And whenever the old man paused, a gleam
From the bowl of his pipe would awhile illume
The silent group in the twilight gloom,
And thoughtful faces, as in a dream;
And for a moment one might mark
What had been hidden by the dark,
That the head of the maiden lay at rest,
Tenderly, on the young man's breast!

IN THE SHIP-YARD

Day by day the vessel grew,
With timbers fashioned strong and true,
Stemson and keelson and sternson-knee,
Till, framed with perfect symmetry,
A skeleton ship rose up to view!
And round the bows and along the side
The heavy hammers and mallets plied,
Till after many a week, at length,
Wonderful for form and strength,
Sublime in its enormous bulk,
Loomed aloft the shadowy hulk!

And around it columns of smoke, upwreathing,
Rose from the boiling, bubbling, seething
Caldron that glowed,
And overflowed
With the black tar, heated for the sheathing.
And amid the clamours
Of clattering hammers,
He who listened heard now and then
The song of the Master and his men:—

'Build me straight, O worthy Master,
   Staunch and strong, a goodly vessel,
That shall laugh at all disaster,
   And with wave and whirlwind wrestle!'

With oaken brace and copper band,
Lay the rudder on the sand,
That, like a thought, should have control
Over the movement of the whole;
And near it the anchor, whose giant hand
Would reach down and grapple with the land,
And immovable and fast
Hold the great ship against the bellowing blast!
And at the bows an image stood,
By a cunning artist carved in wood,
With robes of white, that far behind
Seemed to be fluttering in the wind.
It was not shaped in a classic mould,
Not like a Nymph or Goddess of old,
Or Naiad rising from the water,
But modelled from the Master's daughter!

On many a dreary and misty night
'Twill be seen by the rays of the signal light,
Speeding along through the rain and the dark,
Like a ghost in its snow-white sark,
The pilot of some phantom bark,
Guiding the vessel in its flight
By a path none other knows aright.
Behold, at last,
Each tall and tapering mast
Is swung into its place;
Shrouds and stays
Holding it firm and fast!

Long ago,
In the deer-haunted forests of Maine,
When upon mountain and plain
Lay the snow,
They fell—those lordly pines!
Those grand, majestic pines!
'Mid shouts and cheers
The jaded steers,
Panting beneath the goad,
Dragged down the weary, winding road
Those captive kings so straight and tall,
To be shorn of their streaming hair
And, naked and bare,
To feel the stress and the strain
Of the wind and the reeling main,
Whose roar
Would remind them for evermore
Of their native forest they should not see again.

And everywhere
The slender, graceful spars
Poise aloft in the air,
And at the mast head,
White, blue, and red,
A flag unrolls the stripes and stars.
Ah! when the wanderer, lonely, friendless,
In foreign harbours shall behold
That flag unrolled,
'Twill be as a friendly hand
Stretched out from his native land,
Filling his heart with memories sweet and end·
  less.

THE TWO BRIDALS

All is finished! and at length
Has come the bridal day
Of beauty and of strength.
To-day the vessel shall be launched!
With fleecy clouds the sky is blanched,
And o'er the bay,
Slowly, in all his splendours dight,
The great sun rises to behold the sight.
The ocean old,
Centuries old,
Strong as youth, and as uncontrolled,
Paces restless to and fro
Up and down the sands of gold.
His beating heart is not at rest;
And far and wide,

With ceaseless flow,
His beard of snow
Heaves with the heaving of his breast.

He waits impatient for his bride.
There she stands,
With her foot upon the sands,
Decked with flags and streamers gay
In honour of her marriage day,
Her snow-white signals fluttering, blending,
Round her like a veil descending,
Ready to be
The bride of the grey, old sea.

On the deck another bride
Is standing by her lover's side.
Shadows from the flags and shrouds,
Like the shadows cast by clouds,
Broken by many a sunny fleck,
Fall around them on the deck.

The prayer is said,
The service read,
The joyous bridegroom bows his head,
And in tears the good old Master
Shakes the brown hand of his son,
Kisses his daughter's glowing cheek
In silence, for he cannot speak,
And ever faster
Down his own the tears begin to run.
The worthy pastor—
The shepherd of that wandering flock,

That has the ocean for its wold,
That has the vessel for its fold,
Leaping ever from rock to rock—
Spake, with accents mild and clear,
Words of warning, words of cheer,
But tedious to the bridegroom's ear.
He knew the chart,
Of the sailor's heart,
All its pleasures and its griefs,
All its shallows and rocky reefs,
All those secret currents that flow
With such resistless undertow,
And lift and drift with terrible force,
The will from its moorings and its course.
Therefore he spake, and thus said he:

'Like unto ships far off at sea,
Outward or homeward bound, are we.
Before, behind, and all around,
Floats and swings the horizon's bound,
Seems at its distant rim to rise
And climb the crystal wall of the skies,
And then again to turn and sink,
As if we could slide from its outer brink.
Ah! it is not the sea,
It is not the sea that sinks and shelves,
But ourselves
That rock and rise
With endless and uneasy motion,
Now touching the very skies,
Now sinking into the depths of ocean.

Ah! if our souls but poise and swing
Like the compass in its brazen ring,
Ever level, and ever true
To the toil and the task we have to do,
We shall sail securely, and safely reach
The Fortunate Isles, on whose shining beach
The sights we see, and the sounds we hear,
Will be those of joy and not of fear!'

Then the Master,
With a gesture of command,
Waved his hand;
And at the word,
Loud and sudden there was heard,
All around them and below,
The sound of hammers, blow on blow,
Knocking away the shores and spurs.
And see! she stirs!
She starts—she moves—she seems to feel
The thrill of life along her keel,
And, spurning with her foot the ground,
With one exulting, joyous bound,
She leaps into the ocean's arms!
And lo! from the assembled crowd
There rose a shout, prolonged and loud,
That to the ocean seemed to say,—
'Take her, O bridegroom, old and grey,
Take her to thy protecting arms,
With all her youth and all her charms!'

How beautiful she is! How fair
She lies within those arms, that press

Her form with many a soft caress
Of tenderness and watchful care !
Sail forth into the sea, O ship !
Through wind and wave, right onward steer !
The moistened eye, the trembling lip,
Are not the signs of doubt or fear.

Sail forth into the sea of life,
O gentle, loving, trusting wife,
And safe from all adversity
Upon the bosom of that sea
Thy comings and thy goings be !
For gentleness and love and trust
Prevail o'er angry wave and gust;
And in the wreck of noble lives
Something immortal still survives !

Thou, too, sail on, O ship of State !
Sail on, O Union, strong and great !
Humanity with all its fears,
With all the hopes of future years,
Is hanging breathless on thy fate !
We know what Master laid thy keel,
What Workmen wrought thy ribs of steel,
Who made each mast, and sail, and rope,
What anvils rang, what hammers beat,
In what a forge and what a heat
Were shaped the anchors of thy hope !
Fear not each sudden sound and shock,
'Tis of the wave and not the rock ;
'Tis but the flapping of the sail,

And not a rent made by the gale !
In spite of rock and tempest's roar,
In spite of false lights on the shore,
Sail on, nor fear to breast the sea !
Our hearts, our hopes, are all with thee,
Our hearts, our hopes, our prayers, our tears,
Our faith triumphant o'er our fears,
Are all with thee,—are all with thee !

XC

THE DISCOVERER OF THE NORTH CAPE

OTHERE, the old sea-captain,
  Who dwelt in Helgoland,
To King Alfred, the Lover of Truth,
Brought a snow-white walrus-tooth,
  Which he held in his brown right hand.

His figure was tall and stately,
  Like a boy's his eye appeared;
His hair was yellow as hay,
But threads of a silvery grey
  Gleamed in his tawny beard.

Hearty and hale was Othere,
  His cheek had the colour of oak;
With a kind of laugh in his speech,
Like the sea-tide on a beach,
  As unto the king he spoke.

And Alfred, King of the Saxons,
  Had a book upon his knees,
And wrote down the wondrous tale
Of him who was first to sail
  Into the Arctic seas.

'So far I live to the northward,
  No man lives north of me;
To the east are wild mountain-chains,
And beyond them meres and plains;
  To the westward all is sea.

So far I live to the northward,
    From the harbour of Skeringes-hale;
If you only sailed by day
With a fair wind all the way,
    More than a month would you sail.

I own six hundred reindeer,
    With sheep and swine beside;
I have tribute from the Finns,
Whalebone and reindeer-skins,
    And ropes of walrus-hide.

I ploughed the land with horses,
    But my heart was ill at ease,
For the old seafaring men
Came to me now and then,
    With their sagas of the seas;—

Of Iceland and of Greenland,
    And the stormy Hebrides,
And the undiscovered deep;—
I could not eat nor sleep
    For thinking of those seas.

To the northward stretched the desert,
    How far I fain would know;
So at last I sallied forth,
And three days sailed due north,
    As far as the whale-ships go.

To the west of me was the ocean,
    To the right the desolate shore,
But I did not slacken sail
For the walrus or the whale,
    Till after three days more.

The days grew longer and longer,
　　Till they became as one,
And southward through the haze
I saw the sullen blaze
　　Of the red midnight sun.

And then uprose before me,
　　Upon the water's edge,
The huge and haggard shape
Of that unknown North Cape,
　　Whose form is like a wedge.

The sea was rough and stormy,
　　The tempest howled and wailed,
And the sea-fog, like a ghost,
Haunted that dreary coast,
　　But onward still I sailed.

Four days I steered to eastward,
　　Four days without a night:
Round in a fiery ring
Went the great sun, O King,
　　With red and lurid light.'

Here Alfred, King of the Saxons,
　　Ceased writing for a while;
And raised his eyes from his book,
With a strange and puzzled look,
　　And an incredulous smile.

But Othere, the old sea-captain,
　　He neither paused nor stirred,
Till the King listened, and then
Once more took up his pen,
　　And wrote down every word.

'And now the land,' said Othere,
  'Bent southward suddenly,
And I followed the curving shore,
And ever southward bore
  Into a nameless sea.

And there we hunted the walrus,
  The narwhale, and the seal;
Ha! 'twas a noble game!
And like the lightning's flame
  Flew our harpoons of steel.

There were six of us all together,
  Norsemen of Helgoland;
In two days and no more
We killed of them threescore,
  And dragged them to the strand.'

Here Alfred, the Truth-Teller,
  Suddenly closed his book,
And lifted his blue eyes,
With doubt and strange surmise
  Depicted in their look.

And Othere, the old sea-captain,
  Stared at him wild and weird,
Then smiled till his shining teeth
Gleamed white from underneath
  His tawny, quivering beard.

And to the King of the Saxons,
  In witness of the truth,
Raising his noble head,
He stretched his brown hand, and said,
  'Behold this walrus-tooth!'

XCI

THE CUMBERLAND

At anchor in Hampton Roads we lay,
  On board of the Cumberland, sloop of war;
And at times from the fortress across the bay
      The alarum of drums swept past,
        Or a bugle blast
  From the camp on the shore.

Then far away to the south uprose
  A little feather of snow-white smoke,
And we knew that the iron ship of our foes
      Was steadily steering its course
        To try the force
  Of our ribs of oak.

Down upon us heavily runs,
  Silent and sullen, the floating fort;
Then comes a puff of smoke from her guns,
      And leaps the terrible death,
        With fiery breath,
  From each open port.

We are not idle, but send her straight
  Defiance back in a full-broadside!
As hail rebounds from a roof of slate,
      Rebounds our heavier hail
        From each iron scale
  Of the monster's hide.

'Strike your flag!' the rebel cries,
  In his arrogant old plantation strain.
'Never!' our gallant Morris replies;

'It is better to sink than to yield!'
And the whole air pealed
With the cheers of our men.

Then, like a kraken huge and black,
   She crushed our ribs in her iron grasp!
Down went the Cumberland all a wreck,
   With a sudden shudder of death,
   And the cannon's breath
For her dying gasp.

Next morn, as the sun rose over the bay,
   Still floated our flag at the mainmast head.
Lord, how beautiful was thy day!
   Every waft of the air
   Was a whisper of prayer,
Or a dirge for the dead.

Ho! brave hearts that went down in the seas,
   Ye are at peace in the troubled stream!
Ho! brave land! with hearts like these,
   Thy flag that is rent in twain
   Shall be one again,
And without a seam!

XCII

A DUTCH PICTURE

Simon Danz has come home again,
   From cruising about with his buccaneers;
He has singed the beard of the King of Spain,
And carried away the Dean of Jaen
   And sold him in Algiers.

In his house by the Maes, with its roof of tiles
  And weathercocks flying aloft in air,
There are silver tankards of antique styles,
Plunder of convent and castle, and piles
  Of carpets rich and rare.

In his tulip-garden there by the town,
  Overlooking the sluggish stream,
With his Moorish cap and dressing-gown,
The old sea-captain, hale and brown,
  Walks in a waking dream.

A smile in his grey mustachio lurks
  Whenever he thinks of the King of Spain,
And the listed tulips look like Turks,
And the silent gardener as he works
  Is changed to the Dean of Jaen.

The windmills on the outermost
  Verge of the landscape in the haze,
To him are towers on the Spanish coast
With whiskered sentinels at their post,
  Though this is the river Maes.

But when the winter rains begin,
  He sits and smokes by the blazing brands,
And old seafaring men come in,
Goat-bearded, grey, and with double chin,
  And rings upon their hands.

They sit there in the shadow and shine
  Of the flickering fire of the winter night;
Figures in colour and design
Like those by Rembrandt of the Rhine,
  Half darkness and half light.

And they talk of their ventures lost or won,
    And their talk is ever and ever the same,
While they drink the red wine of Tarragon,
From the cellars of some Spanish Don
    Or convent set on flame.

Restless at times, with heavy strides
    He paces his parlour to and fro;
He is like a ship that at anchor rides,
And swings with the rising and falling tides,
    And tugs at her anchor-tow.

Voices mysterious far and near,
    Sound of the wind and sound of the sea,
Are calling and whispering in his ear,
'Simon Danz! Why stayest thou here?
    Come forth and follow me!'

So he thinks he shall take to the sea again
    For one more cruise with his buccaneers,
To singe the beard of the King of Spain,
And capture another Dean of Jaen
    And sell him in Algiers.

Longfellow.

XCIII

BARBARA FRIETCHIE

Up from the meadows rich with corn,
Clear in the cool September morn,

The clustered spires of Frederick stand
Green-walled by the hills of Maryland.

Round about them orchards sweep,
Apple and peach tree fruited deep,

Fair as a garden of the Lord
To the eyes of the famished rebel horde

On that pleasant morn of the early fall
When Lee marched over the mountain wall,

Over the mountains winding down,
Horse and foot into Frederick town.

Forty flags with their silver stars,
Forty flags with their crimson bars,

Flapped in the morning wind: the sun
Of noon looked down, and saw not one.

Up rose old Barbara Frietchie then,
Bowed with her fourscore years and ten;

Bravest of all in Frederick town,
She took up the flag the men hauled down;

In her attic window the staff she set,
To show that one heart was loyal yet.

Up the street came the rebel tread,
Stonewall Jackson riding ahead.

Under his slouched hat left and right
He glanced; the old flag met his sight.

'Halt!'—the dust-brown ranks stood fast.
'Fire!'—out blazed the rifle-blast.

It shivered the window, pane and sash;
It rent the banner with seam and gash.

Quick, as it fell, from the broken staff
Dame Barbara snatched the silken scarf;

She leaned far out on the window-sill,
And shook it forth with a royal will.

'Shoot, if you must, this old grey head,
But spare your country's flag,' she said.

A shade of sadness, a blush of shame,
Over the face of the leader came;

The nobler nature within him stirred
To life at that woman's deed and word:

'Who touches a hair of yon grey head
Dies like a dog! March on!' he said.

All day long through Frederick street
Sounded the tread of marching feet:

All day long that free flag tost
Over the heads of the rebel host.

Ever its torn folds rose and fell
On the loyal winds that loved it well;

And through the hill-gaps sunset light
Shone over it with a warm good-night.

Whittier.

XCIV

A BALLAD OF THE FLEET

At Flores in the Azores Sir Richard Grenville lay,
And a pinnace, like a fluttered bird, came flying
from far away:

'Spanish ships of war at sea! we have sighted fifty-three!'
Then sware Lord Thomas Howard: ''Fore God I am no coward;
But I cannot meet them here, for my ships are out of gear,
And the half my men are sick. I must fly, but follow quick.
We are six ships of the line; can we fight with fifty-three?'

Then spake Sir Richard Grenville: 'I know you are no coward;
You fly them for a moment to fight with them again.
But I've ninety men and more that are lying sick ashore.
I should count myself the coward if I left them, my Lord Howard,
To these Inquisition dogs and the devildoms of Spain.'

So Lord Howard passed away with five ships of war that day,
Till he melted like a cloud in the silent summer heaven;
But Sir Richard bore in hand all the sick men from the land
Very carefully and slow,
Men of Bideford in Devon,
And we laid them on the ballast down below;
For we brought them all aboard,

And they blest him in their pain, that they were not left to Spain,
To the thumbscrew and the stake, for the glory of the Lord.

He had only a hundred seamen to work the ship and to fight,
And he sailed away from Flores till the Spaniard came in sight,
With his huge sea-castles heaving upon the weather bow.
'Shall we fight or shall we fly?
Good Sir Richard, tell us now,
For to fight is but to die!
There'll be little of us left by the time this sun be set.'
And Sir Richard said again: 'We be all good English men.
Let us bang those dogs of Seville, the children of the devil,
For I never turned my back upon Don or devil yet.'

Sir Richard spoke and he laughed, and we roared a hurrah, and so
The little Revenge ran on sheer into the heart of the foe,
With her hundred fighters on deck, and her ninety sick below;
For half their fleet to the right and half to the left were seen,
And the little Revenge ran on through the long sea-lane between.

Thousands of their soldiers looked down from their decks and laughed,
Thousands of their seamen made mock at the mad little craft
Running on and on, till delayed
By their mountain-like San Philip that, of fifteen hundred tons,
And up-shadowing high above us with her yawning tiers of guns,
Took the breath from our sails, and we stayed.

And while now the great San Philip hung above us like a cloud
Whence the thunderbolt will fall
Long and loud,
Four galleons drew away
From the Spanish fleet that day,
And two upon the larboard and two upon the starboard lay,
And the battle thunder broke from them all.

But anon the great San Philip, she bethought herself and went,
Having that within her womb that had left her ill content;
And the rest they came aboard us, and they fought us hand to hand,
For a dozen times they came with their pikes and musqueteers,
And a dozen times we shook 'em off as a dog that shakes his ears
When he leaps from the water to the land.

And the sun went down, and the stars came out far
  over the summer sea,
But never a moment ceased the fight of the one and
  the fifty-three.
Ship after ship, the whole night long, their high-
  built galleons came,
Ship after ship, the whole night long, with her
  battle-thunder and flame;
Ship after ship, the whole night long, drew back
  with her dead and her shame.
For some were sunk and many were shattered, and
  so could fight us no more—
God of battles, was ever a battle like this in the
  world before?

For he said, 'Fight on! fight on!'
Though his vessel was all but a wreck;
And it chanced that, when half of the short summer
  night was gone,
With a grisly wound to be drest he had left the deck,
But a bullet struck him that was dressing it suddenly
  dead,
And himself he was wounded again in the side and
  the head,
And he said, 'Fight on! fight on!'

And the night went down and the sun smiled out
  far over the summer sea,
And the Spanish fleet with broken sides lay round us
  all in a ring;
But they dared not touch us again, for they feared
  that we still could sting,

So they watched what the end would be.
And we had not fought them in vain,
But in perilous plight were we,
Seeing forty of our poor hundred were slain,
And half of the rest of us maimed for life
In the crash of the cannonades and the desperate strife;
And the sick men down in the hold were most of them stark and cold,
And the pikes were all broken or bent, and the powder was all of it spent;
And the masts and the rigging were lying over the side;

But Sir Richard cried in his English pride:
'We have fought such a fight for a day and a night
As may never be fought again!
We have one great glory, my men!
And a day less or more
At sea or ashore,
We die—does it matter when?
Sink me the ship, Master Gunner—sink her, split her in twain!
Fall into the hands of God, not into the hands of Spain!'

And the gunner said, 'Ay, ay,' but the seamen made reply:
'We have children, we have wives,
And the Lord hath spared our lives.
We will make the Spaniard promise, if we yield, to let us go;

We shall live to fight again and to strike another blow.'
And the lion there lay dying, and they yielded to the foe.

And the stately Spanish men to their flagship bore him then,
Where they laid him by the mast, old Sir Richard caught at last,
And they praised him to his face with their courtly foreign grace;
But he rose upon their decks, and he cried:
'I have fought for Queen and Faith like a valiant man and true;
I have only done my duty as a man is bound to do:
With a joyful spirit I Sir Richard Grenville die!'
And he fell upon their decks and he died.

And they stared at the dead that had been so valiant and true,
And had holden the power and glory of Spain so cheap
That he dared her with one little ship and his English few;
Was he devil or man? He was devil for aught they knew,
But they sank his body with honour down into the deep,
And they manned the Revenge with a swarthier alien crew,
And away she sailed with her loss and longed for her own;

When a wind from the lands they had ruined awoke
    from sleep,
And the water began to heave and the weather to
    moan,
And or ever that evening ended a great gale blew,
And a wave like the wave that is raised by an earth-
    quake grew,
Till it smote on their hulls and their sails and their
    masts and their flags,
And the whole sea plunged and fell on the shot-
    shattered navy of Spain,
And the little Revenge herself went down by the
    island crags
To be lost evermore in the main.

XCV

THE HEAVY BRIGADE

THE charge of the gallant three hundred, the Heavy
    Brigade!
Down the hill, down the hill, thousands of Russians,
Thousands of horsemen, drew to the valley—and
    stayed;
For Scarlett and Scarlett's three hundred were riding
    by
When the points of the Russian lances arose in the
    sky;
And he called, 'Left wheel into line!' and they
    wheeled and obeyed.
Then he looked at the host that had halted he knew
    not why,

And he turned half round, and he bad his trumpeter sound
To the charge, and he rode on ahead, as he waved his blade
To the gallant three hundred whose glory will never die—
'Follow,' and up the hill, up the hill, up the hill,
Followed the Heavy Brigade.

The trumpet, the gallop, the charge, and the might of the fight!
Thousands of horsemen had gathered there on the height,
With a wing pushed out to the left and a wing to the right,
And who shall escape if they close? but he dashed up alone
Through the great grey slope of men,
Swayed his sabre, and held his own
Like an Englishman there and then;
All in a moment followed with force
Three that were next in their fiery course,
Wedged themselves in between horse and horse,
Fought for their lives in the narrow gap they had made—
Four amid thousands! and up the hill, up the hill,
Gallopt the gallant three hundred, the Heavy Brigade.

Fell like a cannon-shot,
Burst like a thunderbolt,
Crashed like a hurricane,

Broke through the mass from below,
Drove through the midst of the foe,
Plunged up and down, to and fro,
Rode flashing blow upon blow,
Brave Inniskillens and Greys
Whirling their sabres in circles of light!
And some of us, all in amaze,
Who were held for a while from the fight,
And were only standing at gaze,
When the dark-muffled Russian crowd
Folded its wings from the left and the right,
And rolled them around like a cloud,—
O mad for the charge and the battle were we,
When our own good redcoats sank from sight,
Like drops of blood in a dark grey sea,
And we turned to each other, whispering, all dismayed,
'Lost are the gallant three hundred of Scarlett's Brigade!'

'Lost one and all' were the words
Muttered in our dismay;
But they rode like Victors and Lords
Through the forest of lances and swords
In the heart of the Russian hordes,
They rode, or they stood at bay—
Struck with the sword-hand and slew,
Down with the bridle-hand drew
The foe from the saddle and threw
Underfoot there in the fray—
Ranged like a storm or stood like a rock
In the wave of a stormy day;

Till suddenly shock upon shock
Staggered the mass from without,
Drove it in wild disarray,
For our men gallopt up with a cheer and a shout,
And the foemen surged, and wavered and reeled
Up the hill, up the hill, up the hill, out of the field,
And over the brow and away.

Glory to each and to all, and the charge that they made!
Glory to all the three hundred, and all the Brigade!
Tennyson.

XCVI

THE PRIVATE OF THE BUFFS

Last night, among his fellow roughs,
   He jested, quaffed, and swore;
A drunken private of the Buffs,
   Who never looked before.
To-day, beneath the foeman's frown,
   He stands in Elgin's place,
Ambassador from Britain's crown
   And type of all her race.

Poor, reckless, rude, low-born, untaught,
   Bewildered, and alone,
A heart, with English instinct fraught,
   He yet can call his own.

Ay, tear his body limb from limb,
  Bring cord, or axe, or flame:
He only knows, that not through *him*
  Shall England come to shame.

Far Kentish hop-fields round him seemed,
  Like dreams, to come and go;
Bright leagues of cherry-blossom gleamed,
  One sheet of living snow;
The smoke, above his father's door,
  In grey soft eddyings hung:
Must he then watch it rise no more,
  Doomed by himself, so young?

Yes, honour calls!—with strength like steel
  He put the vision by.
Let dusky Indians whine and kneel;
  An English lad must die.
And thus, with eyes that would not shrink,
  With knee to man unbent,
Unfaltering on its dreadful brink,
  To his red grave he went.

Vain, mightiest fleets of iron frames;
  Vain, those all-shattering guns;
Unless proud England keep, untamed,
  The strong heart of her sons.
So, let his name through Europe ring—
  A man of mean estate,
Who died, as firm as Sparta's king,
  Because his soul was great.

XCVII

THE RED THREAD OF HONOUR

Eleven men of England
  A breastwork charged in vain;
Eleven men of England
  Lie stripped, and gashed, and slain.
Slain; but of foes that guarded
  Their rock-built fortress well,
Some twenty had been mastered,
  When the last soldier fell.

Whilst Napier piloted his wondrous way
  Across the sand-waves of the desert sea,
Then flashed at once, on each fierce clan, dismay,
  Lord of their wild Truckee.
These missed the glen to which their steps were bent,
  Mistook a mandate, from afar half heard,
And, in that glorious error, calmly went
  To death without a word.

The robber-chief mused deeply
  Above those daring dead;
'Bring here,' at length he shouted,
  'Bring quick, the battle thread.
Let Eblis blast for ever
  Their souls, if Allah will:
But we must keep unbroken
  The old rules of the Hill.

Before the Ghiznee tiger
  Leapt forth to burn and slay;

Before the holy Prophet
  Taught our grim tribes to pray;
Before Secunder's lances
  Pierced through each Indian glen;
The mountain laws of honour
  Were framed for fearless men.

Still, when a chief dies bravely,
  We bind with green *one* wrist—
Green for the brave, for heroes
  ONE crimson thread we twist.
Say ye, Oh gallant Hillmen,
  For these, whose life has fled,
Which is the fitting colour,
  The green one or the red?'

'Our brethren, laid in honoured graves, may wear
  Their green reward,' each noble savage said;
'To these, whom hawks and hungry wolves shall tear,
  Who dares deny the red?'

Thus conquering hate, and steadfast to the right,
  Fresh from the heart that haughty verdict came;
Beneath a waning moon, each spectral height
  Rolled back its loud acclaim.

Once more the chief gazed keenly
  Down on those daring dead;
From his good sword their heart's blood
  Crept to that crimson thread.
Once more he cried, 'The judgment,
  Good friends, is wise and true,

But though the red *be* given,
    Have we not more to do?

These were not stirred by anger,
    Nor yet by lust made bold;
Renown they thought above them,
    Nor did they look for gold.
To them their leader's signal
    Was as the voice of God:
Unmoved, and uncomplaining,
    The path it showed they trod.

As, without sound or struggle,
    The stars unhurrying march,
Where Allah's finger guides them,
    Through yonder purple arch,
These Franks, sublimely silent,
    Without a quickened breath,
Went in the strength of duty
    Straight to their goal of death.

'If I were now to ask you
    To name our bravest man,
Ye all at once would answer,
    They called him Mehrab Khan.
He sleeps among his fathers,
    Dear to our native land,
With the bright mark he bled for
    Firm round his faithful hand.

'The songs they sing of Rustum
    Fill all the past with light;
If truth be in their music,
    He was a noble knight.

But were those heroes living
  And strong for battle still,
Would Mehrad Khan or Rustum
  Have climbed, like these, the hill?'

And they replied, 'Though Mehrab Khan was brave,
  As chief, he chose himself what risks to run;
Prince Rustum lied, his forfeit life to save,
  Which these had never done.'

'Enough!' he shouted fiercely;
  Doomed though they be to hell,
Bind fast the crimson trophy
  Round BOTH wrists—bind it well.
Who knows but that great Allah
  May grudge such matchless men,
With none so decked in heaven,
  To the fiends' flaming den?'

Then all those gallant robbers
  Shouted a stern 'Amen!'
They raised the slaughtered sergeant,
  They raised his mangled ten.
And when we found their bodies
  Left bleaching in the wind,
Around BOTH wrists in glory
  That crimson thread was twined.

Then Napier's knightly heart, touched to the core,
  Rung, like an echo, to that knightly deed,
He bade its memory live for evermore,
  That those who run may read.

XCVIII

HOME THOUGHTS FROM THE SEA

Nobly, nobly Cape St. Vincent to the North-west died away;
Sunset ran, one glorious blood-red, reeking into Cadiz Bay;
Bluish 'mid the burning water, full in face Trafalgar lay;
In the dimmest North-east distance dawned Gibraltar grand and grey;
'Here and here did England help me: how can I help England?'—say,
Whoso turns as I, this evening, turn to God to praise and pray,
While Jove's planet rises yonder, silent over Africa.

XCIX

HERVÉ RIEL

On the sea and at the Hogue, sixteen hundred ninety-two,
   Did the English fight the French,—woe to France!
And, the thirty-first of May, helter-skelter thro' the blue,
Like a crowd of frightened porpoises a shoal of sharks pursue,
   Came crowding ship on ship to St. Malo on the Rance,
With the English fleet in view.

'Twas the squadron that escaped, with the victor in full chase;
  First and foremost of the drove, in his great ship, Damfreville;
    Close on him fled, great and small,
    Twenty-two good ships in all;
And they signalled to the place
' Help the winners of a race!
  Get us guidance, give us harbour, take us quick—
    or, quicker still,
  Here's the English can and will!'

Then the pilots of the place put out brisk and leapt on board;
  'Why, what hope or chance have ships like these to pass?' laughed they:
'Rocks to starboard, rocks to port, all the passage scarred and scored,
Shall the *Formidable* here with her twelve and eighty guns
  Think to make the river-mouth by the single narrow way,
Trust to enter where 'tis ticklish for a craft of twenty tons,
    And with flow at full beside?
    Now, 'tis slackest ebb of tide.
  Reach the mooring? Rather say,
While rock stands or water runs,
Not a ship will leave the bay!'

Then was called a council straight.
Brief and bitter the debate:

'Here's the English at our heels; would you have them take in tow
All that's left us of the fleet, linked together stern and bow,
For a prize to Plymouth Sound?
Better run the ships aground!'
   (Ended Damfreville his speech).
Not a minute more to wait!
   'Let the Captains all and each
   Shove ashore, then blow up, burn the vessels on the beach!
France must undergo her fate.

Give the word!' But no such word
Was ever spoke or heard;
   For up stood, for out stepped, for in struck amid all these
— A Captain? A Lieutenant? A Mate — first, second, third?
   No such man of mark, and meet
   With his betters to compete!
   But a simple Breton sailor pressed by Tourville for the fleet,
A poor coasting-pilot he, Hervé Riel the Croisickese.

And, 'What mockery or malice have we here?' cries Hervé Riel:
   'Are you mad, you Malouins? Are you cowards, fools, or rogues?
Talk to me of rocks and shoals, me who took the soundings, tell
On my fingers every bank, every shallow, every swell

'Twixt the offing here and Grève where the river disembogues?
Are you bought by English gold? Is it love the lying's for?
   Morn and eve, night and day,
   Have I piloted your bay,
Entered free and anchored fast at the foot of Solidor.

  Burn the fleet and ruin France? That were worse than fifty Hogues!
    Sirs, they know I speak the truth! Sirs, believe me there's a way!
Only let me lead the line,
   Have the biggest ship to steer,
   Get this *Formidable* clear,
Make the others follow mine,
And I lead them, most and least, by a passage I know well,
   Right to Solidor past Grève,
   And there lay them safe and sound;
   And if one ship misbehave,
   —Keel so much as grate the ground,
Why, I've nothing but my life,—here's my head!' cries Hervé Riel.

Not a minute more to wait.
'Steer us in, then, small and great!
   Take the helm, lead the line, save the squadron!' cried his chief.
'Captains, give the sailor place!
   He is Admiral, in brief.

Still the north-wind, by God's grace!
See the noble fellow's face,
As the big ship with a bound,
Clears the entry like a hound,
Keeps the passage as its inch of way were the wide seas profound!
  See, safe thro' shoal and rock,
  How they follow in a flock,
Not a ship that misbehaves, not a keel that grates the ground,
  Not a spar that comes to grief!
The peril, see, is past,
All are harboured to the last,
And just as Hervé Riel hollas 'Anchor!'—sure as fate
Up the English come, too late!

So, the storm subsides to calm:
  They see the green trees wave
  On the o'erlooking Grève.
Hearts that bled are stanched with balm.
'Just our rapture to enhance,
  Let the English rake the bay,
Gnash their teeth and glare askance,
  As they cannonade away!
'Neath rampired Solidor pleasant riding on the Rance!'
How hope succeeds despair on each Captain's countenance!
Out burst all with one accord,
  'This is Paradise for Hell!

    Let France, let France's King
      Thank the man that did the thing!'
What a shout, and all one word,
  'Hervé Riel!'
As he stepped in front once more,
    Not a symptom of surprise
    In the frank blue Breton eyes,
Just the same man as before.

Then said Damfreville, 'My friend,
I must speak out at the end,
    Though I find the speaking hard.
Praise is deeper than the lips:
You have saved the King his ships,
    You must name your own reward.
'Faith our sun was near eclipse!
Demand whate'er you will,
France remains your debtor still.
Ask to heart's content and have! or my name's not
        Damfreville.'

Then a beam of fun outbroke
On the bearded mouth that spoke,
As the honest heart laughed through
Those frank eyes of Breton blue:
'Since I needs must say my say,
    Since on board the duty's done,
    And from Malo Roads to Croisic Point, what is it
        but a run?—
Since 'tis ask and have, I may—
    Since the others go ashore—
Come! A good whole holiday!

>   Leave to go and see my wife, whom I call the
>   Belle Aurore!'
> That he asked and that he got,—nothing more.
>
> Name and deed alike are lost:
> Not a pillar nor a post
>   In his Croisic keeps alive the feat as it befell;
> Not a head in white and black
> On a single fishing smack,
> In memory of the man but for whom had gone to
>   wrack
>   All that France saved from the fight whence
>   England bore the bell.
> Go to Paris: rank on rank
>   Search the heroes flung pell-mell
> On the Louvre, face and flank!
>   You shall look long enough ere you come to
>   Hervé Riel.
> So, for better and for worse,
> Hervé Riel, accept my verse!
> In my verse, Hervé Riel, do thou once more
> Save the squadron, honour France, love thy wife, the
>   Belle Aurore!

Browning.

C

THE DYING FIREMAN

I AM the mashed fireman with breast-bone broken,
Tumbling walls buried me in their débris,
Heat and smoke I inspired, I heard the yelling
  shouts of my comrades,

I heard the distant click of their picks and shovels,
They have cleared the beams away, they tenderly lift me forth.

I lie in the night air in my red shirt, the pervading hush is for my sake,
Painless after all I lie, exhausted but not so unhappy,
White and beautiful are the faces around me, the heads are bared of their fire-caps,
The kneeling crowd fades with the light of the torches.

CI

A SEA-FIGHT

Would you hear of an old-time sea-fight?
Would you learn who won by the light of the moon and stars?
List to the yarn, as my grandmother's father the sailor told it to me.

'Our foe was no skulk in his ship, I tell you (said he),
His was the surly English pluck, and there is no tougher or truer, and never was, and never will be;
Along the lowered eve he came horribly raking us.

We closed with him, the yards entangled, the cannon touched,
My captain lashed fast with his own hands.

We had received some eighteen-pound shots under the water,
On our lower-gun-deck two large pieces had burst at the first fire, killing all around and blowing up overhead.

Fighting at sun-down, fighting at dark,
Ten o'clock at night, the full moon well up, our leaks on the gain, and five feet of water reported,
The master-at-arms loosing the prisoners confined in the after-hold to give them a chance for themselves.

The transit to and from the magazine is now stopt by the sentinels,
They see so many strange faces they do not know whom to trust.

Our frigate takes fire,
The other asks if we demand quarter?
If our colours are struck and the fighting done?

Now I laugh content, for I hear the voice of my little captain,
"We have not struck," he composedly cries, "we have just begun our part of the fighting."

Only three guns are in use,
One is directed by the captain himself against the enemy's main-mast,
Two well served with grape and canister silence his musketry and clear his decks.

The tops alone second the fire of this little battery, especially the main-top,
They hold out bravely during the whole of the action.

Not a moment's cease,
The leaks gain fast on the pumps, the fire eats toward the powder-magazine.

One of the pumps had been shot away, it is generally
> thought we are sinking.

Serene stands the little captain,
He is not hurried, his voice is neither high nor low,
His eyes give more light to us than our battle-
> lanterns.

Toward twelve, there in the beams of the moon, they
> surrender to us.'

CII

BEAT! BEAT! DRUMS!

Beat! beat! drums!—blow! bugles! blow!
Through the windows—through doors—burst like a
> ruthless force,
Into the solemn church, and scatter the congregation,
Into the school where the scholar is studying;
Leave not the bridegroom quiet—no happiness must
> he have now with his bride,
Nor the peaceful farmer any peace, ploughing his
> field or gathering his grain,
So fierce you whirr and pound, you drums—so shrill,
> you bugles, blow.

Beat! beat! drums!—blow! bugles! blow!
Over the traffic of cities—over the rumble of wheels
> in the streets;
Are beds prepared for sleepers at night in the
> houses? no sleepers must sleep in those beds,
No bargainers' bargains by day—no brokers or
> speculators—would they continue?

Would the talkers be talking? would the singer
 attempt to sing?
Would the lawyer rise in the court to state his case
 before the judge?
Then rattle quicker, heavier, drums—you bugles,
 wilder blow.

Beat! beat! drums!—blow! bugles! blow!
Make no parley—stop for no expostulation,
Mind not the timid—mind not the weeper or prayer,
Mind not the old man beseeching the young man,
Let not the child's voice be heard, nor the mother's
 entreaties,
Make even the trestle to shake the dead where they
 lie awaiting the hearses,
So strong you thump, O terrible drums—so loud, you
 bugles, blow.

CIII

TWO VETERANS

THE last sunbeam
Lightly falls from the finished Sabbath,
On the pavement here, and there beyond it is looking
 Down a new-made double grave.

Lo! the moon ascending,
Up from the east the silvery round moon,
Beautiful over the house-tops, ghastly, phantom
 moon,
    Immense and silent moon.

I see a sad procession,
And I hear the sound of coming full-keyed bugles,
All the channels of the city streets they're flooding,
    As with voices and with tears.

I hear the great drums pounding,
And the small drums steady whirring,
And every blow of the great convulsive drums
    Strikes me through and through.

For the son is brought with the father,
(In the foremost ranks of the fierce assault they fell,
Two veterans son and father dropt together,
    And the double grave awaits them).

Now nearer blow the bugles,
And the drums strike more convulsive,
And the daylight o'er the pavement quite has faded,
    And the strong dead-march enwraps me.

In the eastern sky up-buoying,
The sorrowful vast phantom moves illumined,
('Tis some mother's large transparent face
    In heaven brighter growing).

O strong dead-march you please me!
O moon immense with your silvery face you soothe me!
O my soldiers twain! O my veterans passing to burial!
    What I have I also give you.

The moon gives you light,
And the bugles and the drums give you music,
And my heart, O my soldiers, my veterans,
    My heart gives you love.

CIV

THE PLEASANT ISLE OF AVÈS

Oh England is a pleasant place for them that's rich
   and high,
But England is a cruel place for such poor folks as I;
And such a port for mariners I ne'er shall see again
As the pleasant Isle of Avès, beside the Spanish
   main.

There were forty craft in Avès that were both swift
   and stout,
All furnished well with small arms and cannons
   round about;
And a thousand men in Avès made laws so fair and
   free
To choose their valiant captains and obey them
   loyally.

Thence we sailed against the Spaniard with his
   hoards of plate and gold,
Which he wrung with cruel tortures from Indian
   folk of old;
Likewise the merchant captains, with hearts as hard
   as stone,
Who flog men and keel-haul them, and starve them
   to the bone.

O the palms grew high in Avès, and fruits that
   shone like gold,
And the colibris and parrots they were gorgeous to
   behold;

And the negro maids to Avès from bondage fast did flee,
To welcome gallant sailors, a-sweeping in from sea.

O sweet it was in Avès to hear the landward breeze,
A-swing with good tobacco in a net between the trees,
With a negro lass to fan you, while you listened to the roar
Of the breakers on the reef outside, that never touched the shore.

But Scripture saith, an ending to all fine things must be;
So the King's ships sailed on Avès, and quite put down were we.
All day we fought like bulldogs, but they burst the booms at night;
And I fled in a piragua, sore wounded, from the fight.

Nine days I floated starving, and a negro lass beside,
Till, for all I tried to cheer her, the poor young thing she died;
But as I lay a-gasping, a Bristol sail came by,
And brought me home to England here, to beg until I die.

And now I'm old and going—I'm sure I can't tell where;
One comfort is, this world's so hard, I can't be worse off there:
If I might but be a sea-dove, I'd fly across the main,
To the pleasant Isle of Avès, to look at it once again.

CV

A WELCOME

Welcome, wild North-easter.
　Shame it is to see
Odes to every zephyr;
　Ne'er a verse to thee.
Welcome, black North-easter!
　O'er the German foam;
O'er the Danish moorlands,
　From thy frozen home.
Tired we are of summer,
　Tired of gaudy glare,
Showers soft and steaming,
　Hot and breathless air.
Tired of listless dreaming,
　Through the lazy day:
Jovial wind of winter
　Turns us out to play!
Sweep the golden reed-beds;
　Crisp the lazy dyke;
Hunger into madness
　Every plunging pike.
Fill the lake with wild-fowl;
　Fill the marsh with snipe;
While on dreary moorlands
　Lonely curlew pipe.
Through the black fir-forest
　Thunder harsh and dry,
Shattering down the snow-flakes
　Off the curdled sky.

Hark! The brave North-easter!
  Breast-high lies the scent,
On by holt and headland,
  Over heath and bent.
Chime, ye dappled darlings,
  Through the sleet and snow.
Who can over-ride you?
  Let the horses go!
Chime, ye dappled darlings,
  Down the roaring blast;
You shall see a fox die
  Ere an hour be past.
Go! and rest to-morrow,
  Hunting in your dreams,
While our skates are ringing
  O'er the frozen streams.
Let the luscious South-wind
  Breathe in lovers' sighs,
While the lazy gallants
  Bask in ladies' eyes.
What does he but soften
  Heart alike and pen?
'Tis the hard grey weather
  Breeds hard English men.
What's the soft South-wester?
  'Tis the ladies' breeze,
Bringing home their true-loves
  Out of all the seas:
But the black North-easter,
  Through the snowstorm hurled,
Drives our English hearts of oak
  Seaward round the world.

Come, as came our fathers,
   Heralded by thee,
Conquering from the eastward,
   Lords by land and sea.
Come; and strong within us
   Stir the Vikings' blood;
Bracing brain and sinew;
   Blow, thou wind of God!

Kingsley.

CVI

THE BIRKENHEAD

AMID the loud ebriety of War,
With shouts of 'la Republique' and 'la Gloire,'
The Vengeur's crew, 'twas said, with flying flag
And broadside blazing level with the wave
Went down erect, defiant, to their grave
Beneath the sea.—'Twas but a Frenchman's brag,
Yet Europe rang with it for many a year.
Now we recount no fable; Europe, hear!
And when they tell thee 'England is a fen
Corrupt, a kingdom tottering to decay,
Her nerveless burghers lying an easy prey
For the first comer,' tell how the other day
A crew of half a thousand Englishmen
Went down into the deep in Simon's Bay!

Not with the cheer of battle in the throat,
Or cannon-glare and din to stir their blood,
But, roused from dreams of home to find their boat

Fast sinking, mustered on the deck they stood,
Biding God's pleasure and their chief's command.
Calm was the sea, but not less calm that band
Close ranged upon the poop, with bated breath
But flinching not though eye to eye with Death!
　　Heroes!

Who were those Heroes? Veterans steeled
To face the King of Terrors mid the scaith
Of many an hurricane and trenchèd field?
Far other: weavers from the stocking-frame;
Boys from the plough; cornets with beardless chin,
But steeped in honour and in discipline!

Weep, Britain, for the Cape whose ill-starred name,
Long since divorced from Hope suggests but shame,
Disaster, and thy Captains held at bay
By naked hordes; but as thou weepest, thank
Heaven for those undegenerate sons who sank
Aboard the Birkenhead in Simon's Bay!

Yule.

CVII

APOLLO

Through the black, rushing smoke-bursts
Thick breaks the red flame;
All Etna heaves fiercely
Her forest-clothed frame.

Not here, O Apollo!
Are haunts meet for thee.
But, where Helicon breaks down
In cliff to the sea,

Where the moon-silvered inlets
Send far their light voice
Up the still vale of Thisbe,
O speed, and rejoice!

On the sward at the cliff-top
Lie strewn the white flocks.
On the cliff-side the pigeons
Roost deep in the rocks.

In the moonlight the shepherds,
Soft lulled by the rills,
Lie wrapt in their blankets
Asleep on the hills.

—What forms are these coming
So white through the gloom?
What garments out-glistening
The gold-flowered broom?

What sweet-breathing presence
Out-perfumes the thyme?
What voices enrapture
The night's balmy prime?—

'Tis Apollo comes leading
His choir, the Nine.
—The leader is fairest,
But all are divine.

They are lost in the hollows!
They stream up again!
What seeks on this mountain
The glorified train?—

They bathe on this mountain,
In the spring by the road;
Then on to Olympus,
Their endless abode.

—Whose praise do they mention?
Of what is it told?—
What will be for ever;
What was from of old.

First hymn they the Father
Of all things; and then,
The rest of immortals,
The action of men.

The day in his hotness,
The strife with the palm;
The night in her silence,
The stars in their calm.

CVIII

THE DEATH OF SOHRAB

THE DUEL

He spoke, and Sohrab kindled at his taunts,
And he too drew his sword; at once they rushed
Together, as two eagles on one prey
Come rushing down together from the clouds,
One from the east, one from the west; their shields
Dashed with a clang together, and a din
Rose, such as that the sinewy woodcutters
Make often in the forest's heart at morn,

Of hewing axes, crashing trees—such blows
Rustum and Sohrab on each other hailed.
And you would say that sun and stars took part
In that unnatural conflict; for a cloud
Grew suddenly in Heaven, and darkened the sun
Over the fighters' heads; and a wind rose
Under their feet, and moaning swept the plain,
And in a sandy whirlwind wrapped the pair.
In gloom they twain were wrapped, and they alone;
For both the on-looking hosts on either hand
Stood in broad daylight, and the sky was pure,
And the sun sparkled on the Oxus stream.
But in the gloom they fought, with bloodshot eyes
And labouring breath; first Rustum struck the shield
Which Sohrab held stiff out; the steel-spiked spear
Rent the tough plates, but failed to reach the skin,
And Rustum plucked it back with angry groan.
Then Sohrab with his sword smote Rustum's helm,
Nor clove its steel quite through; but all the crest
He shore away, and that proud horsehair plume,
Never till now defiled, sank to the dust;
And Rustum bowed his head; but then the gloom
Grew blacker, thunder rumbled in the air,
And lightnings rent the cloud; and Ruksh, the horse,
Who stood at hand, uttered a dreadful cry;—
No horse's cry was that, most like the roar
Of some pained desert-lion, who all day
Hath trailed the hunter's javelin in his side,
And comes at night to die upon the sand.
The two hosts heard that cry, and quaked for fear,
And Oxus curdled as it crossed his stream.

But Sohrab heard, and quailed not, but rushed on,
And struck again; and again Rustum bowed
His head; but this time all the blade, like glass,
Sprang in a thousand shivers on the helm,
And in the hand the hilt remained alone.
Then Rustum raised his head; his dreadful eyes
Glared, and he shook on high his menacing spear,
And shouted: *Rustum!*—Sohrab heard that shout,
And shrank amazed; back he recoiled one step,
And scanned with blinking eyes the advancing form;
And then he stood bewildered; and he dropped
His covering shield, and the spear pierced his side.
He reeled, and staggering back, sank to the ground;
And then the gloom dispersed, and the wind fell,
And the bright sun broke forth, and melted all
The cloud; and the two armies saw the pair—
Saw Rustum standing, safe upon his feet,
And Sohrab, wounded, on the bloody sand.

SOHRAB

Then with a bitter smile, Rustum began:—
'Sohrab, thou thoughtest in thy mind to kill
A Persian lord this day, and strip his corpse,
And bear thy trophies to Afrasiab's tent.
Or else that the great Rustum would come down
Himself to fight, and that thy wiles would move
His heart to take a gift, and let thee go.
And then that all the Tartar host would praise
Thy courage or thy craft, and spread thy fame,
To glad thy father in his weak old age.

Fool, thou art slain, and by an unknown man!
Dearer to the red jackels shalt thou be
Than to thy friends, and to thy father old.'

   And, with a fearless mien, Sohrab replied:—
'Unknown thou art; yet thy fierce vaunt is vain.
Thou dost not slay me, proud and boastful man!
No! Rustum slays me, and this filial heart.
For were I matched with ten such men as thee,
And I were that which till to-day I was,
They should be lying here, I standing there.
But that beloved name unnerved my arm—
That name, and something, I confess, in thee,
Which troubles all my heart, and made my shield
Fall; and thy spear transfix an unarmed foe.
And now thou boastest, and insultest my fate.
But hear thou this, fierce man, tremble to hear:
The mighty Rustum shall avenge my death!
My father, whom I seek through all the world,
He shall avenge my death, and punish thee!'

   As when some hunter in the spring hath found
A breeding eagle sitting on her nest,
Upon the craggy isle of a hill-lake,
And pierced her with an arrow as she rose,
And followed her to find her where she fell
Far off;—anon her mate comes winging back
From hunting, and a great way off decries
His huddling young left-sole; at that he checks
His pinion, and with short uneasy sweeps
Circles above his eyry, with loud screams
Chiding his mate back to her nest; but she
Lies dying, with the arrow in her side,

In some far stony gorge out of his ken,
A heap of fluttering feathers—never more
Shall the lake glass her, flying over it;
Never the black and dripping precipices
Echo her stormy scream as she sails by—
As that poor bird flies home, nor knows his loss,
So Rustum knew not his own loss, but stood
Over his dying son, and knew him not.

   But, with a cold, incredulous voice he said:
'What prate is this of fathers and revenge?
The mighty Rustum never had a son.'

   And with a failing voice Sohrab replied:
'Ah yes, he had! and that lost son am I,
Surely the news will one day reach his ear,
Reach Rustum, where he sits, and tarries long,
Somewhere, I know not where, but far from here;
And pierce him like a stab, and make him leap
To arms, and cry for vengeance upon thee.
Fierce man, bethink thee, for an only son!
What will that grief, what will that vengeance be?
O could I live, till I that grief had seen!
Yet him I pity not so much, but her,
My mother, who in Ader-baijan dwells
With that old king, her father, who grows grey
With age, and rules over the valiant Koords.
Her most I pity, who no more will see
Sohrab returning from the Tartar camp,
With spoils and honour, when the war is done.
But a dark rumour will be bruited up,
From tribe to tribe, until it reach her ear;
And then will that defenceless woman learn

That Sohrab will rejoice her sight no more,
But that in battle with a nameless foe,
By the far-distant Oxus, he is slain.'

THE RECOGNITION

He spoke, and as he ceased he wept aloud,
Thinking of her he left, and his own death.
He spoke; but Rustum listened plunged in thought.
Nor did he yet believe it was his son
Who spoke, although he called back names he knew;
For he had had sure tidings that the babe,
Which was in Ader-baijan born to him,
Had been a puny girl, no boy at all—
So that sad mother sent him word, for fear
Rustum should seek the boy, to train in arms.
And as he deemed that either Sohrab took,
By a false boast, the style of Rustum's son;
Or that men gave it him, to swell his fame.
So deemed he; yet he listened plunged in thought;
And his soul set to grief, as the vast tide
Of the bright rocking Ocean sets to shore
At the full moon; tears gathered in his eyes;
For he remembered his own early youth,
And all its bounding rapture; as, at dawn,
The shepherd from his mountain-lodge descries
A far, bright city, smitten by the sun,
Through many rolling clouds—so Rustum saw
His youth; saw Sohrab's mother, in her bloom;
And that old king, her father, who loved well
His wandering guest, and gave him his fair child
With joy; and all the pleasant life they led,

They three, in that long-distant summer-time—
The castle, and the dewy woods, and hunt
And hound, and morn on those delightful hills
In Ader-baijan. And he saw that Youth,
Of age and looks to be his own dear son,
Piteous and lovely, lying on the sand,
Like some rich hyacinth which by the scythe
Of an unskilful gardener has been cut,
Mowing the garden grass-plots near its bed,
And lies, a fragrant tower of purple bloom,
On the mown, dying grass—so Sohrab lay,
Lovely in death, upon the common sand.
And Rustum gazed on him in grief, and said:
  'O Sohrab, thou indeed art such a son
Whom Rustum, wert thou his, might well have loved.
Yet here thou errest, Sohrab, or else men
Have told thee false—thou art not Rustum's son.
For Rustum had no son; one child he had—
But one—a girl; who with her mother now
Plies some light female task, nor dreams of us—
Of us she dreams not, nor of wounds, nor war.'
  But Sohrab answered him in wrath; for now
The anguish of the deep-fixed spear grew fierce,
And he desirèd to draw forth the steel,
And let the blood flow free, and so to die—
But first he would convince his stubborn foe;
And, rising sternly on one arm, he said:
  'Man, who art thou who dost deny my words?
Truth sits upon the lips of dying men,
And falsehood, while I lived, was far from mine.
I tell thee, pricked upon this arm I bear

That seal which Rustum to my mother gave,
That she might prick it on the babe she bore.'

He spoke; and all the blood left Rustum's cheeks,
And his knees tottered, and he smote his hand
Against his breast, his heavy mailèd hand,
That the hard iron corselet clanked aloud;
And to his heart he pressed the other hand,
And in a hollow voice he spake and said:

'Sohrab, that were a proof that could not lie!
If thou show this, then art thou Rustum's son.'

Then with weak hasty fingers Sohrab loosed
His belt, and near the shoulder bared his arm,
And showed a sign in faint vermilion points
Pricked; as a cunning workman, in Pekin,
Pricks with vermilion some clear porcelain vase,
An emperor's gift—at early morn he paints,
And all day long, and, when night comes, the lamp
Lights up his studious forehead and thin hands—
So delicately pricked the sign appeared
On Sohrab's arm, the sign of Rustum's seal.
It was that griffin, which of old reared Zal,
Rustum's great father, whom they left to die,
A helpless babe, among the mountain rocks;
Him that kind creature found, and reared, and loved—
Then Rustum took it for his glorious sign.
And Sohrab bared that image on his arm,
And himself scanned it long with mournful eyes,
And then he touched it with his hand and said:—

'How sayest thou? Is that sign the proper sign
Of Rustum's son, or of some other man's?'

RUKSH THE HORSE

He spoke; but Rustum gazed, and gazed, and stood
Speechless; and then he uttered one sharp cry:
O boy—thy father!—and his voice choked there.
And then a dark cloud passed before his eyes,
And his head swam, and he sank down to earth.
But Sohrab crawled to where he lay, and cast
His arms about his neck, and kissed his lips,
And with fond faltering fingers stroked his cheeks,
Trying to call him back to life; and life
Came back to Rustum, and he oped his eyes,
And they stood wide with horror; and he seized
In both his hands the dust which lay around,
And threw it on his head, and smirched his hair,—
His hair, and face, and beard, and glittering arms;
And strong convulsive groanings shook his breast,
And his sobs choked him; and he clutched his sword,
To draw it, and for ever let life out.
But Sohrab saw his thought, and held his hands,
And with a soothing voice he spake, and said:
    'Father, forbear! for I but meet to-day
The doom which at my birth was written down
In Heaven, and thou art Heaven's unconscious hand.
Surely my heart cried out that it was thou,
When first I saw thee; and thy heart spoke too,
I know it! but fate trod these promptings down
Under its iron heel; fate, fate engaged
The strife, and hurled me on my father's spear.
But let us speak no more of this! I find
My father; let me feel that I have found!

Come, sit beside me on this sand, and take
My head betwixt thy hands, and kiss my cheeks,
And wash them with thy tears, and say: *My son!*
Quick! quick! for numbered are my sands of life,
And swift; for like the lightning to this field
I came, and like the wind I go away—
Sudden, and swift, and like a passing wind.
But it was writ in Heaven that this should be.'

    So said he, and his voice released the heart
Of Rustum, and his tears broke forth; he cast
His arms round his son's neck, and wept aloud,
And kissed him. And awe fell on both the hosts,
When they saw Rustum's grief; and Ruksh the horse,
With his head bowing to the ground and mane
Sweeping the dust, came near, and in mute woe
First to the one, then to the other moved
His head, as if inquiring what their grief
Might mean; and from his dark, compassionate eyes,
The big warm tears rolled down, and caked the sand.
But Rustum chid him with stern voice, and said:—

    'Ruksh, now thou grievest; but, O Ruksh, thy feet
Should first have rotted on their nimble joints,
Or ere they brought thy master to this field!'

    But Sohrab looked upon the horse and said:
'Is this, then, Ruksh? How often in past days,
My mother told me of thee, thou brave steed,
My terrible father's terrible horse! and said,
That I should one day find thy lord and thee.
Come, let me lay my hand upon thy mane!
O Ruksh, thou art more fortunate than I;

For thou hast gone where I shall never go,
And snuffed the breezes of my father's home.
And thou hast trod the sands of Seistan,
And seen the river of Helmund, and the Lake
Of Zirrah; and the aged Zal himself
Has often stroked thy neck, and given thee food,
Corn in a golden platter soaked with wine,
And said: *O Ruksh! bear Rustum well!*—but I
Have never known my grandsire's furrowed face,
Nor seen his lofty house in Seistan,
Nor slaked my thirst at the clear Helmund stream;
But lodged among my father's foes, and seen
Afrasiab's cities only, Samarcand,
Bokhara, and lone Khiva in the waste,
And the black Toorkman tents; and only drunk
The desert rivers, Moorghab and Tejend,
Kohik, and where the Kalmuks feed their sheep,
The northern Sir; and this great Oxus stream,
The yellow Oxus, by whose brink I die.'

RUSTUM

Then with a heavy groan, Rustum bewailed:
'O that its waves were flowing over me!
O that I saw its grains of yellow silt
Roll tumbling in the current o'er my head!'
But with a grave mild voice, Sohrab replied:—
'Desire not that, my father! thou must live.
For some are born to do great deeds, and live,
As some are born to be obscured, and die.
Do thou the deeds I die too young to do,

And reap a second glory in thine age;
Thou art my father, and thy gain is mine.
But come! thou seest this great host of men
Which follow me; I pray thee, slay not these!
Let me entreat for them; what have they done?
They followed me, my hope, my fame, my star.
Let them all cross the Oxus back in peace.
But me thou must bear hence, not send with them,
But carry me with thee to Seistan,
And place me on a bed, and mourn for me,
Thou, and the snow-haired Zal, and all thy friends.
And thou must lay me in that lovely earth,
And heap a stately mound above my bones,
And plant a far-seen pillar over all.
That so the passing horseman on the waste
May see my tomb a great way off, and cry:
Sohrab, the mighty Rustum's son, lies here,
Whom his great father did in ignorance kill!
And I be not forgotten in my grave.'

And, with a mournful voice, Rustum replied:
'Fear not! as thou hast said, Sohrab, my son,
So shall it be; for I will burn my tents,
And quit the host, and bear thee hence with me,
And carry thee away to Seistan,
And place thee on a bed, and mourn for thee,
With the snow-headed Zal, and all my friends.
And I will lay thee in that lovely earth,
And heap a stately mound above thy bones,
And plant a far-seen pillar over all,
And men shall not forget thee in thy grave.

And I will spare thy host; yea, let them go!
Let them all cross the Oxus back in peace!
What should I do with slaying any more?
For would that all whom I have ever slain
Might be once more alive—my bitterest foes,
And they who were called champions in their time,
And through whose death I won that fame I have—
And I were nothing but a common man,
A poor, mean soldier, and without renown,
So thou mightest live too, my son, my son!
Or rather would that I, even I myself,
Might now be lying on this bloody sand,
Near death, and by an ignorant stroke of thine,
Not thou of mine! and I might die, not thou;
And I, not thou, be borne to Seistan;
And Zal might weep above my grave, not thine;
And say: *O Son, I weep thee not too sore,*
For willingly, I know, thou met'st thine end!
But now in blood and battles was my youth,
And full of blood and battles is my age,
And I shall never end this life of blood.'

Then at the point of death, Sohrab replied:
'A life of blood indeed, thou dreadful man!
But thou shalt yet have peace; only not now,
Not yet! but thou shalt have it on that day,
When thou shalt sail in a high-masted ship,
Thou and the other peers of Kai Khosroo
Returning home over the salt blue sea,
From laying thy dear master in his grave.'

NIGHT

And Rustum gazed in Sohrab's face, and said:
'Soon be that day, my son, and deep that sea!
Till then, if fate so wills, let me endure.'
    He spoke; and Sohrab smiled on him, and took
The spear, and drew it from his side, and eased
His wound's imperious anguish; but the blood
Came welling from the open gash, and life
Flowed with the stream;—all down his cold white side
The crimson torrent ran, dim now and soiled,
Like the soiled tissue of white violets
Left, freshly gathered, on their native bank,
By children whom their nurses call with haste
Indoors from the sun's eye; his head dropped low,
His limbs grew slack; motionless, white, he lay—
White, with eyes closed; only when heavy gasps,
Deep heavy gasps quivering through all his frame,
Convulsed him back to life, he opened them,
And fixed them feebly on his father's face;
Till now all strength was ebbed, and from his limbs
Unwillingly the spirit fled away,
Regretting the warm mansion which it left,
And youth, and bloom, and this delightful world.
    So, on the bloody sand, Sohrab lay dead;
And the great Rustum drew his horseman's cloak
Down o'er his face, and sate by his dead son.
As those black granite pillars once high-reared
By Jemshid in Persepolis, to bear
His house, now 'mid their broken flights of steps

Lie prone, enormous, down the mountain side,
So in the sand lay Rustum by his son.

And night came down over the solemn waste,
And the two gazing hosts, and that sole pair,
And darkened all; and a cold fog, with night,
Crept from the Oxus. Soon a hum arose,
As of a great assembly loosed, and fires
Began to twinkle through the fog; for now
Both armies moved to camp, and took their meal;
The Persians took it on the open sands
Southward, the Tartars by the river marge;
And Rustum and his son were left alone.

But the majestic river floated on,
Out of the mist and hum of that low land,
Into the frosty starlight, and there moved,
Rejoicing, through the hushed Chorasmian waste,
Under the solitary moon;—he flowed
Right for the polar star, past Orgunjè,
Brimming, and bright, and large; then sands begin
To hem his watery march, and dam his streams,
And split his currents; that for many a league
The shorn and parcelled Oxus strains along
Through beds of sand and matted rushy isles—
Oxus, forgetting the bright speed he had
In his high mountain cradle in Pamere
A foiled circuitous wanderer—till at last
The longed-for dash of waves is heard, and wide
His luminous home of waters opens, bright
And tranquil, from whose floor the new-bathed stars
Emerge, and shine upon the Aral Sea.

CIX

FLEE FRO' THE PRESS

O BORN in days when wits were fresh and clear
   And life ran gaily as the sparkling Thames;
     Before this strange disease of modern life,
With its sick hurry, its divided aims,
     Its heads o'ertaxed, its palsied hearts, was rife—
       Fly hence, our contact fear!
Still fly, plunge deeper in the bowering wood!
   Averse, as Dido did with gesture stern
   From her false friend's approach in Hades turn,
Wave us away and keep thy solitude!

Still nursing the unconquerable hope,
   Still clutching the inviolable shade,
     With a free, onward impulse brushing through,
By night, the silvered branches of the glade—
     Far on the forest-skirts, where none pursue,
       On some mild pastoral slope
Emerge, and resting on the moonlit pales
   Freshen thy flowers as in former years
   With dew, or listen with enchanted ears,
From the dark dingles, to the nightingales!

But fly our paths, our feverish contact fly!
   For strong the infection of our mental strife,
     Which, though it gives no bliss, yet spoils for rest;
And we should win thee from thy own fair life,

Like us distracted, and like us unblest.
    Soon, soon thy cheer would die,
Thy hopes grow timorous, and unfixed thy powers,
    And thy clear aims be cross and shifting made;
    And then thy glad perennial youth would fade,
Fade, and grow old at last, and die like ours.

Then fly our greetings, fly our speech and smiles!
    As some grave Tyrian trader, from the sea,
    Descried at sunrise an emerging prow
Lifting the cool-haired creepers stealthily,
    The fringes of a southward-facing brow
        Among the Ægæan isles;
And saw the merry Grecian coaster come,
    Freighted with amber grapes, and Chian wine,
    Green, bursting figs, and tunnies steeped in brine—
And knew the intruders on his ancient home,

The young light-hearted masters of the waves—
    And snatched his rudder, and shook out more sail;
    And day and night held on indignantly
O'er the blue Midland waters with the gale,
    Betwixt the Syrtes and soft Sicily,
        To where the Atlantic raves
Outside the western straits; and unbent sails
    There, where down cloudy cliffs, through sheets of foam,
    Shy traffickers, the dark Iberians come;
And on the beach undid his corded bales.

CX

SCHOOL FENCIBLES

We come in arms, we stand ten score,
   Embattled on the castle green;
We grasp our firelocks tight, for war
   Is threatening, and we see our Queen.
And 'Will the churls last out till we
   Have duly hardened bones and thews
For scouring leagues of swamp and sea
   Of braggart mobs and corsair crews?'
We ask; we fear not scoff or smile
   At meek attire of blue and grey,
For the proud wrath that thrills our isle
   Gives faith and force to this array.
So great a charm is England's right,
   That hearts enlarged together flow,
And each man rises up a knight
   To work the evil-thinkers woe.
And, girt with ancient truth and grace,
   We do our service and our suit,
And each can be, whate'er his race,
   A Chandos or a Montacute.
Thou, Mistress, whom we serve to-day,
   Bless the real swords that we shall wield,
Repeat the call we now obey
   In sunset lands, on some fair field.
Thy flag shall make some Huron rock
   As dear to us as Windsor's keep,
And arms thy Thames hath nerved shall mock
   The surgings of th' Ontarian deep.

The stately music of thy Guards,
  Which times our march beneath thy ken,
Shall sound, with spells of sacred bards,
  From heart to heart, when we are men.
And when we bleed on alien earth,
  We'll call to mind how cheers of ours
Proclaimed a loud uncourtly mirth
  Amongst thy glowing orange bowers.
And if for England's sake we fall,
  So be it, so thy cross be won,
Fixed by kind hands on silvered pall,
  And worn in death, for duty done.
Ah! thus we fondle Death, the soldier's mate,
  Blending his image with the hopes of youth
To hallow all; meanwhile the hidden fate
  Chills not our fancies with the iron truth.
Death from afar we call, and Death is here,
  To choose out him who wears the loftiest mien;
And Grief, the cruel lord who knows no peer,
  Breaks through the shield of love to pierce our Queen.

CXI

THE TWO CAPTAINS

When George the Third was reigning a hundred years ago,
He ordered Captain Farmer to chase the foreign foe.
'You're not afraid of shot,' said he, 'you're not afraid of wreck,
So cruise about the west of France in the frigate called *Quebec*.

Quebec was once a Frenchman's town, but twenty years ago
King George the Second sent a man called General Wolfe, you know,
To clamber up a precipice and look into Quebec,
As you'd look down a hatchway when standing on the deck.

If Wolfe could beat the Frenchmen then so you can beat them now.
Before he got inside the town he died, I must allow.
But since the town was won for us it is a lucky name,
And you'll remember Wolfe's good work, and you shall do the same.'

Then Farmer said, 'I'll try, sir,' and Farmer bowed so low
That George could see his pigtail tied in a velvet bow.
George gave him his commission, and that it might be safer,
Signed 'King of Britain, King of France,' and sealed it with a wafer.

Then proud was Captain Farmer in a frigate of his own,
And grander on his quarter-deck than George upon the throne.
He'd two guns in his cabin, and on the spar-deck ten,
And twenty on the gun-deck, and more than ten score men.

And as a huntsman scours the brakes with sixteen brace of dogs,
With two-and-thirty cannon the ship explored the fogs.

From Cape la Hogue to Ushant, from Rochefort to Belleisle,
She hunted game till reef and mud were rubbing on her keel.

The fogs are dried, the frigate's side is bright with melting tar,
The lad up in the foretop sees square white sails afar;
The east wind drives three square-sailed masts from out the Breton bay,
And 'Clear for action!' Farmer shouts, and reefers yell 'Hooray!'

The Frenchman's captain had a name I wish I could pronounce;
A Breton gentleman was he, and wholly free from bounce,
One like those famous fellows who died by guillotine
For honour and the fleurs-de-lys and Antoinette the Queen.

The Catholic for Louis, the Protestant for George,
Each captain drew as bright a sword as saintly smiths could forge;
And both were simple seamen, but both could understand
How each was bound to win or die for flag and native land.

The French ship was *la Surveillante*, which means the watchful maid;
She folded up her head-dress and began to cannonade.

Her hull was clean, and ours was foul; we had to spread more sail.
On canvas, stays, and topsail yards her bullets came like hail.

Sore smitten were both captains, and many lads beside,
And still to cut our rigging the foreign gunners tried.
A sail-clad spar came flapping down athwart a blazing gun;
We could not quench the rushing flames, and so the Frenchman won.

Our quarter-deck was crowded, the waist was all aglow;
Men hung upon the taffrail half scorched, but loth to go;
Our captain sat where once he stood, and would not quit his chair.
He bade his comrades leap for life, and leave him bleeding there.

The guns were hushed on either side, the Frenchmen lowered boats,
They flung us planks and hencoops, and everything that floats.
They risked their lives, good fellows! to bring their rivals aid.
'Twas by the conflagration the peace was strangely made.

La Surveillante was like a sieve; the victors had no rest.
They had to dodge the east wind to reach the port of Brest.

And where fhe waves leapt lower, and the riddled
  ship went slower,
In triumph, yet in funeral guise, came fisher-boats to
  tow her.

They dealt with us as brethren, they mourned for
  Farmer dead;
And as the wounded captives passed each Breton
  bowed the head.
Then spoke the French Lieutenant, ''Twas fire that
  won, not we.
You never struck your flag to us; you'll go to
  England free.'

'Twas the sixth day of October, seventeen hundred
  seventy-nine,
A year when nations ventured against us to com-
  bine,
Quebec was burnt and Farmer slain, by us re-
  membered not;
But thanks be to the French book wherein they're
  not forgot.

Now you, if you've to fight the French, my youngster,
  bear in mind
Those seamen of King Louis so chivalrous and
  kind;
Think of the Breton gentlemen who took our lads to
  Brest,
And treat some rescued Breton as a comrade and a
  guest.

CXII

THE HEAD OF BRAN

WHEN the head of Bran
    Was firm on British shoulders,
God made a man!
    Cried all beholders.

Steel could not resist
    The weight his arm would rattle;
He with naked fist
    Has brained a knight in battle.

He marched on the foe,
    And never counted numbers;
Foreign widows know
    The hosts he sent to slumbers.

As a street you scan
    That's towered by the steeple,
So the head of Bran
    Rose o'er his people.

    'Death's my neighbour,'
        Quoth Bran the blest;
    'Christian labour
        Brings Christian rest.

From the trunk sever
    The head of Bran,
That which never
    Has bent to man!

That which never
    To men has bowed
Shall live ever
    To shame the shroud:
Shall live ever
    To face the foe;
Sever it, sever,
    And with one blow.

Be it written,
    That all I wrought
Was for Britain,
    In deed and thought:
Be it written,
    That, while I die,
"Glory to Britain!"
    Is my last cry.

"Glory to Britain!"
    Death echoes me round.
Glory to Britain!
    The world shall resound.
Glory to Britain!
    In ruin and fall,
Glory to Britain!
    Is heard over all.'

Burn, Sun, down the sea!
Bran lies low with thee.

Burst, Morn, from the main!
Bran so shall rise again.

Blow, Wind, from the field!
Bran's Head is the Briton's shield.

Beam, Star, in the west!
Bright burns the Head of Bran the Blest.

Crimson-footed like the stork,
  From great ruts of slaughter,
Warriors of the Golden Torque
  Cross the lifting water.
Princes seven, enchaining hands,
  Bear the live Head homeward.
Lo! it speaks, and still commands;
  Gazing far out foamward.

Fiery words of lightning sense
  Down the hollows thunder;
Forest hostels know not whence
  Comes the speech, and wonder.
City-castles, on the steep
  Where the faithful Severn
House at midnight, hear in sleep
  Laughter under heaven.

Lilies, swimming on the mere,
  In the castle shadow,
Under draw their heads, and Fear
  Walks the misty meadow;
Tremble not, it is not Death
  Pledging dark espousal:
'Tis the Head of endless breath,
  Challenging carousal!

Brim the horn! a health is drunk,
    Now, that shall keep going:
Life is but the pebble sunk,
    Deeds, the circle growing!
Fill, and pledge the Head of Bran!
    While his lead they follow,
Long shall heads in Britain plan
    Speech Death cannot swallow.

George Meredith.

CXIII

THE SLAYING OF THE NIBLUNGS

HOGNI

YE shall know that in Atli's feast-hall on the side that joined the house
Were many carven doorways whose work was glorious
With marble stones and gold-work, and their doors of beaten brass:
Lo now, in the merry morning how the story cometh to pass!
—While the echoes of the trumpet yet fill the people's ears,
And Hogni casts by the war-horn, and his Dwarf-wrought sword uprears,
All those doors aforesaid open, and in pour the streams of steel,
The best of the Eastland champions, the bold men of Atli's weal:

They raise no cry of battle nor cast forth threat of woe,
And their helmed and hidden faces from each other none may know:
Then a light in the hall ariseth, and the fire of battle runs
All adown the front of the Niblungs in the face of the mighty-ones;
All eyes are set upon them, hard drawn is every breath,
Ere the foremost points be mingled and death be blent with death.
—All eyes save the eyes of Hogni; but e'en as the edges meet,
He turneth about for a moment to the gold of the kingly seat,
Then aback to the front of battle; there then, as the lightning-flash
Through the dark night showeth the city when the clouds of heaven clash,
And the gazer shrinketh backward, yet he seeth from end to end
The street and the merry market, and the windows of his friend,
And the pavement where his footsteps yester'en returning trod,
Now white and changed and dreadful 'neath the threatening voice of God;
So Hogni seeth Gudrun, and the face he used to know,

Unspeakable, unchanging, with white unknitted brow
With half-closed lips untrembling, with deedless hands and cold
Laid still on knees that stir not, and the linen's moveless fold.

Turned Hogni unto the spear-wall, and smote from where he stood,
And hewed with his sword two-handed as the axe-man in a wood:
Before his sword was a champion, and the edges clave to the chin,
And the first man fell in the feast-hall of those that should fall therein.
Then man with man was dealing, and the Niblung host of war
Was swept by the leaping iron, as the rock anigh the shore
By the ice-cold waves of winter: yet a moment Gunnar stayed
As high in his hand unblooded he shook his awful blade;
And he cried: 'O Eastland champions, do ye behold it here,
The sword of the ancient Giuki? Fall on and have no fear,
But slay and be slain and be famous, if your master's will it be!
Yet are we the blameless Niblungs, and bidden guests are we:

So forbear, if ye wander hood-winked, nor for nothing slay and be slain;
For I know not what to tell you of the dead that live again.'

So he saith in the midst of the foemen with his war-flame reared on high,
But all about and around him goes up a bitter cry
From the iron men of Atli, and the bickering of the steel
Sends a roar up to the roof-ridge, and the Niblung war-ranks reel
Behind the steadfast Gunnar: but lo! have ye seen the corn,
While yet men grind the sickle, by the wind-streak overborne
When the sudden rain sweeps downward, and summer groweth black,
And the smitten wood-side roareth 'neath the driving thunder-wrack?
So before the wise-heart Hogni shrank the champions of the East,
As his great voice shook the timbers in the hall of Atli's feast.
There he smote, and beheld not the smitten, and by nought were his edges stopped;
He smote, and the dead were thrust from him; a hand with its shield he lopped;
There met him Alti's marshal, and his arm at the shoulder he shred;
Three swords were upreared against him of the best of the kin of the dead;

And he struck off a head to the rightward, and his
    sword through a throat he thrust,
But the third stroke fell on his helm-crest, and he
    stooped to the ruddy dust,
And uprose as the ancient Giant, and both his hands
    were wet:
Red then was the world to his eyen, as his hand to
    the labour he set;
Swords shook and fell in his pathway, huge bodies
    leapt and fell,
Harsh grided shield and war-helm like the tempest-
    smitten bell,
And the war-cries ran together, and no man his
    brother knew,
And the dead men loaded the living, as he went
    the war-wood through;
And man 'gainst man was huddled, till no sword
    rose to smite,
And clear stood the glorious Hogni in an island of
    the fight,
And there ran a river of death 'twixt the Niblung
    and his foes,
And therefrom the terror of men and the wrath of
    the Gods arose.

GUNNAR

Now fell the sword of Gunnar, and rose up red in
    the air,
And hearkened the song of the Niblung, as his voice
    rang glad and clear,

And rejoiced and leapt at the Eastmen, and cried as it met the rings
Of a Giant of King Atli and a murder-wolf of kings;
But it quenched its thirst in his entrails, and knew the heart in his breast,
And hearkened the praise of Gunnar, and lingered not to rest,
But fell upon Atli's brother, and stayed not in his brain;
Then he fell, and the King leapt over, and clave a neck atwain,
And leapt o'er the sweep of a pole-axe, and thrust a lord in the throat,
And King Atli's banner-bearer through shield and hauberk smote;
Then he laughed on the huddled East-folk, and against their war-shields drave
While the white swords tossed about him, and that archer's skull he clave
Whom Atli had bought in the Southlands for many a pound of gold;
And the dark-skinned fell upon Gunnar, and over his war-shield rolled,
And cumbered his sword for a season, and the many blades fell on,
And sheared the cloudy helm-crest and rents in his hauberk won,
And the red blood ran from Gunnar; till that Giuki's sword outburst,
As the fire-tongue from the smoulder that the leafy heap hath nursed,

And unshielded smote King Gunnar, and sent the Niblung song
Through the quaking stems of battle in the hall of Atli's wrong:
Then he rent the knitted war-hedge till by Hogni's side he stood,
And kissed him amidst of the spear-hail, and their cheeks were wet with blood.

Then on came the Niblung bucklers, and they drave the East-folk home,
As the bows of the oar-driven long-ship beat off the waves in foam:
They leave their dead behind them, and they come to the doors and the wall,
And a few last spears from the fleeing amidst their shield-hedge fall:
But the doors clash to in their faces, as the fleeing rout they drive,
And fain would follow after; and none is left alive
In the feast-hall of King Atli, save those fishes of the net,
And the white and silent woman above the slaughter set.

Then biddeth the heart-wise Hogni, and men to the windows climb,
And uplift the war-grey corpses, dead drift of the stormy time,
And cast them adown to their people: thence they come aback and say
That scarce shall ye see the houses, and no whit the wheel-worn way

For the spears and shields of the Eastlands that the merchant city throng;
And back to the Niblung burg-gate the way seemed weary-long.

Yet passeth hour on hour, and the doors they watch and ward
But a long while hear no mail-clash, nor the ringing of the sword;
Then droop the Niblung children, and their wounds are waxen chill,
And they think of the burg by the river, and the builded holy hill,
And their eyes are set on Gudrun as of men who would beseech;
But unlearned are they in craving, and know not dastard's speech.
Then doth Giuki's first-begotten a deed most fair to be told,
For his fair harp Gunnar taketh, and the warp of silver and gold;
With the hand of a cunning harper he dealeth with the strings,
And his voice in their midst goeth upward, as of ancient days he sings,
Of the days before the Niblungs, and the days that shall be yet;
Till the hour of toil and smiting the warrior hearts forget,
Nor hear the gathering foemen, nor the sound of swords aloof:

Then clear the song of Gunnar goes up to the dusky roof,
And the coming spear-host tarries, and the bearers of the woe
Through the cloisters of King Atli with lingering footsteps go.

But Hogni looketh on Gudrun, and no change in her face he sees,
And no stir in her folded linen and the deedless hands on her knees:
Then from Gunnar's side he hasteneth; and lo! the open door,
And a foeman treadeth the pavement, and his lips are on Atli's floor,
For Hogni is death in the doorway: then the Niblungs turn on the foe,
And the hosts are mingled together, and blow cries out on blow.

GUDRUN

Still the song goeth up from Gunnar, though his harp to earth be laid;
But he fighteth exceeding wisely, and is many a warrior's aid,
And he shieldeth and delivereth, and his eyes search through the hall,
And woe is he for his fellows, as his battle-brethren fall;
For the turmoil hideth little from that glorious folk-king's eyes,
And o'er all he beholdeth Gudrun, and his soul is waxen wise,

And he saith: 'We shall look on Sigurd, and Sigmund of old days,
And see the boughs of the Branstock o'er the ancient Volsung's praise.'

Woe's me for the wrath of Hogni! From the door he giveth aback
That the Eastland slayers may enter to the murder and the wrack:
Then he rageth and driveth the battle to the golden kingly seat,
And the last of the foes he slayeth by Gudrun's very feet,
That the red blood splasheth her raiment; and his own blood therewithal
He casteth aloft before her, and the drops on her white hands fall:
But nought she seeth or heedeth, and again he turns to fight,
Nor heedeth stroke nor wounding so he a foe may smite:
Then the battle opens before him, and the Niblungs draw to his side;
As death in the world first fashioned, through the feast-hall doth he stride.
And so once more do the Niblungs sweep that murder-flood of men
From the hall of toils and treason, and the doors swing to again.
Then again is there peace for a little within the fateful fold;

But the Niblungs look about them, and but few folk they behold
Upright on their feet for the battle: now they climb aloft no more,
Nor cast the dead from the windows; but they raise a rampart of war,
And its stones are the fallen East-folk, and no lowly wall is that.

Therein was Gunnar the mighty: on the shields of men he sat,
And the sons of his people hearkened, for his hand through the harp-strings ran,
And he sang in the hall of his foeman of the Gods and the making of man,
And how season was sundered from season in the days of the fashioning,
And became the Summer and Autumn, and became the Winter and Spring;
He sang of men's hunger and labour, and their love and their breeding of broil,
And their hope that is fostered of famine, and their rest that is fashioned of toil:
Fame then and the sword he sang of, and the hour of the hardy and wise,
When the last of the living shall perish, and the first of the dead shall arise,
And the torch shall be lit in the daylight, and God unto man shall pray,
And the heart shall cry out for the hand in the fight of the uttermost day.

So he sang, and beheld not Gudrun, save as long ago he saw
His sister, the little maiden of the face without a flaw:
But wearily Hogni beheld her, and no change in her face there was,
And long thereon gazed Hogni, and set his brows as the brass,
Though the hands of the King were weary, and weak his knees were grown,
And he felt as a man unholpen in a waste land wending alone.

THE SONS OF GIUKI

Now the noon was long passed over when again the rumour arose,
And through the doors cast open flowed in the river of foes:
They flooded the hall of the murder, and surged round that rampart of dead;
No war-duke ran before them, no lord to the onset led,
But the thralls shot spears at adventure, and shot out shafts from afar,
Till the misty hall was blinded with the bitter drift of war:
Few and faint were the Niblung children, and their wounds were waxen acold,
And they saw the Hell-gates open as they stood in their grimly hold:
Yet thrice stormed out King Hogni, thrice stormed out Gunnar the King,

Thrice fell they aback yet living to the heart of
    the fated ring;
And they looked and their band was little, and no
    man but was wounded sore,
And the hall seemed growing greater, such hosts of
    foes it bore,
So tossed the iron harvest from wall to gilded wall;
And they looked and the white-clad Gudrun sat
    silent over all.

Then the churls and thralls of the Eastland howled
    out as wolves accurst,
But oft gaped the Niblungs voiceless, for they choked
    with anger and thirst;
And the hall grew hot as a furnace, and men drank
    their flowing blood,
Men laughed and gnawed on their shield-rims, men
    knew not where they stood,
And saw not what was before them; as in the dark
    men smote,
Men died heart-broken, unsmitten; men wept with
    the cry in the throat,
Men lived on full of war-shafts, men cast their
    shields aside
And caught the spears to their bosoms; men rushed
    with none beside,
And fell unarmed on the foemen, and tore and slew
    in death:
And still down rained the arrows as the rain across
    the heath;
Still proud o'er all the turmoil stood the Kings of
    Giuki born,

Nor knit were the brows of Gunnar, nor his song-speech overworn;
But Hogni's mouth kept silence, and oft his heart went forth
To the long, long day of the darkness, and the end of worldly worth.

Loud rose the roar of the East-folk, and the end was coming at last:
Now the foremost locked their shield-rims and the hindmost over them cast,
And nigher they drew and nigher, and their fear was fading away,
For every man of the Niblungs on the shaft-strewn pavement lay,
Save Gunnar the King and Hogni: still the glorious King up-bore
The cloudy shield of the Niblungs set full of shafts of war;
But Hogni's hands had fainted, and his shield had sunk adown,
So thick with the Eastland spearwood was that rampart of renown;
And hacked and dull were the edges that had rent the wall of foes:
Yet he stood upright by Gunnar before that shielded close,
Nor looked on the foeman's faces as their wild eyes drew anear,
And their faltering shield-rims clattered with the remnant of their fear;

But he gazed on the Niblung woman, and the
daughter of his folk,
Who sat o'er all unchanging ere the war-cloud over
them broke.

Now nothing might men hearken in the house of
Atli's weal,
Save the feet slow tramping onward, and the rattling
of the steel,
And the song of the glorious Gunnar, that rang as
clearly now
As the speckled storm-cock singeth from the scant-
leaved hawthorn-bough,
When the sun is dusking over and the March snow
pelts the land.
There stood the mighty Gunnar with sword and
shield in hand,
There stood the shieldless Hogni with set unangry
eyes,
And watched the wall of war-shields o'er the dead
men's rampart rise,
And the white blades flickering nigher, and the
quavering points of war.
Then the heavy air of the feast-hall was rent with a
fearful roar,
And the turmoil came and the tangle, as the wall
together ran:
But aloft yet towered the Niblungs, and man toppled
over man,
And leapt and struggled to tear them; as whiles
amidst the sea

The doomed ship strives its utmost with mid-ocean's
    mastery,
And the tall masts whip the cordage, while the
    welter whirls and leaps,
And they rise and reel and waver, and sink amid
    the deeps:
So before the little-hearted in King Atli's murder-hall
Did the glorious sons of Giuki 'neath the shielded
    onrush fall:
Sore wounded, bound and helpless, but living yet,
    they lie
Till the afternoon and the even in the first of night
    shall die.

William Morris.

CXIV

IS LIFE WORTH LIVING

Is life worth living? Yes, so long
   As Spring revives the year,
And hails us with the cuckoo's song,
   To show that she is here;
So long as May of April takes,
   In smiles and tears, farewell,
And windflowers dapple all the brakes,
   And primroses the dell;
While children in the woodlands yet
   Adorn their little laps
With ladysmock and violet,
   And daisy-chain their caps;
While over orchard daffodils
   Cloud-shadows float and fleet,

And ousel pipes and laverock trills,
  And young lambs buck and bleat;
So long as that which bursts the bud
  And swells and tunes the rill
Makes springtime in the maiden's blood,
  Life is worth living still.

Life not worth living! Come with me,
  Now that, through vanishing veil,
Shimmers the dew on lawn and lea,
  And milk foams in the pail;
Now that June's sweltering sunlight bathes
  With sweat the striplings lithe,
As fall the long straight scented swathes
  Over the crescent scythe;
Now that the throstle never stops
  His self-sufficing strain,
And woodbine-trails festoon the copse,
  And eglantine the lane;
Now rustic labour seems as sweet
  As leisure, and blithe herds
Wend homeward with unweary feet,
  Carolling like the birds;
Now all, except the lover's vow,
  And nightingale, is still;
Here, in the twilight hour, allow,
  Life is worth living still.

When Summer, lingering half-forlorn,
  On Autumn loves to lean,
And fields of slowly yellowing corn
  Are girt by woods still green;

When hazel-nuts wax brown and plump,
   And apples rosy-red,
And the owlet hoots from hollow stump,
   And the dormouse makes its bed;
When crammed are all the granary floors,
   And the Hunter's moon is bright,
And life again is sweet indoors,
   And logs again alight;
Ay, even when the houseless wind
   Waileth through cleft and chink,
And in the twilight maids grow kind,
   And jugs are filled and clink;
When children clasp their hands and pray
   'Be done Thy Heavenly will!'
Who doth not lift his voice, and say,
   'Life is worth living still'?

Is life worth living? Yes, so long
   As there is wrong to right,
Wail of the weak against the strong,
   Or tyranny to fight;
Long as there lingers gloom to chase,
   Or streaming tear to dry,
One kindred woe, one sorrowing face
   That smiles as we draw nigh;
Long as at tale of anguish swells
   The heart, and lids grow wet,
And at the sound of Christmas bells
   We pardon and forget;
So long as Faith with Freedom reigns,
   And loyal Hope survives,

And gracious Charity remains
  To leaven lowly lives;
While there is one untrodden tract
  For Intellect or Will,
And men are free to think and act
  Life is worth living still.

Not care to live while English homes
  Nestle in English trees,
And England's Trident-Sceptre roams
  Her territorial seas!
Not live while English songs are sung
  Wherever blows the wind,
And England's laws and England's tongue
  Enfranchise half mankind!
So long as in Pacific main,
  Or on Atlantic strand,
Our kin transmit the parent strain,
  And love the Mother-land;
So long as flashes English steel,
  And English trumpets shrill,
He is dead already who doth not feel
  Life is worth living still.

Austin.

CXV

THEOLOGY IN EXTREMIS

Oft in the pleasant summer years,
  Reading the tales of days bygone,
I have mused on the story of human tears,
  All that man unto man has done,

Massacre, torture, and black despair;
Reading it all in my easy-chair.

Passionate prayer for a minute's life;
    Tortured crying for death as rest;
Husband pleading for child or wife,
    Pitiless stroke upon tender breast.
Was it all real as that I lay there
Lazily stretched on my easy-chair?

Could I believe in those hard old times,
    Here in this safe luxurious age?
Were the horrors invented to season rhymes,
    Or truly is man so fierce in his rage?
What could I suffer, and what could I dare?
I who was bred to that easy-chair.

They were my fathers, the men of yore,
    Little they recked of a cruel death;
They would dip their hands in a heretic's gore,
    They stood and burnt for a rule of faith.
What would I burn for, and whom not spare?
I, who had faith in an easy-chair.

Now do I see old tales are true,
    Here in the clutch of a savage foe;
Now shall I know what my fathers knew,
    Bodily anguish and bitter woe,
Naked and bound in the strong sun's glare,
Far from my civilised easy-chair.

Now have I tasted and understood
    That old-world feeling of mortal hate;

For the eyes all round us are hot with blood;
  They will kill us coolly—they do but wait;
While I, I would sell ten lives, at least,
For one fair stroke at that devilish priest.

Just in return for the kick he gave,
  Bidding me call on the prophet's name;
Even a dog by this may save
  Skin from the knife and soul from the flame;
My soul! if he can let the prophet burn it,
But life is sweet if a word may earn it.

A bullock's death, and at thirty years!
  Just one phrase, and a man gets off it;
Look at that mongrel clerk in his tears
  Whining aloud the name of the prophet;
Only a formula easy to patter,
And, God Almighty, what *can* it matter?

'Matter enough,' will my comrade say
  Praying aloud here close at my side,
'Whether you mourn in despair alway,
  Cursed for ever by Christ denied;
Or whether you suffer a minute's pain
All the reward of Heaven to gain.'

Not for a moment faltereth he,
  Sure of the promise and pardon of sin;
Thus did the martyrs die, I see,
  Little to lose and muckle to win;
Death means Heaven, he longs to receive it,
But what shall I do if I don't believe it?

Life is pleasant, and friends may be nigh,
   Fain would I speak one word and be spared;
Yet I could be silent and cheerfully die,
   If I were only sure God cared;
If I had faith, and were only certain
That light is behind that terrible curtain.

But what if He listeth nothing at all,
   Of words a poor wretch in his terror may say?
That mighty God who created all
   To labour and live their appointed day;
Who stoops not either to bless or ban,
Weaving the woof of an endless plan.

He is the Reaper, and binds the sheaf,
   Shall not the season its order keep?
Can it be changed by a man's belief?
   Millions of harvests still to reap;
Will God reward, if I die for a creed,
Or will He but pity, and sow more seed?

Surely He pities who made the brain,
   When breaks that mirror of memories sweet,
When the hard blow falleth, and never again
   Nerve shall quiver nor pulse shall beat;
Bitter the vision of vanishing joys;
Surely He pities when man destroys.

Here stand I on the ocean's brink,
   Who hath brought news of the further shore?
How shall I cross it? Sail or sink,
   One thing is sure, I return no more;
Shall I find haven, or aye shall I be
Tossed in the depths of a shoreless sea?

They tell fair tales of a far-off land,
   Of love rekindled, of forms renewed;
There may I only touch one hand
   Here life's ruin will little be rued;
But the hand I have pressed and the voice I have heard,
To lose them for ever, and all for a word!

Now do I feel that my heart must break
   All for one glimpse of a woman's face;
Swiftly the slumbering memories wake
   Odour and shadow of hour and place;
One bright ray through the darkening past
Leaps from the lamp as it brightens last,

Showing me summer in western land
   Now, as the cool breeze murmureth
In leaf and flower—And here I stand
   In this plain all bare save the shadow of death;
Leaving my life in its full noonday,
And no one to know why I flung it away.

Why? Am I bidding for glory's roll?
   I shall be murdered and clean forgot;
Is it a bargain to save my soul?
   God, whom I trust in, bargains not;
Yet for the honour of English race,
May I not live or endure disgrace.

Ay, but the word, if I could have said it,
   I by no terrors of hell perplext;
Hard to be silent and have no credit
   From man in this world, or reward in the next;

None to bear witness and reckon the cost
Of the name that is saved by the life that is lost.

I must be gone to the crowd untold
   Of men by the cause which they served unknown,
Who moulder in myriad graves of old;
   Never a story and never a stone
Tells of the martyrs who die like me,
Just for the pride of the old countree.
Lyall.

CXVI

THE OBLATION

Ask nothing more of me, sweet;
   All I can give you I give.
     Heart of my heart, were it more,
More would be laid at your feet:
   Love that should help you to live,
     Song that should spur you to soar.

All things were nothing to give
   Once to have sense of you more,
     Touch you and taste of you, sweet,
Think you and breathe you and live,
   Swept of your wings as they soar,
     Trodden by chance of your feet.

I that have love and no more
   Give you but love of you, sweet:
     He that hath more, let him give;
He that hath wings, let him soar;
   Mine is the heart at your feet
     Here, that must love you to live.

CXVII

ENGLAND

ENGLAND, queen of the waves, whose green inviolate girdle enrings thee round,
Mother fair as the morning, where is now the place of thy foemen found?
Still the sea that salutes us free proclaims them stricken, acclaims thee crowned.
Time may change, and the skies grow strange with signs of treason, and fraud, and fear:
Foes in union of strange communion may rise against thee from far and near:
Sloth and greed on thy strength may feed as cankers waxing from year to year.

Yet, though treason and fierce unreason should league and lie and defame and smite,
We that know thee, how far below thee the hatred burns of the sons of night,
We that love thee, behold above thee the witness written of life in light.

Life that shines from thee shows forth signs that none may read not by eyeless foes:
Hate, born blind, in his abject mind grows hopeful now but as madness grows:
Love, born wise, with exultant eyes adores thy glory, beholds and glows.
Truth is in thee, and none may win thee to lie, forsaking the face of truth:

Freedom lives by the grace she gives thee, born
    again from thy deathless youth:
Faith should fail, and the world turn pale, wert thou
    the prey of the serpent's tooth.

Greed and fraud, unabashed, unawed, may strive to
    sting thee at heel in vain;
Craft and fear and mistrust may leer and mourn and
    murmur and plead and plain:
Thou art thou: and thy sunbright brow is hers that
    blasted the strength of Spain.

Mother, mother beloved, none other could claim in
    place of thee England's place:
Earth bears none that beholds the sun so pure of
    record, so clothed with grace:
Dear our mother, nor son nor brother is thine, as
    strong or as fair of face,
How shalt thou be abased? or how shalt fear take
    hold of thy heart? of thine,
England, maiden immortal, laden with charge of life
    and with hopes divine?
Earth shall wither, when eyes turned hither behold
    not light in her darkness shine.

England, none that is born thy son, and lives by
    grace of thy glory, free,
Lives and yearns not at heart and burns with hope
    to serve as he worships thee;
None may sing thee: the sea-wind's wing beats
    down our songs as it hails the sea.

CXVIII

A JACOBITE IN EXILE

The weary day rins down and dies,
    The weary night wears through:
And never an hour is fair wi' flower,
    And never a flower wi' dew.

I would the day were night for me,
    I would the night were day:
For then would I stand in my ain fair land,
    As now in dreams I may.

O lordly flow the Loire and Seine,
    And loud the dark Durance:
But bonnier shine the braes of Tyne
    Than a' the fields of France;
And the waves of Till that speak sae still
    Gleam goodlier where they glance.

O weel were they that fell fighting
    On dark Drumossie's day:
They keep their hame ayont the faem
    And we die far away.

O sound they sleep, and saft, and deep,
    But night and day wake we;
And ever between the sea banks green
    Sounds loud the sundering sea.

And ill we sleep, sae sair we weep
    But sweet and fast sleep they:
And the mool that haps them roun' and laps them
    Is e'en their country's clay;

But the land we tread that are not dead
   Is strange as night by day.

Strange as night in a strange man's sight,
   Though fair as dawn it be:
For what is here that a stranger's cheer
   Should yet wax blithe to see?

The hills stand steep, the dells lie deep,
   The fields are green and gold:
The hill-streams sing, and the hill-sides ring,
   As ours at home of old.

But hills and flowers are nane of ours,
   And ours are over sea:
And the kind strange land whereon we stand,
   It wotsna what were we
Or ever we came, wi' scathe and shame,
   To try what end might be.

Scathe and shame, and a waefu' name,
   And a weary time and strange,
Have they that seeing a weird for dreeing
   Can die, and cannot change.

Shame and scorn may we thole that mourn,
   Though sair be they to dree:
But ill may we bide the thoughts we hide,
   Mair keen than wind and sea.

Ill may we thole the night's watches,
   And ill the weary day:
And the dreams that keep the gates of sleep,
   A waefu' gift gie they;
For the songs they sing us, the sights they bring us,
   The morn blaws all away.

On Aikenshaw the sun blinks braw,
   The burn rins blithe and fain:
There's nought wi' me I wadna gie
   To look thereon again.

On Keilder-side the wind blaws wide:
   There sounds nae hunting-horn
That rings sae sweet as the winds that beat
   Round banks where Tyne is born.

The Wansbeck sings with all her springs
   The bents and braes give ear;
But the wood that rings wi' the sang she sings
   I may not see nor hear;
For far and far thae blithe burns are,
   And strange is a' thing near.

The light there lightens, the day there brightens,
   The loud wind there lives free:
Nae light comes nigh me or wind blaws by me
   That I wad hear or see.

But O gin I were there again,
   Afar ayont the faem,
Cauld and dead in the sweet saft bed
   That haps my sires at hame!

We'll see nae mair the sea-banks fair,
   And the sweet grey gleaming sky,
And the lordly strand of Northumberland,
   And the goodly towers thereby;
And none shall know but the winds that blow
   The graves wherein we lie.

CXIX

THE REVEILLÉ

Hark! I hear the tramp of thousands,
  And of armèd men the hum;
Lo! a nation's hosts have gathered
  Round the quick alarming drum,—
      Saying, 'Come,
      Freemen, come!
Ere your heritage be wasted,' said the quick alarming drum.

'Let me of my heart take counsel:
  War is not of life the sum;
Who shall stay and reap the harvest
  When the autumn days shall come?
      But the drum
      Echoed, 'Come!
Death shall reap the braver harvest,' said the solemn-sounding drum.

'But when won the coming battle,
  What of profit springs therefrom?
What if conquest, subjugation,
  Even greater ills become?'
      But the drum
      Answered, 'Come!
You must do the sum to prove it,' said the Yankee-answering drum.

'What if, 'mid the cannons' thunder,
  Whistling shot and bursting bomb,

When my brothers fall around me,
   Should my heart grow cold and numb?'
      But the drum
      Answered, 'Come!
Better there in death united, than in life a recreant,
   —Come!'

Thus they answered,—hoping, fearing,
   Some in faith, and doubting some,
Till a trumpet-voice proclaiming,
   Said, 'My chosen people, come!'
      Then the drum,
      Lo! was dumb,
For the great heart of the nation, throbbing, answered,
   'Lord, we come!'

CXX

WHAT THE BULLET SANG

   O Joy of creation
      To be!
   O rapture to fly
      And be free!
   Be the battle lost or won
   Though its smoke shall hide the sun,
   I shall find my love—the one
      Born for me!

   I shall know him where he stands,
      All alone,
   With the power in his hands
      Not o'erthrown;

I shall know him by his face,
By his god-like front and grace;
I shall hold him for a space
    All my own!

It is he—O my love!
    So bold!
It is I—All thy love
    Foretold!
It is I. O love! what bliss!
Dost thou answer to my kiss?
O sweetheart! what is this
    Lieth there so cold?

Bret Harte.

CXXI

A BALLAD OF THE ARMADA

King Philip had vaunted his claims;
  He had sworn for a year he would sack us;
With an army of heathenish names
  He was coming to fagot and stack us;
  Like the thieves of the sea he would track us,
And shatter our ships on the main;
  But we had bold Neptune to back us—
And where are the galleons of Spain?

His carackes were christened of dames
  To the kirtles whereof he would tack us;
With his saints and his gilded stern-frames
  He had thought like an egg-shell to crack us;

Now Howard may get to his Flaccus,
And Drake to his Devon again,
   And Hawkins bowl rubbers to Bacchus—
For where are the galleons of Spain?

Let his Majesty hang to St. James
   The axe that he whetted to hack us;
He must play at some lustier games
   Or at sea he can hope to out-thwack us;
   To his mines of Peru he would pack us
To tug at his bullet and chain;
   Alas! that his Greatness should lack us!—
But where are the galleons of Spain?

ENVOY

   GLORIANA!—the Don may attack us
Whenever his stomach be fain;
   He must reach us before he can rack us, . . .
And where are the galleons of Spain?

Dobson.

CXXII

THE WHITE PACHA

VAIN is the dream! However Hope may rave,
He perished with the folk he could not save,
And though none surely told us he is dead,
And though perchance another in his stead,
Another, not less brave, when 'all was done,
Had fled unto the southward and the sun,
Had urged a way by force, or won by guile
To streams remotest of the secret Nile,

Had raised an army of the Desert men,
And, waiting for his hour, had turned again
And fallen on that False Prophet, yet we know
Gordon is dead, and these things are not so!
Nay, not for England's cause, nor to restore
Her trampled flag—for he loved Honour more—
Nay, not for Life, Revenge, or Victory,
Would he have fled, whose hour had dawned to die
He will not come again, whate'er our need,
He will not come, who is happy, being freed
From the deathly flesh and perishable things,
And lies of statesmen and rewards of kings.
Nay, somewhere by the sacred River's shore
He sleeps like those who shall return no more,
No more return for all the prayers of men—
Arthur and Charles—they never come again!
They shall not wake, though fair the vision seem:
Whate'er sick Hope may whisper, vain the dream!
Lang.

CXXIII

MOTHER AND SON

It is not yours, O mother, to complain,
Not, mother, yours to weep,
Though nevermore your son again
Shall to your bosom creep,
Though nevermore again you watch your baby sleep

Though in the greener paths of earth
Mother and child, no more
We wander; and no more the birth

Of me whom once you bore,
Seems still the brave reward that once it seemed of yore;

Though as all passes, day and night,
The seasons and the years,
From you, O mother, this delight,
This also disappears—
Some profit yet survives of all your pangs and tears.

The child, the seed, the grain of corn,
The acorn on the hill,
Each for some separate end is born
In season fit, and still
Each must in strength arise to work the Almighty will.

So from the hearth the children flee,
By that Almighty hand
Austerely led; so one by sea
Goes forth, and one by land;
Nor aught of all men's sons escapes from that command.

So from the sally each obeys
The unseen Almighty nod;
So till the ending all their ways
Blind-folded loth have trod:
Nor knew their task at all, but were the tools of God.

And as the fervent smith of yore
Beat out the glowing blade,
Nor wielded in the front of war

The weapons that he made,
But in the tower at home still plied his ringing
    trade;

So like a sword the son shall roam
On nobler missions sent;
And as the smith remained at home
In peaceful turret pent,
So sits the while at home the mother well content.

Stevenson.

CXXIV

PRAYERS

God who created me
　Nimble and light of limb,
In three elements free,
　To run, to ride, to swim:
Not when the sense is dim,
　But now from the heart of joy,
I would remember Him:
　Take the thanks of a boy.

Jesu, King and Lord,
　Whose are my foes to fight,
Gird me with Thy sword
　Swift and sharp and bright.
Thee would I serve if I might;
　And conquer if I can,
From day-dawn till night,
　Take the strength of a man.

Spirit of Love and Truth,
  Breathing in grosser clay,
The light and flame of youth,
  Delight of men in the fray,
Wisdom in strength's decay;
  From pain, strife, wrong to be free
This best gift I pray,
  Take my spirit to Thee.

Beeching.

CXXV

A BALLAD OF EAST AND WEST

KAMAL is out with twenty men to raise the Border side,
And he has lifted the Colonel's mare that is the Colonel's pride:
He has lifted her out of the stable-door between the dawn and the day,
And turned the calkins upon her feet, and ridden her far away.
Then up and spoke the Colonel's son that led a troop of the Guides:
'Is there never a man of all my men can say where Kamal hides?'
Then up and spoke Mahommed Khan, the son of the Ressaldar,
'If ye know the track of the morning-mist, ye know where his pickets are.
At dusk he harries the Abazai—at dawn he is into Bonair—
But he must go by Fort Bukloh to his own place to fare,

So if ye gallop to Fort Bukloh as fast as a bird can fly,
By the favour of God ye may cut him off ere he win to the Tongue of Jagai.
But if he be passed the Tongue of Jagai, right swiftly turn ye then,
For the length and the breadth of that grisly plain are sown with Kamal's men.'
The Colonel's son has taken a horse, and a raw rough dun was he,
With the mouth of a bell and the heart of Hell and the head of the gallows-tree.
The Colonel's son to the Fort has won, they bid him stay to eat—
Who rides at the tail of a Border thief, he sits not long at his meat.
He's up and away from Fort Bukloh as fast as he can fly,
Till he was aware of his father's mare in the gut of the Tongue of Jagai,
Till he was aware of his father's mare with Kamal upon her back,
And when he could spy the white of her eye, he made the pistol crack.
He has fired once, he has fired twice, but the whistling ball went wide.
'Ye shoot like a soldier,' Kamal said. 'Show now if ye can ride.'
It's up and over the Tongue of Jagai, as blown dust-devils go,
The dun he fled like a stag of ten, but the mare like a barren doe.

The dun he leaned against the bit and slugged his
    head above,
But the red mare played with the snaffle-bars as a
    lady plays with a glove.
They have ridden the low moon out of the sky, their
    hoofs drum up the dawn,
The dun he went like a wounded bull, but the mare
    like a new-roused fawn.
The dun he fell at a water-course—in a woful heap
    fell he,—
And Kamal has turned the red mare back, and
    pulled the rider free.
He has knocked the pistol out of his hand—small
    room was there to strive—
' 'Twas only by favour of mine,' quoth he, 'ye rode
    so long alive;
There was not a rock for twenty mile, there was
    not a clump of tree,
But covered a man of my own men with his rifle
    cocked on his knee.
If I had raised my bridle-hand, as I have held it low,
The little jackals that flee so fast were feasting all
    in a row;
If I had bowed my head on my breast, as I have
    held it high,
The kite that whistles above us now were gorged
    till she could not fly.'
Lightly answered the Colonel's son:—' Do good to
    bird and beast,
But count who come for the broken meats before
    thou makest a feast.

If there should follow a thousand swords to carry
  my bones away,
Belike the price of a jackal's meal were more than
  a thief could pay.
They will feed their horse on the standing crop,
  their men on the garnered grain,
The thatch of the byres will serve their fires when
  all the cattle are slain.
But if thou thinkest the price be fair, and thy
  brethren wait to sup,
The hound is kin to the jackal-spawn,—howl, dog,
  and call them up!
And if thou thinkest the price be high, in steer
  and gear and stack,
Give me my father's mare again, and I'll fight my
  own way back!'
Kamal has gripped him by the hand and set him upon
  his feet.
'No talk shall be of dogs,' said he, 'when wolf and
  grey wolf meet.
May I eat dirt if thou hast hurt of me in deed or breath.
What dam of lances brought thee forth to jest at the
  dawn with Death?'
Lightly answered the Colonel's son:—'I hold by the
  blood of my clan;
Take up the mare for my father's gift—By God she
  has carried a man!'
The red mare ran to the Colonel's son, and nuzzled
  her nose in his breast,
'We be two strong men,' said Kamal then, 'but she
  loveth the younger best.

So she shall go with a lifter's dower, my turquoise studded rein,
My broidered saddle and saddle-cloth, and silver stirrups twain.'
The Colonel's son a pistol drew and held it muzzle-end,
'Ye have taken the one from a foe,' said he; 'will ye take the mate from a friend?'
'A gift for a gift,' said Kamal straight; 'a limb for the risk of a limb.
Thy father has sent his son to me, I'll send my son to him!'
With that he whistled his only son, who dropped from a mountain-crest—
He trod the ling like a buck in spring and he looked like a lance in rest.
'Now here is thy master,' Kamal said, 'who leads a troop of the Guides,
And thou must ride at his left side as shield to shoulder rides.
Till Death or I cut loose the tie, at camp and board and bed,
Thy life is his—thy fate it is to guard him with thy head.
And thou must eat the White Queen's meat, and all her foes are thine,
And thou must harry thy father's hold for the peace of the Border-line,
And thou must make a trooper tough and hack thy way to power—
Belike they will raise thee to Ressaldar when I am hanged in Peshawur.'

They have looked each other between the eyes,
   and there they found no fault,
They have taken the Oath of the Brother-in-Blood
   on leavened bread and salt;
They have taken the Oath of the Brother-in-Blood
   on fire and fresh-cut sod,
On the hilt and the haft of the Khyber knife, and
   the Wondrous Names of God.
The Colonel's son he rides the mare and Kamal's boy
   the dun,
And two have come back to Fort Bukloh where there
   went forth but one.
And when they drew to the Quarter-Guard, full
   twenty swords flew clear—
There was not a man but carried his feud with the
   blood of the mountaineer.
 Ha' done! ha' done!' said the Colonel's son. ' Put
   up the steel at your sides!
Last night ye had struck at a Border thief—to-
   night 'tis a man of the Guides!'

Oh, east is east, and west is west, and never the
   two shall meet
Till earth and sky stand presently at God's great
   Judgment Seat.
But there is neither east nor west, border or breed
   or birth,
When two strong men stand face to face, though
   they come from the ends of the earth.

CXXVI

THE FLAG OF ENGLAND

Winds of the World, give answer! They are whimpering to and fro—
And what should they know of England who only England know?—
The poor little street-bred people that vapour and fume and brag,
They are lifting their heads in the stillness to yelp at the English Flag.

Must we borrow a clout from the Boer—to plaster anew with dirt?
An Irish liar's bandage, or an English coward's shirt?
We may not speak of England; her Flag's to sell or share.
What is the Flag of England? Winds of the World, declare!

The North Wind blew:—'From Bergen my steel-shod vanguards go;
I chase your lazy whalers home from the Disko floe;
By the great North Lights above me I work the will of God,
And the liner splits on the ice-fields or the Dogger fills with cod.

I barred my gates with iron, I shuttered my doors with flame,
Because to force my ramparts your nutshell navies came;

I took the sun from their presence, I cut them
  down with my blast,
And they died, but the Flag of England blew free
  ere the spirit passed.

The lean white bear hath seen it in the long, long
  Arctic night,
The musk-ox knows the standard that flouts the
  Northern Light:
What is the Flag of England? Ye have but my
  bergs to dare,
Ye have but my drifts to conquer. Go forth, for
  it is there!'

The South Wind sighed:—'From the Virgins my
  mid-sea course was ta'en
Over a thousand islands lost in an idle main,
Where the sea-egg flames on the coral and the
  long-backed breakers croon
Their endless ocean legends to the lazy, locked
  lagoon.

Strayed amid lonely islets, mazed amid outer keys,
I waked the palms to laughter—I tossed the scud
  in the breeze—
Never was isle so little, never was sea so lone,
But over the scud and the palm-trees an English
  flag was flown.

I have wrenched it free from the halliard to hang
  for a wisp on the Horn;
I have chased it north to the Lizard—ribboned
  and rolled and torn;

I have spread its fold o'er the dying, adrift in a hopeless sea;
I have hurled it swift on the slaver, and seen the slave set free.

My basking sunfish know it, and wheeling albatross,
Where the lone wave fills with fire beneath the Southern Cross.
What is the Flag of England? Ye have but my reefs to dare,
Ye have but my seas to furrow. Go forth, for it is there!'

The East Wind roared:—'From the Kuriles, the Bitter Seas, I come,
And me men call the Home-Wind, for I bring the English home.
Look—look well to your shipping! By the breath of my mad typhoon
I swept your close-packed Praya and beached your best at Kowloon!

The reeling junks behind me and the racing seas before,
I raped your richest roadstead—I plundered Singapore!
I set my hand on the Hoogli; as a hooded snake she rose,
And I heaved your stoutest steamers to roost with the startled crows.

Never the lotos closes, never the wild-fowl wake,
But a soul goes out on the East Wind that died for England's sake—

Man or woman or suckling, mother or bride or maid—
Because on the bones of the English the English Flag is stayed.

The desert-dust hath dimmed it, the flying wild-ass knows,
The scared white leopard winds it across the taintless snows.
What is the Flag of England? Ye have but my sun to dare,
Ye have but my sands to travel. Go forth, for it is there!'

The West Wind called:—'In squadrons the thoughtless galleons fly
That bear the wheat and cattle lest street-bred people die.
They make my might their porter, they make my house their path,
And I loose my neck from their service and whelm them all in my wrath.

I draw the gliding fog-bank as a snake is drawn from the hole,
They bellow one to the other, the frighted ship-bells toll:
For day is a drifting terror till I raise the shroud with my breath,
And they see strange bows above them and the two go locked to death.

But whether in calm or wrack-wreath, whether by dark or day
I heave them whole to the conger or rip their plates away,
First of the scattered legions, under a shrieking sky,
Dipping between the rollers, the English Flag goes by.

The dead dumb fog hath wrapped it—the frozen dews have kissed—
The morning stars have hailed it, a fellow-star in the mist.
What is the Flag of England? Ye have but my breath to dare,
Ye have but my waves to conquer. Go forth, for it is there!'

NOTES

I

THIS descant upon one of the most glorious feats of arms that even England has achieved is selected and pieced together from the magnificent verse assigned to the Chorus—'*Enter* RUMOUR *painted full of tongues*'—to *King Henry V.*, the noble piece of pageantry produced in 1598, and a famous number from the *Poems Lyrick and Pastorall* (*circ.* 1605) of Michael Drayton. 'Look,' says Ben Jonson, in his *Vision on the Muses of his Friend, Michael Drayton:*—

> Look how we read the Spartans were inflamed
> With bold Tyrtæus' verse; when thou art named
> So shall our English youths urge on, and cry
> An AGINCOURT! an AGINCOURT! or die.

This, it is true, was in respect of another *Agincourt*, but we need not hesitate to appropriate it to our own: in respect of which—'To the Cambro-Britons and their Harp, His *Ballad of Agincourt*,' is the poet's own description—it is to note that Drayton had no model for it; that it remains wellnigh unique in English letters for over two hundred years; and that, despite such lapses into doggerel as the third stanza, and some curious infelicities of diction which need not here be specified, it remains, with a certain Sonnet, its author's chief title to fame. Compare the ballads of *The Brave Lord Willoughby* and *The Honour of Bristol* in the seventeenth century, the song of *The Arethusa* in the eighteenth, and in the nineteenth a choice of such Tyrtæan music as *The Battle of the Baltic*, Lord Tennyson's *Ballad of the Fleet*, and *The Red Thread of Honour* of the late Sir Francis Doyle.

II

Originally *The True Character of a Happy Life:* written and printed about 1614, and reprinted by Percy (1765) from the *Reliquiæ Wottonianæ* of 1651. Says Drummond of Ben Jonson, 'Sir Edward (*sic*) Wotton's verses of a Happy Life he hath by heart.' Of Wotton himself it was reserved for Cowley to remark that

> He did the utmost bounds of knowledge find,
> And found them not so large as was his mind;
>   *   *   *   *   *   *
> And when he saw that he through all had passed
> He died—lest he should idle grow at last.

See Izaak Walton, *Lives.*

III, IV

From *Underwoods* (1640). The first, *An Ode*, is addressed to an innominate not yet, I believe, identified. The second is part of that *Ode to the Immortal Memory of that Heroic Pair, Sir Lucius Cary and Sir Henry Morrison*, which is the first true Pindaric in the language. Gifford ascribes it to 1629, when Sir Henry died, but it seems not to have been printed before 1640. Sir Lucius Cary is the Lord Falkland of Clarendon and Horace Walpole.

V

From *The Mad Lover* (produced about 1618: published in 1640). Compare the wooden imitations of Dryden in *Amboyna* and elsewhere.

VI

First printed, Mr. Bullen tells me, in 1640. Compare X. (Shirley, *post*, p. 20), and the cry from Raleigh's *History of the World*: 'O Eloquent, Just, and Mighty Death! Whom none could advise, thou hast persuaded; what none hath dared, thou hast done; and whom all the World hath flattered, thou only hast cast out of the World and despised: thou hast drawn together all the far-stretched Greatness, all the Pride, Cruelty, and Ambition of Man, and covered it all over with these two narrow words, "*Hic Jacet*."'

VII, VIII

This pair of 'noble numbers,' of brilliant and fervent lyrics, is from *Hesperides, or, The Works both Human and Divine of Robert Herrick, Esq.* (1648).

IX

No. 61, '*Vertue*,' in *The Temple: Sacred Poems and Private Ejaculations*, 1632-33. Compare Herbert to Christopher Farrer, as reported by Izaak Walton:—'Tell him that I do not repine, but am pleased with my want of health; and tell him, my heart is fixed on that place where true joy is only to be found, and that I long to be there, and do wait for my appointed change with hope and patience.'

X

From *The Contention of Ajax and Ulysses*, printed 1659. Compare VI. (Beaumont, *ante*, p. 15), and Bacon, *Essays*, 'On Death':

NOTES

'But, above all, believe it, the sweetest canticle is *Nunc dimittis*, when a man hath attained worthy ends and expectations.'

XI

Written in the November of 1637, and printed next year in the *Obsequies to the Memorie of Mr. Edward King*. 'In this Monody,' the title runs, 'the Author bewails a Learned Friend unfortunately drowned in his passage from Chester on the Irish Seas, 1637. And by occasion foretells the ruine of our corrupted Clergie, then in their height.' King, who died at five- or six-and-twenty, was a personal friend of Milton's, but the true accents of grief are inaudible in *Lycidas*, which is, indeed, an example as perfect as exists of Milton's capacity for turning whatever he touched into pure poetry: an arrangement, that is, of 'the best words in the best order'; or, to go still further than Coleridge, the best words in the prescribed or inevitable sequence that makes the arrangement art. For the innumerable allusions see Professor Masson's edition of Milton (Macmillan, 1890), i. 187-201, and iii. 254-276.

XII

The Eighth Sonnet (Masson): 'When the Assault was Intended to the City.' Written in 1642, with Rupert and the King at Brentford, and printed in the edition of 1645.

XIII

The Sixteenth Sonnet (Masson): 'To the Lord General Cromwell, May, 1652: On the Proposals of Certain Ministers at the Committee for Propagation of the Gospel.' Printed by Philips, *Life of Milton*, 1694. In defence of the principle of Religious Voluntaryism, and against the intolerant Fifteen Proposals of John Owen and the majority of the Committee.

XIV

The Eighteenth Sonnet (Masson). 'Written in 1655,' says Masson, and referring 'to the persecution instituted, in the early part of the year, by Charles Emmanuel II., Duke of Savoy and Prince of Piedmont, against his Protestant subjects of the valleys of the Cottian Alps.' In January, an edict required them to turn Romanists or quit the country out of hand; it was enforced with such barbarity that Cromwell took the case of the sufferers in hand; and so vigorous was his action that the Edict was withdrawn and a convention was signed (August 1655) by which the Vaudois were permitted to worship as they would. Printed in 1673.

XV

The Nineteenth Sonnet (Masson) 'may have been written any time between 1652 and 1655,' the first years of Milton's blindness, 'but it follows the Sonnet on the Piedmontese Massacre in Milton's own volume of 1673.'

XVI, XVII

From the choric parts of *Samson Agonistes* (*i.e.* the Agonist, or Wrestler), first printed in 1671.

XVIII

Of uncertain date; first printed by Watson 1706-11. The version given here is Emerson's (which is shorter than the original), with the exception of the last stanza, which is Napier's (*Montrose*, i. Appendices). Napier is at great pains to prove that the ballad is allegorical, and that Montrose's 'dear and only love' was that unhappy King whose Epitaph, the famous *Great, Good, and Just*, he is said—falsely—to have written with his sword. Be this as it may, the verses have a second part, which has dropped into oblivion. For the Great Marquis, who reminded De Retz of the men in Plutarch's *Lives*, was not averse from the practice of poetry, and wrote, besides these numbers, a prayer ('Let them bestow on every airth a limb'), a 'pasquil,' a pleasant string of conceits in praise of woman, a set of vehement and fiery memorial stanzas on the King, and one copy of verses more.

XIX, XX

To Lucasta going to the Wars and *To Althea from Prison* are both, I believe, from Lovelace's *Lucasta* (1645).

XXI

First printed by Captain Thomson, *Works* (1776), from a copy he held, on what seems excellent authority, to be in Marvell's hand. The true title is *A Horatian Ode on Cromwell's Return from Ireland* (1650). It is always ascribed to Marvell (whose verse was first collected and printed by his widow in 1681), but there are faint doubts as to the authorship.

XXII

Poems (1681). This elegant and romantic lyric appears to have been inspired by a passage in the life of John Oxenbridge, of whom, 'religionis causa oberrantem,' it is enough to note that, after migrating to Bermudas, where he had a church, and being 'ejected' at the Restoration from an English cure, he went to Surinam (1662-67), to Barbadoes (1667), and to New England (1669), where he was made pastor of 'the First Church of Boston' (1670), and where he died in 1674. These details are from Mr. Grosart's *Marvell* (1875), i. 82-85, and ii. 5-8.

XXIII

Dryden's second Ode for Saint Cecilia's Day, *Alexander's Feast, or the Power of Sound*, as it is called, was written and printed in 1697. As it was designed for music (it was set by Jeremiah Clarke), the closing lines of every strophe are repeated by way of chorus. I have removed these repetitions as impertinent to the effect of the poem in print, and as interrupting the rushing vehemency of the narrative. The incident described is the burning of Persepolis.

XXIV

Written early in 1782, in memory of Robert Levett: 'an old and faithful friend,' says Johnson, and withal 'a very useful and very blameless man.' Excepting for the perfect odes of Cowper (*post*, pp. 85, 86), in these excellent and affecting verses the 'classic' note is audible for the last time in this book until we reach the *Iphigeneia* of Walter Savage Landor, who was a lad of seven at the date of their composition. They were written seventeen years after the publication of the *Reliques* (1765), and a full quarter century after the appearance of *The Bard* (1757); but in style they proceed from the age of Pope. For the rest, the Augustan Muse was an utter stranger to the fighting inspiration. Her gait was pedestrian, her purpose didactic, her practice neat and formal: and she prosed of England's greatest captain, the victor of Blenheim, as tamely as himself had been 'a parson in a tye-wig'—himself, and not the amiable man of letters who acted as her amanuensis for the nonce.

XXV

Chevy Chase is here preferred to *Otterbourne* as appealing more directly to Englishmen. The text is Percy's, and the movement, like that of all the English ballads, is jog-trot enough. Sidney's confession—that he never heard it, even from a blind fiddler, but it stirred him like the sound of a trumpet—refers, no doubt, to an earlier version than the present, which appears to date from the first quarter of the seventeenth century. Compare *The Brave Lord Willoughby* and *The Honour of Bristol* (*post*, pp. 60, 73).

XXVI

First printed by Percy. The text I give is, with some few variants, that of the vastly better version in *The Minstrelsy of the Scottish Border* (1802-3). Of the 'history' of the ballad the less said the better. The argument is neatly summarised by Mr. Allingham, p. 376 of *The Ballad Book* ('Golden Treasury,' 1879).

skeely = *skilful*	gurly = *rough*	wap = *warp*
white monie = *silver*	lap = *sprang*	flattered = '*fluttered*,
gane = *would suffice*	bout = *bolt*	or rather, floated'
half-fou = *the eighth*	twine = *thread*,	(Scott)
part of a peck	*i.e.* canvas	kaims = *combs*

XXVII

Printed by Percy, 'from an old black-letter copy; with some conjectural emendations.' At the suggestion of my friend, the Rev. Mr. Hunt, I have restored the original readings, as in truer consonancy with the vainglorious, insolent, and swaggering ballad spirit. As for the hero, Peregrine Bertie, Lord Willoughby of Eresby, described as 'one of the Queen's best swordsmen' and 'a great master of the art military,' he succeeded Leicester in the command in the Low Countries in 1587, distinguished himself repeatedly in fight with the Spaniards, and died in 1601. 'Both Norris and Turner were famous among the military men of that age' (Percy). In the Roxburgh Ballads the full title of the broadside—which is 'printed for S. Coles in Vine St., near Hatton Garden,'—is as follows:—'*A true relation of a famous and bloudy Battell fought in Flanders by the noble and valiant Lord Willoughby with* 1500 *English against* 40,000 *Spaniards, wherein the English obtained a notable victory for the glory and renown of our nation.* Tune: *Lord Willoughby.*'

XXVIII

First printed by Tom D'Urfey, *Wit and Mirth, etc.* (1720), vi. 289-91; revised by Robert Burns for *The Scots Musical Magazine*, and again by Allan Cunningham for *The Songs of Scotland;* given with many differences, 'long current in Selkirkshire,' in the *Minstrelsy of the Scottish Border*. The present version is a *rifaccimento* from Burns and Scott. It is worth noting that Græme (pronounced 'Grime'), and Graham are both forms of one name, which name was originally Grimm, and that, according to some, the latter orthography is the privilege of the chief of the clan.

XXIX

First printed in the *Minstrelsy*. This time the 'history' is authentic enough. It happened early in 1596, when Salkeld, the

NOTES

Deputy Warden of the Western Marches, seized under truce the person of William Armstrong of Kinmont—elsewhere described as 'Will Kinmonde the common thieffe'—and haled him to Carlisle Castle, whence he was rescued—'with shouting and crying and sound of trumpet'—by the Laird of Buccleuch, Keeper of Liddesdale, and a troop of two hundred horse. 'The Queen of England,' says Spottiswoode, 'having notice sent her of what was done, stormed not a little'; but see the excellent summary compiled by Scott (who confesses to having touched up the ballad) for the *Minstrelsy*.

Haribee = *the gallows hill at Carlisle*
reiver = *a border thief*, one of a class which lived sparely, fought stoutly, entertained the strictest sense of honour and justice, went ever on horseback, and carried the art of cattle-lifting to the highest possible point of perfection (*National Observer*, 30*th May*, 1891)

yett = *gate*
lawing = *reckoning*
basnet = *helmet*
curch = *coif or cap*
lightly = *to scorn*
in a lowe = *on fire*
slocken = *to slake*
splent = *shoulder-piece*
spauld = *shoulder*
broken men = *outlaws*

marshal men = *officers of law*
rank reiver = *common thief*
herry = *harry*
corbie = *crow*
lear = *learning*
row-footed = *rough-shod*
spait = *flood*
garred = *made*
slogan = *battle-cry*

stear = *stir*
saft = *light*
fleyed = *frightened*
bairns = *children*
spier = *ask*
hente = *lifted, haled*
maill = *rent*
furs = *furrows*
trew = *trust*
Christentie = *Christendom*

XXX

Communicated by Mr. Hunt,—who dates it about 1626—from Seyer's *Memoirs, Historical and Topographical, of Bristol and its Neighbourhood* (1821-23). The full title is *The Honour of Bristol; shewing how the Angel Gabriel of Bristol fought with three ships, who boarded as many times, wherein we cleared our decks and killed five hundred of their men, and wounded many more, and made them fly into Cales, when we lost but three men, to the Honour of the Angel Gabriel of Bristol*. To the tune *Our Noble King in his Progress*. Cales (13), pronounced as a dissyllable, is of course Cadiz. It is fair to add that this spirited and amusing piece of doggerel has been severely edited.

XXXI

From the *Minstrelsy*, where it is 'given, without alteration or improvement, from the most accurate copy that could be recovered.' The story runs that Helen Irving (or Helen Bell), of

348 NOTES

Kirkconnell in Dumfriesshire, was beloved by Adam Fleming, and (as some say) Bell of Blacket House; that she favoured the first, but her people encouraged the second; that she was thus constrained to tryst with Fleming by night in the churchyard, 'a romantic spot, almost surrounded by the river Kirtle'; that they were here surprised by the rejected suitor, who fired at his rival from the far bank of the stream; that Helen, seeking to shield her lover, was shot in his stead; and that Fleming, either there and then, or afterwards in Spain, avenged her death on the body of her slayer. Wordsworth has told the story in a copy of verses which shows, like so much more of his work, how dreary a poetaster he could be.

XXXII

This epic-in-little, as tremendous an invention as exists in verse, is from the *Minstrelsy*: 'as written down from tradition by a lady' (C. Kirkpatrick Sharpe).

corbies = *crows* fail-dyke = *wall of* hause-bane = *breast-*
theek = *thatch* *turf* *bone*

XXXIII

Begun in 1755, and finished and printed (with *The Progress of Poetry*) in 1757. 'Founded,' says the poet, 'on a tradition current in Wales, that Edward the First, when he concluded the conquest of that country, ordered all the bards that fell into his hands to be put to death.' The 'agonising king' (line 56) is Edward II.; the 'she-wolf of France' (57), Isabel his queen; the 'scourge of heaven' (60), Edward III.; the 'sable warrior' (67), Edward the Black Prince. Lines 75-82 commemorate the rise and fall of Richard II.; lines 83-90, the Wars of the Roses, the murders in the Tower, the 'faith' of Margaret of Anjou, the 'fame' of Henry V., the 'holy head' of Henry VI. The 'bristled boar' (93) is symbolical of Richard III.; 'half of thy heart' (99) of Eleanor of Castile, 'who died a few years after the conquest of Wales.' Line 110 celebrates the accession of the House of Tudor in fulfilment of the prophecies of Merlin and Taliessin; lines 115-20, Queen Elizabeth; lines 128-30, Shakespeare; lines 131-32, Milton; and the 'distant warblings' of line 133, 'the succession of poets after Milton's time' (Gray).

XXXIV, XXXV

Written, the one in September 1782 (in the August of which year the *Royal George* (108 guns) was overset in Portsmouth Harbour with the loss of close on a thousand souls), and the other 'after reading Hume's *History* in 1780' (Benham).

NOTES

XXXVI

It is worth recalling that at one time Walter Scott attributed this gallant lyric, which he printed in the *Minstrelsy*, to a 'greater Graham'—the Marquis of Montrose.

XXXVII, XXXVIII

Of these, the first, *Blow High, Blow Low*, was sung in *The Seraglio* (1776), a forgotten opera; the second, said to have been inspired by the death of the author's brother, a naval officer, in *The Oddities* (1778)—a 'table-entertainment,' where Dibdin was author, actor, singer, musician, accompanist, everything but audience and candle-snuffer. They are among the first in time of his sea-ditties.

XXXIX

It is told (*Life*, W. H. Curran, 1819) that Curran met a deserter, drank a bottle, and talked of his chances, with him, and put his ideas and sentiments into this song.

XL

The *Arethusa*, Mr. Hannay tells me, being attached to Keppel's fleet at the mouth of the Channel, was sent to order the *Belle Poule*, which was cruising with some smaller craft in search of Keppel's ships, to come under his stern. The *Belle Poule* (commanded by M. Chadeau de la Clocheterie) refusing, the *Arethusa* (Captain Marshall) opened fire. The ships were fairly matched, and in the action which ensued the *Arethusa* appears to have got the worst of it. In the end, after about an hour's fighting, Keppel's liners came up, and the *Belle Poule* made off. She was afterwards driven ashore by a superior English force, and it is an odd coincidence that in 1789 the *Arethusa* ran ashore off Brest during her action (10th March) with *l'Aigrette*. As for the French captain, he lived to command *l'Hercule*, De Grasse's leading ship in the great sea-fight (12th April 1782) with Rodney off Dominica, where he was killed.

XLI

From the *Songs of Experience* (1794).

XLII

Scots Musical Museum, 1788. Adapted from, or rather suggested by, the *Farewell*, which Macpherson, a cateran 'of great personal strength and musical accomplishment,' is said to have played and sung at the gallows foot; thereafter breaking his violin across his knee and submitting his neck to the hangman.

    spring = *a melody in quick time*   sturt = *molestation*

XLIII

Museum, 1796. Burns told Thomson and Mrs. Dunlop that this noble and most moving song was old; but nobody believed him then, and nobody believes him now.

pint-stoup = *pint-mug*
braes = *hill-sides*
gowans = *daisies*
paidl't = *paddled*
burn = *brook*
fiere = *friend, companion*
guid-willie = *well-meant, full of good-will*
waught = *draught*

XLIV

The first four lines are old. The rest were written apparently in 1788, when the poet sent this song and *Auld Lang Syne* to Mrs. Dunlop. It appeared in the *Museum*, 1790.

tassie = *a cup; Fr.* 'tasse'

XLV

About 1777–80: printed 1801. 'One of my juvenile works,' says Burns. 'I do not think it very remarkable, either for its merits or demerits.' But Hazlitt thought the world of it, and now it passes for one of Burns's masterpieces.

trysted = *appointed*   stoure = *dust and din*

XLVI

Museum, 1796. Attributed, in one shape or another, to a certain Captain Ogilvie. Sharpe, too, printed a broadside in which the third stanza (used more than once by Sir Walter) is found as here. But Scott Douglas (*Burns*, iii. 173) has 'no doubt that this broadside was printed after 1796,' and as it stands the thing is assuredly the work of Burns. The refrain and the metrical structure have been used by Scott (*Rokeby*, IV. 28), Carlyle, Charles Kingsley (*Dolcino to Margaret*), and Mr. Swinburne (*A Reiver's Neck Verse*), among others.

XLVII—LII

Of the first four numbers, the high-water mark of Wordsworth's achievement, all four were written in 1802; the second and third were published in 1803; the first and fourth in 1807. The *Ode to Duty* was written in 1805, and published in 1807, to which year belongs that *Song for the Feast of Brougham Castle*, from which I have extracted the excellent verses here called *Two Victories*.

LIII—LXII

The first three numbers are from *Marmion* (1808): I. Introduction; V. 12; and VI. 18-20, 25-27, and 33-34. The next is from *The Lady of the Lake* (1810), I. 1-9; *The Outlaw* is from

Rokeby (1813), III. 16; the *Pibroch* was published in 1816; *The Omnipotent* and *The Red Harlaw* are from *The Antiquary* (1816), and the *Farewell* from *The Pirate* (1821). As for *Bonny Dundee*, that incomparable ditty, it was written as late as 1825. 'The air of Bonny Dundee running in my head to-day,' he writes under date of 22d December (*Diary*, 1890, i. 61), 'I wrote a few verses to it before dinner, taking the key-note from the story of Clavers leaving the Scottish Convention of Estates in 1688-9. *I wonder if they are good.*' See *The Doom of Devorgoil* (1830), Note A, Act II. sc. 2.

LXIII

This unsurpassed piece of art, in which a music the most exquisite is used to body forth a set of suggestions that seem dictated by the very Spirit of Romance, was produced, under the influence of 'an anodyne,' as early as 1797. Coleridge, who calls it *Kubla Khan: A Vision within a Dream*, avers that, having fallen asleep in his chair over a sentence from Purchas's Pilgrimage—'Here the Khan Kubla commanded a palace to be built and a stately garden thereto; and thus ten miles of ground were enclosed with a wall,'—he remained unconscious for about three hours, 'during which time he had the most vivid confidence that he could not have composed less than three hundred lines'; 'if that,' he adds, 'can be called composition, in which all the images rose up before him as things, with a parallel production of the correspondent expressions, without any sensation or consciousness of effort.' On awakening, he proceeded to write out his 'composition,' and had set down as much of it as is printed here, when 'he was unfortunately called out by a person on business from Porlock,' whose departure, an hour after, left him wellnigh oblivious of the rest. This confession, which is dated 1816, has been generally accepted as true; but Coleridge had a trick of dreaming dreams about himself which makes doubt permissible.

LXIV

From the *Hellenics* (written in Latin, 1814-20, and translated into English at the instance of Lady Blessington), 1846. See Colvin, *Landor* ('English Men of Letters'), pp. 189, 190.

LXV—LXVII

Of the first, 'Napoleon and the British Sailor' (*The Pilgrim of Glencoe*, 1842), Campbe writes that the 'anecdote has been published in several public journals, both French and English.' 'My belief,' he continues, ' in its authenticity was confirmed by an Englishman, long resident in Boulogne, lately telling me that he remembered the circumstance to have been generally talked of in the place.' Authentic or not, I have preferred the story to *Hohenlinden*, as less hackneyed, for one thing, and, for another, less pretentious and rhetorical. The second (*Gertrude of Wyoming*, 1809) is truly one of 'the glories of our birth and state.' The third (*idem*) I have ventured to shorten by three stanzas: a proceeding which, however culpable it seem, at least gets rid of the chief who gave a country's wounds relief by stopping a battle, eliminates the mermaid and her song (the song that 'condoles'), and ends the lyric on as sonorous and romantic a word as even Shakespeare ever used.

LXVIII

Corn Law Rhymes, 1831.

LXIX

From that famous and successful forgery, Cromek's *Remains of Nithsdale and Galloway Song* (1810), written when Allan was a working mason in Dumfriesshire. I have omitted a stanza as inferior to the rest.

LXXI

English Songs and other Small Poems, 1834.

LXXII—LXXVIII

The first is from the *Hebrew Melodies* (1815); the next is selected from *The Siege of Corinth* (1816), 22-33; *Alhama* (*idem*) is a spirited yet faithful rendering of the *Romance muy Doloroso del Sitio y Toma de Alhama*, which existed both in Spanish and in Arabic, and whose effect was such that 'it was forbidden to be sung by the Moors on the pain of death in Granada' (Byron); No. LXXV., surely one of the bravest songs in the language, was addressed (*idem*) to Thomas Moore; the tremendous *Race with Death* is lifted out of the *Ode in Venice* (1819); for the next number see *Don Juan*, III. (1821); the last of all, 'Stanzas inscribed *On this day I completed my Thirty-sixth year*' (1824), is the last verse that Byron wrote.

LXXIX

Napier has described the terrific effect of Napoleon's pursuit; but in the operations before Corunna he was distanced, if not outgeneralled, by Sir John Moore, and ere the first days of 1809 he gave his command to Soult, who pressed us vainly through the hill-country between Leon and Gallicia, and got beaten at Corunna for his pains. Wolfe, who was an Irish parson and died of consumption, wrote some spirited verses on the flight of Busaco, but this admirable elegy—'I will show you,' said

NOTES

Byron to Shelley (Medwin, ii. 154) 'one you have never seen, that I consider little if at all inferior to the best, the present prolific age has brought forth '—remains his passport to immortality. It was printed, not by the author, in an Irish newspaper; was copied all over Britain; was claimed by liar after liar in succession; and has been reprinted more often, perhaps, than any poem of the century.

LXXX

From *Snarleyow, or the Dog Fiend* (1837). Compare Nelson to Collingwood: '*Victory*, 25th June, 1805,—May God bless you and send you alongside the *Santissima Trinidad.*'

LXXXI, LXXXII

The story of Casabianca is, I believe, untrue; but the intention of the singer, alike in this number and in the next, is excellent. Each indeed is, in its way, a classic. The *Mayflower* sailed from Southampton in 1626.

LXXXIII

This magnificent sonnet, *On First Reading Chapman's Homer*, was printed in 1817. The 'Cortez' of the eleventh verse is a mistake; the discoverer of the Pacific being Nuñez de Balboa.

LXXXIV—LXXXVII

The *Lays* are dated 1824; they have passed through edition after edition; and if Matthew Arnold disliked and contemned them (see Sir F. H. Doyle, *Reminiscences and Opinions*, pp. 178–87), the general is wise enough to know them by heart. But a book that is 'a catechism to fight' (in Jonson's phrase) would have sinned against itself had it taken no account of them, and I have given *Horatius* in its integrity: if only, as Landor puts it,

> To show the British youth, who ne'er
> Will lag behind, what Romans were,
> When all the Tuscans and their Lars
> Shouted, and shook the towers of Mars.

As for *The Armada*, I have preferred it to *The Battle of Naseby*, first, because it is neither vicious nor ugly, and the other is both; and, second, because it is so brilliant an outcome of that capacity for dealing with proper names which Macaulay, whether poet or not, possesses in common with none but certain among the greater poets. For *The Last Buccaneer* (a curious anticipation of some effects of Mr. Rudyard Kipling), and that noble thing, the *Jacobite's Epitaph*, they are dated 1839 and 1845 respectively.

354   NOTES

LXXXVIII

The Poetical Works of Robert Stephen Hawker (Kegan Paul, 1879). By permission of Mrs. R. S. Hawker. 'With the exception of the choral lines—

> And shall Trelawney die?
> There's twenty thousand Cornishmen
> Will know the reason why!—

and which have been, ever since the imprisonment by James II. of the Seven Bishops—one of them Sir Jonathan Trelawney—a popular proverb throughout Cornwall, the whole of this song was composed by me in the year 1825. I wrote it under a stag-horned oak in Sir Beville's Walk in Stowe Wood. It was sent by me anonymously to a Plymouth paper, and there it attracted the notice of Mr. Davies Gilbert, who reprinted it at his private press at Eastbourne under the avowed impression that it was the original ballad. It had the good fortune to win the eulogy of Sir Walter Scott, who also deemed it to be the ancient song. It was praised under the same persuasion by Lord Macaulay and Mr. Dickens.'—*Author's Note.*

LXXXIX—XCII

From *The Sea Side and the Fire Side*, 1851; *Birds of Passage, Flight the First*, and *Flight the Second;* and *Flower de Luce*, 1866. Of these four examples of the picturesque and taking art of Longfellow, I need say no more than that all are printed in their integrity, with the exception of the first. This I leave the lighter by a moral and an application, both of which, superfluous or not, are remote from the general purpose of this book: a confession in which I may include the following number, Mr. Whittier's *Barbara Frietchie* (*In War-Time*, 1863).

XCIV

Nineteenth Century, March 1878; *Ballads and other Poems*, 1880. By permission of Messrs. Macmillan, to whom I am indebted for some of my choicest numbers. For the story of Sir Richard Grenville's heroic death, 'in the last of August,' 1591—after the Revenge had endured the onset of 'fifteen several armadas,' and received some 'eight hundred shot of great artillerie,'—see Hakluyt (1598–1600), ii. 169–176, where you will find it told with singular animation and directness by Sir Walter Raleigh, who held a brief against the Spaniards in Sir Richard's case as always. To Sir Richard's proposal to blow up the ship the master gunner 'readily condescended,' as did 'divers others'; but the captain was of 'another opinion,' and in the end Sir Richard was taken aboard the ship of the Spanish admiral, Don Alfonso de Bazan, who used him well and honourably until he died: leaving to his friends the 'comfort that being dead he hath not outlived his own honour,' and that he had nobly

NOTES

shown how false and vain, and therefore how contrary to God's will, the 'ambitious and bloudie practices of the Spaniards' were.

XCV

Tiresias and Other Poems, 1885. By permission of Messrs. Macmillan. Included at Lord Tennyson's own suggestion. For the noble feat of arms (25th October 1854) thus nobly commemorated, see Kinglake (v. i. 102–66). 'The three hundred of the Heavy Brigade who made this famous charge were the Scots Greys and the second squadron of Enniskillings, the remainder of the "Heavy Brigade" subsequently dashing up to their support. The "three" were Scarlett's aide-de-camp, Elliot, and the trumpeter, and Shegog the orderly, who had been close behind him.'—*Author's Note*.

XCVI, XCVII

The Return of the Guards, and other Poems, 1866. By permission of Messrs. Macmillan. As to the first, which deals with an incident of the war with China, and is presumably referred to in 1860, 'Some Seiks and a private of the Buffs (or East Kent Regiment) having remained behind with the grog-carts, fell into the hands of the Chinese. On the next morning they were brought before the authorities and commanded to perform the *Ko tou*. The Seiks obeyed; but Moyse, the English soldier, declaring that he would not prostrate himself before any Chinaman alive, was immediately knocked upon the head and his body thrown upon a dunghill.'—Quoted by the author from *The Times*. The Elgin of line 6 is Henry Bruce, eighth Lord Elgin (1811–1863), then Ambassador to China, and afterwards Governor-General of India. Compare *Theology in Extremis* (*post*, p. 309). Of the second, which Mr. Saintsbury describes 'as one of the most lofty, insolent, and passionate things concerning this matter that our time has produced,' Sir Francis notes that the incident—no doubt a part of the conquest of Sindh—was told him by Sir Charles Napier, and that 'Truckee' (line 12)= 'a stronghold in the Desert, supposed to be unassailable and impregnable.'

XCVIII, XCIX

By permission of Messrs. Smith, Elder, and Co. *Dramatic Lyrics*, 1845; *Cornhill Magazine*, June 1871, and *Pacchiarotto*, 1876, Works, iv. and xiv. I can find nothing about Hervé Riel.

C—CIII

The two first are from the 'Song of Myself,' *Leaves of Grass* (1855); the others from *Drum Taps* (1865). See *Leaves of Grass* (Philadelphia, 1884), pp. 60, 62–63, 222, and 246.

CIV, CV

By permission of Messrs. Macmillan. Dated severally 1857 and 1859.

CVI

Edinburgh Courant, 1852. Compare *The Loss of the 'Birkenhead'* in *The Return of the Guards, and other Poems* (Macmillan, 1883), pp. 256-58. Of the troopship *Birkenhead* I note that she sailed from Queenstown on the 7th January 1852, with close on seven hundred souls on board; that the most of these were soldiers—of the Twelfth Lancers, the Sixtieth Rifles, the Second, Sixth, Forty-third, Forty-fifth, Seventy-third, Seventy-fourth, and Ninety-first Regiments; that she struck on a rock (26th February 1852) off Simon's Bay, South Africa; that the boats would hold no more than a hundred and thirty-eight, and that, the women and children being safe, the men that were left—four hundred and fifty-four, all told—were formed on deck by their officers, and went down with the ship, true to colours and discipline till the end.

CVII—CIX

By permission of Messrs. Macmillan. From *Empedocles on Etna* (1853). As regards the second number, it may be noted that Sohrab, being in quest of his father Rustum, to whom he is unknown, offers battle as one of the host of the Tartar King Afrasiab, to any champion of the Persian Kai Khosroo. The challenge is accepted by Rustum, who fights as a nameless knight (like Wilfrid of Ivanhoe at the Gentle and Joyous Passage of Ashby), and so becomes the unwitting slayer of his son. For the story of the pair the poet refers his readers to Sir John Malcom's *History of Persia*. See *Poems*, by Matthew Arnold (Macmillan), i. 268, 269.

CX, CXI

Ionica (Allen, 1891). By permission of the Author. *School Fencibles* (1861) was 'printed, not published, in 1877.' *The Ballad for a Boy*, Mr. Cory writes, 'was never printed till this year.'

CXII

By permission of the Author. This ballad, which was suggested, Mr. Meredith tells me, by the story of Bendigeid Vran, the son of Llyr, in the *Mabinogion* (iii. 121-9), is reprinted from *Modern Love* (1862), but it originally appeared (*circ.* 1860) in *Once a Week*, a forgotten print the source of not a little unforgotten stuff—as *Evan Harrington* and the first part of *The Cloister and the Hearth*.

CXIII

From the fourth and last book of *Sigurd the Volsung*, 1877. By permission of the Author. Hogni and Gunnar, being the guests of King Atli, husband to their sister Gudrun, refused to tell him the whereabouts of the treasure of Fafnir, whom Sigurd slew; and this is the manner of their taking and the beginning of King Atli's vengeance.

CXIV

English Illustrated Magazine, January 1890, and *Lyrical Poems* (Macmillan, 1891). By permission of the Author: with whose sanction I have omitted four lines from the last stanza.

CXV

By permission of Sir Alfred Lyall. *Cornhill Magazine*, September 1868, and *Verses Written in India* (Kegan Paul, 1889). The second title is: *A Soliloquy that may have been delivered in India, June* 1857; and this is further explained by the following 'extract from an Indian newspaper':—'They would have spared life to any of their English prisoners who should consent to profess Mahometanism by repeating the usual short formula; but only one half-caste cared to save himself that way.' Then comes the description, *Moriturus Loquitur*, and next the poem.

CXVI—CXVIII

From *Songs before Sunrise* (Chatto and Windus, 1877), and the third series of *Poems and Ballads* (Chatto and Windus, 1889). By permission of the Author.

CXIX, CXX

The Complete Poetical Works of Bret Harte (Chatto and Windus, 1886). By permission of Author and Publisher. *The Reveillé* was spoken before a Union Meeting at San Francisco at the beginning of the Civil War and appeared in a volume of the Author's poems in 1867. *What the Bullet Sang* is much later work: dating, thinks Mr. Harte, from '79 or '80.

CXXI

St. James's Magazine, October 1877, and *At the Sign of the Lyre* (Kegan Paul, 1889). By permission of the Author.

CXXII

St. James's Gazette, 20th July 1888, and *Grass of Parnassus* (Longmans, 1888). By permission of Author and Publisher. Written in memory of Gordon's betrayal and death, but while there were yet hopes and rumours of escape.

CXXIII

Underwoods (Chatto and Windus, 1886). By permission of the Publishers.

NOTES

CXXIV

Love's Looking-Glass (Percival, 1891). By permission of the Author.

CXXV

Macmillan's Magazine, November 1889. By permission of the Author. Kamal Khan is a Pathan; and the scene of this exploit —which, I am told, is perfectly consonant with the history and tradition of Guides and Pathans both—is the North Frontier country in the Peshawar-Kohat region, say, between Abazai and Bonair, behind which is stationed the Punjab Irregular Frontier Force— 'the steel head of the lance couched for the defence of India.' As for the Queen's Own Corps of Guides, to the general 'God's Own Guides' (from its exclusiveness and gallantry), it comprehends both horse and foot, is recruited from Sikhs, Pathans, Rajputs, Afghans, all the fighting races, is officered both by natives and by Englishmen, and in all respects is worthy of this admirable ballad.

> Ressaldar = *the native leader of a* ressala *or troop of horse*
> Tongue = *a barren and naked strath*—' what geologists call a fan '
> Gut of the Tongue = *the narrowest part of the strath*
> dust-devils = *dust-clouds blown by a whirlwind*

CXXVI

National Observer, 4th April 1891. At the burning of the Court-House at Cork, ' Above the portico a flagstaff bearing the Union Jack remained fluttering in the air for some time, but ultimately when it fell the crowds rent the air with shouts, and seemed to see significance in the incident.'—DAILY PAPERS. *Author's Note.*

INDEX

	PAGE
A good sword and a trusty hand	207
All is finished! and at length	217
Alone stood brave Horatius	196
Amid the loud ebriety of war	264
And Rustum gazed in Sohrab's face, and said	280
Arm, arm, arm, arm! the scouts are all come in	3
As I was walking all alane	79
Ask nothing more of me, sweet	316
As the spring-tides, with heavy plash	153
At anchor in Hampton Roads we lay	227
At Flores in the Azores Sir Richard Grenville lay	232
Attend, all ye who list to hear our noble England's praise	200
Attend you, and give ear awhile	73
Avenge, O Lord, thy slaughtered saints, whose bones	28
A wet sheet and a flowing sea	148
Beat! beat! drums!—blow! bugles! blow!	257
Bid me to live, and I will live	18
Blow high, blow low, let tempests tear	89
Build me straight, O worthy Master	208
But by the yellow Tiber	183
But see! look up—on Flodden bent	116
By this, though deep the evening fell	119
Captain, or Colonel, or Knight in Arms	27
Come, all ye jolly sailors bold	92

INDEX

	PAGE
Condemned to Hope's delusive mine	45
Cromwell, our chief of men, who through a cloud	28
Darkly, sternly, and all alone	156
Day by day the vessel grew	214
Day, like our souls, is fiercely dark	146
Eleven men of England	244
England, queen of the waves, whose green inviolate girdle enrings thee round	317
Erle Douglas on his milke-white steede	49
Fair stood the wind for France	6
Farewell! farewell! the voice you hear	133
Farewell, ye dungeons dark and strong	95
Get up! get up for shame! The blooming morn	15
God prosper long our noble king	47
God who created me	328
Go fetch to me a pint o' wine	97
Good Lord Scroope to the hills is gane	64
Hame, hame, hame, hame fain wad I be	147
Hark! I hear the tramp of thousands	322
He has called him forty Marchmen bold	69
Here, a sheer hulk, lies poor Tom Bowling	90
He spoke, and as he ceased he wept aloud	272
He spoke, and Sohrab kindled at his taunts	267
He spoke; but Rustum gazed, and gazed, and stood	275
High-spirited friend	12
How happy is he born or taught	11
I am the mashed fireman with breast-bone broken	254
If doughty deeds my lady please	88
If sadly thinking	91
I love contemplating, apart	140

INDEX

	PAGE
In the ship-yard stood the Master	210
In Xanadu did Kubla Khan	136
Iphigeneia, when she heard her doom	138
I said, when evil men are strong	105
Is life worth living? Yes, so long	308
It is not growing like a tree	13
It is not to be thought of that the Flood	101
It is not yours, O mother, to complain	326
It was a' for our rightfu' King	99
I wish I were where Helen lies	77
Kamal is out with twenty men to raise the Border side	329
King Philip had vaunted his claims	324
Lars Porsena of Clusium	179
Last night, among his fellow-roughs	242
Milton! thou shouldst be living at this hour	102
Mortality, behold and fear	15
Much have I travelled in the realms of gold	179
My boat is on the shore	164
My dear and only love, I pray	31
Next morn the Baron climbed the tower	114
Nobly, nobly Cape St. Vincent to the north-west died away	248
Not a drum was heard, not a funeral note	172
Now all the youth of England are on fire	2
Now entertain conjecture of a time	4
Now fell the sword of Gunnar, and rose up red in the air	297
Now the noon was long passed over when again the rumour arose	304
Now we bear the king	10
Now while the Three were tightening	189
Now word is gane to the bold Keeper	67

INDEX

	PAGE
O born in days when wits were fresh and clear	282
O Brignall banks are wild and fair	126
O England is a pleasant place for them that's rich and high	260
Of Nelson and the North	144
O for a Muse of fire, that would ascend	1
Oft in the pleasant summer years	311
O have ye na heard o' the fause Sakelde	66
O how comely it is, and how reviving	31
O joy of creation	323
O Mary, at thy window be	98
Once did She hold the gorgeous East in fee	100
On the sea and at the Hogue, sixteen hundred and ninety-two	248
Othere, the old sea-captain	223
Our English archers bent their bowes	51
O Venice! Venice! when thy marble walls	165
O, young Lochinvar is come out of the west	112
Pibroch of Donuil Dhu	129
Ruin seize thee, ruthless King	80
Should auld acquaintance be forgot	96
Simon Danz has come home again	228
Stern Daughter of the Voice of God	103
Still the song goeth up from Gunnar, though his harp to earth be laid	301
Sweet day, so cool, so calm, so bright	19
Tell me not, Sweet, I am unkind	32
The Assyrian came down like the wolf on the fold	150
The boy stood on the burning deck	175
The breaking waves dashed high	177
The captain stood on the carronade: 'First Lieutenant,' says he	174

INDEX

	PAGE
The charge of the gallant three hundred, the Heavy Brigade	239
The fifteenth day of July	60
The forward youth that would appear	34
The glories of our birth and state	20
The herring loves the merry moonlight	131
The isles of Greece, the isles of Greece	167
The King sits in Dunfermline town	57
The last sunbeam	258
The Moorish King rides up and down	160
The newes was brought to Eddenborrow	56
The night is past, and shines the sun	151
The Sea! the Sea, the open Sea	149
The stag at eve had drunk his fill	121
The weary day rins down and dies	319
The winds were yelling, the waves were swelling	205
Then speedilie to wark we gaed	71
Then with a bitter smile, Rustum began	269
Then with a heavy groan, Rustum bewailed	277
This, this is he; softly a while	30
Through the black, rushing smoke bursts	265
Thus with imagined wing our swift scene flies	3
Tiger, tiger, burning bright	94
'Tis time this heart should be unmoved	171
Toll for the Brave	85
To mute and to material things	107
To my true king I offered free from stain	206
To the Lords of Convention 'twas Claver'se who spoke	134
'Twas at the royal feast for Persia won	40
Up from the meadows rich with corn	230
Vain is the dream! However Hope may rave	325
We come in arms, we stand ten score	284
Welcome, wild north-easter	262

INDEX

	PAGE
When George the Third was reigning a hundred years ago	285
When I consider how my light is spent	29
When I have borne in memory what has tamed	101
When Love with unconfinèd wings	33
When the British warrior queen	86
When the head of Bran	290
Where the remote Bermudas ride	39
Why sitt'st thou by that ruined hall	130
Winds of the World, give answer! They are whimpering to and fro	335
With stout Erle Percy, there was slaine	54
Would you hear of an old-time sea-fight	255
Ye Mariners of England	143
Ye shall know that in Atli's feast-hall on the side that joined the house	293
Yet once more, O ye laurels, and once more	21